Descartes

PHILOSOPHICAL WRITINGS

*A selection translated
and edited by*
Elizabeth Anscombe
and Peter Thomas Geach
With an Introduction by
Alexandre Koyré

Nelson's University Paperbacks
The Open University

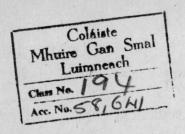
Thomas Nelson and Sons Ltd.
Lincoln Way Windmill Road
Sunbury–on–Thames Middlesex
TW16 7HP
P.O. Box 73146 Nairobi Kenya
Thomas Nelson (Australia) Ltd.
19-39 Jeffcott Street West
Melbourne Victoria 3003
Thomas Nelson and Sons (Canada) Ltd.
81 Curlew Drive Don Mills Ontario
Thomas Nelson (Nigeria) Ltd.
8 Ilupeju Bypass PMB 1303 Ikeja Lagos

First published 1954 in The Nelson Philosophical Texts series
(General Editor: Professor Raymond Klibansky)
This revised edition published
in Nelson's University Paperbacks
for The Open University 1970
Reprinted 1971, 1972, 1975, 1976, 1977
This translation © Elizabeth Anscombe and Peter Thomas Geach 1954
Introduction © Alexandre Koyré 1954

ISBN 0 17 712037 1

Printed in Hong Kong

CONTENTS

CONTENTS

[1] *Much abridged.*

Note: In the text, footnotes signed 'Ed' have been added by the General Editor, Professor Klibansky; those signed 'Tr' are by the translators, Professors Anscombe and Geach.

INTRODUCTION

Three centuries separate us from Descartes: three
centuries of uninterrupted and ever quickening progress
that utterly transformed the framework and the conditions
of human existence.

Three centuries, especially three centuries of progress,
are a long stretch of time—long enough to throw back into
the dead past most of the subjects and some of the problems
that stirred the minds of our forgotten ancestors of three
hundred years ago. And yet nobody, when reading
Descartes, will feel that he is dealing with dead texts. On
the contrary: they are still living and sparkling; we can
still enjoy the deceptive simplicity and apparent carelessness
of the *Discourse*; we can still learn something of value from
the carefully veiled intensity of the *Meditations*. Philosophical progress has not made them obsolete, as scientific
progress has made obsolete Descartes's *Meteors* and large
parts of his *Dioptrics*.

Philosophy—we must frankly confess—moves slowly,
and makes little progress. It deals with simple things.
It deals with being, with knowledge, with man. The
questions it asks, moreover, are simple questions: simple,
and therefore permanently alive; simple, and thus im-
mensely difficult to grasp. It follows that the attempts
of great philosophers to solve these simple questions remain
important, and ' modern ', for hundreds and even for
thousands of years. Thus what is living in philosophy
extends as far back as the history of philosophy itself:
there is no thought, perhaps, more alive today than that
of Descartes.[1] Except, of course, that of Plato.

[1] Edmund Husserl's phenomenology is a conscious revival of the
Cartesian tradition; the *cogito* of Descartes contained more than he
himself was aware of.

Yet, in spite of this perennial aliveness of philosophical questions and answers—or because of it—no philosophy, at least no authentic one, can be ' abstracted ' from its context in time. Not only does philosophy speak the language and use the concepts of its time—as it must in order to be understood by its contemporaries—it grows from the deepest reflection on the specific, burning problems of the age. Thus it belongs to an epoch and shares its climate and its background, and these we must study in order fully to understand the philosopher's message. It is therefore first of all to the spiritual climate and mental background of the beginning of the seventeenth century that we must turn our attention.

The Renaissance had brought with it an unprecedented enlargement of the historical, geographical, scientific image of man and the world; a chaotic and fecund effervescence of new ideas, and of old ideas renewed; the revival of a forgotten world and the birth of a new one; the self-assertion of man aware of his might, his freedom and his dignity; a joyful admiration of the colourful multiplicity of things. But these had as their counterpart a spirit of criticism which first undermined, then finally destroyed the old beliefs, the old conceptions, the traditional truths that had enabled mankind to find certainty in knowledge and security in action. These processes are, as a matter of fact, inevitably bound together: human thought starts usually with negation and polemic, and the new truth establishes itself on the tomb of the old.

This applies particularly to the thought of the sixteenth century. It attacked everything: it undermined everything; and nearly everything crumbled: the political, religious, spiritual unity of Europe; the certainty of science together with that of faith; the authority of the Bible as well as that of Aristotle; the prestige of the Church and the glamour of the State.

Deprived of his traditional patterns and rules of judgment and of choice, man finally feels himself lost in an alien and uncertain world, a world in which nothing is certain and everything is possible. Little by little, doubt stirs and awakens. If everything is possible, nothing is true. If nothing is assured, the only certainty is error.

The disenchantment which succeeded the magnificent effort of the Renaissance is not an invention of modern historians. Thinkers of the Renaissance — Agrippa, Sanchez, and Montaigne—amply attest it in their own day.

As far back as 1527, having passed in review all the fields of human knowledge, Agrippa announces *the uncertainty and vanity of human wisdom.* In 1562, having submitted to a searching and careful examination our very faculty of knowing and reaching the truth, Sanchez reiterates and even reinforces the conclusion: *Nothing is known.* Nothing can be known. Neither the world, *nor ourselves.* And finally, Montaigne sums up: man lacks certain knowledge, for he lacks true being.

The case of Montaigne is particularly illuminating. In point of fact, that great sceptic accomplishes his destructive work despite himself. What he really had set out to destroy was superstition, prejudice and error, the narrow-minded fanaticism of private opinion that offers itself for truth and without reason claims for itself an exclusive right. It is not his fault if his radical criticism wins a pyrrhic victory and leaves him with nothing in hand: in an uncertain world where everything is possible no distinction can be drawn between truth and mere opinion. Having gone so far, Montaigne tries to turn round, tries to perform the Socratic inversion, the classical strategy of philosophy at bay.

He abandons the external world—uncertain object of uncertain opinion—and tries to fall back upon himself in order to find *in himself* the foundation of certainty, the firm principles of *judgment*—that is, of a *discriminating discernment between the true and the false.*

For this reason he proceeds to study, to describe, to analyse himself: in the world of his own being, ' fluctuating and changeful ', he looks for the firm foundation which would substantiate the norms of judgment. Alas ! he finds nothing but perpetual change, instability, void.

Montaigne—and that is his greatness—acknowledges his failure. He accepts himself for what he is, or for what, at any rate, his bold attempt has revealed him to be. He does not attempt to conceal the results—he is too honest, too lucid, too fearless. For him, there is no way out of the maze. We have to accept things as they are. It is useless to try to go back, to try to restore the veil of illusions that has been torn away: we have to renounce the hope with which we started. We have to abide by doubt. This is the last word of wisdom. The *Essais* are by no means a treatise of despair. They are a treatise of renunciation.

And yet, scepticism is not an attitude that can be easily sustained in life. In the long run it is intolerable. We must not deceive ourselves: the ' soft pillow of doubt ' that Montaigne offers to us is very hard. Man cannot abandon, once and for ever, his hope of encompassing certainty and ' assurance of judgment '. He cannot renounce the quest of truth.

Thus, against the sceptical trend that culminates in Montaigne a threefold reaction takes place: Pierre Charron, Francis Bacon, Descartes. In other words: faith, experience, reason.

Pierre Charron—who was only the most outspoken and honest of contemporary religious thinkers—does not indeed have much to oppose to Montaigne; no more per- haps than the clear recognition that the situation revealed by him is, in the full sense of the term, unbearable for man and finally leads to despair. If human reason cannot reach absolute truth, so much the worse for it. Yet, perhaps, so much the better for us who can establish ourselves on the firm rock of faith that even Montaigne did not shake.

The sceptical criticism has, it is true, undermined the foundations of scholastic philosophy and theology, destroyed the bases of traditional proofs of religious and moral truths. This, after all, is not surprising : natural reason, the reason of man, an ephemeral and fallible being, is not made for certainty. We possess it in order to be able to muddle through in this life, not in order to apprehend Being or God. Sceptical criticism is, therefore, self-destructive : the proofs of the theologian (existence of God, immortality of the soul, and so on) are worthless : but the reasons marshalled against them have just as little value. Thus to *the uncertainty of natural reason* Charron opposes the *supernatural certainty of faith.*

The sceptical fideism of Charron had, in his day, much less success than it has in ours. People who had not been troubled in their faith did not need him. As for the others, they wanted *proofs* and not an appeal to authority. As Descartes has so neatly said in his *Epistle to the Doctors of the Sorbonne,* 'though it is absolutely true that one must believe in God because it is so taught in the Holy Writ, and, on the other hand, that one has to believe in the Holy Writ because it comes from God . . . one cannot, nevertheless, propose this to the infidels [Descartes means the sceptics and libertines] who might imagine that in so doing one commits the fallacy which the logicians call a circle '. Thus the *Wisdom* of Pierre Charron did not put an end to the sceptical trend. Quite on the contrary; it became its text-book.

Pierre Charron was a churchman. Francis Bacon was a statesman. His chief interest is not religious truth and

the eternal destiny of man in the other world—this is a
matter of faith, of supernatural revelation which is outside
the realm of man's reason—but the progress of knowledge
and of useful inventions, the temporal destiny of man in
this world. He is concerned not with blessedness, but with
well-being. Thus it is not in an appeal to some transcen-
dent authority, or in a return to the wisdom of the ancients,
but in the achievements of the present and the promise of the
future, that he seeks a remedy and guidance for his time.

Sceptical criticism is accepted and even perfected by
Bacon: nobody has better classified the types of human
errors, the fallacies and idols of our mind; nobody has
more successfully uncovered their roots and their origins,
natural as well as social, particular as well as general;
nobody has less confidence in the spontaneous and un-
fettered exercise of our reason.

Human reason, discursive, theoretical reason, is not
only perverted and diseased, but is in itself fallacious, weak,
unstable. But the cure is at hand: not to try using
reason where it cannot be used, and for purposes for which
it is unsuited. We are endowed with reason not for the
sake of speculation or of spinning out theories about things
that are beyond our reach: we possess reason for the
sake of action. For man's essence is action and not mere
thought. Thus it is in action, in practice, in experience,
that man finds the very foundations of knowledge, of the
only knowledge that is available and important to him.
Theoretical reason is fanciful and chimerical. It runs
wildly astray whenever it leaves the firm ground of experience. Thus we must not allow it to wander at will;
we must shackle or enchain it by precise and numerous
rules of procedure, we must restrict and restrain it to its
only legitimate use, the empirical one. Experience, then,
is the remedy that Bacon offers to mankind. The *Novum
Organon* has no other goal than to set against the sterile

uncertainty of reason left to itself the fruitful certitude of well-ordered *experience*. And Bacon's challenging work *On the Advancement of Learning* is a reply, as much by its title as by its contents, to the disillusioned work of Agrippa.

The Baconian solution was a tremendous success. Unfortunately it was a purely literary and social one; for, as a matter of fact, this new science—an active, operative, experiential science that the herald of the new learning announced to the world—was not produced by him. And nobody, not even Boyle and Hooke, was able to fulfil the promise, for the simple reason that it was quite impossible to do so. Pure empiricism does not lead us anywhere—not even to experience; much less, of course, to experiment. An experiment, indeed, is a question we put to nature. It presupposes, therefore, a language in which we formulate our questions; in other words, experiment is not the basis of theory, but only a way of testing it. Science does not result from an accumulation of facts; there are no facts that do not imply concepts. It was because he did not understand this, and wanted to follow ' the order of things and not that of ideas ' that Bacon failed in his attempted reformation of the intellect. Unlike Bacon, Descartes fully understood it. Going beyond common sense and classification (which Bacon aimed at just as intently as Aristotle), he followed ' the order of ideas, not that of things '. It was for this reason that the Cartesian revolution succeeded.

II

From Descartes's point of view at any rate, the sixteenth-century landscape is completely dominated by the sceptical element; and among the influences that Descartes has to contend with in the first place, that of Montaigne is paramount. There were, of course, Aristotle and the

Scholastics: yet, for Descartes, they have not the over-
whelming importance that historians (myself included)
have so often attributed to them; they have to be replaced,
not fought against. Montaigne, on the other hand, is not
to be set aside, but to be used and absorbed. Thus,
Descartes not only opposes Montaigne, he learns from him;
he is his best pupil.[1]

It is obvious that Descartes considers Montaigne
perfectly justified in his destructive criticism of the false
scholastic rationalism and of all the ' superstitions ',
' preconceptions ', and ' prejudices ' that clutter up the
mind and obscure its natural light. The fault of Montaigne,
in Descartes's opinion, is not, however, that he is too
radical; on the contrary, it is that he is not radical
enough. The only way to deal with Montaigne is to go
beyond him. It is because Montaigne was too timid that
he could not find the way out of the labyrinth; and it
was because of Descartes's own fearless decision not to stop,
not to yield, but to pursue his way to the end, that he
succeeded in breaking through into the realm of pure
mind—a realm which Montaigne could not reach; and
thus, whereas Montaigne stopped at the finitude of the
human soul, Descartes discovered the fullness of spiritual
freedom, the certainty of intellectual truth, the reality of
the infinite God.

The Discourse on Method, which could be called the
Cartesian *Confessions* or his *Itinerarium Mentis in Veritatem*,
his *Journey of mind towards Truth*, is simply the story of this
successful break-through. It is a reply to the *Essais*.
To the sad story told by Montaigne, the story of a defeat,
Descartes opposes his own, the story of a decisive victory.

I will not attempt to follow, step by step, this pilgrim's
progress. Yet I would like to point out some moments of
this eventful, and yet uneventful journey; and, first of all,

[1] *Cf.* Léon Brunschvicg, *Descartes et Pascal lecteurs de Montaigne*, 1944

at the starting point, the utter deception, bewilderment, and discouragement of the young graduate of the world-famous Jesuit school of La Flèche.

He had been a good student; he had been told that he must study ' letters and arts ' because ' by means of them one could acquire a clear and assured knowledge of all that is useful for life '. He believed this and had worked as hard as he could. Yet now, being ' admitted among the ranks of the learned ', he finds himself ' embarrassed by doubts and errors ' and forced to recognise that ' there was no such learning in the world as he had been led to hope '.

Much of this teaching was not, indeed, completely worthless. ' Languages '—he means Greek and Latin— ' are necessary for the understanding of ancient literature . . . the gracefulness of the fables stimulates the mind . . . the memorable deeds related in historical works elevate it and help to form one's judgment if they are read with discretion . . . Eloquence has points of incomparable strength and beauty . . . poetry contains passages of entrancing sweetness and delicacy; mathematics contains very subtle inventions . . . theology teaches how to attain heaven . . . philosophy enables one to talk plausibly on all subjects and win the admiration of people less learned than oneself . . . jurisprudence and medicine . . . bring honours and wealth to those who cultivate them.' All that, undoubtedly, was not without profit. Still, it was something quite different that had been promised him: he had been made to hope for *clear* and *certain* knowledge; a knowledge indispensable in order that he might *judge and direct himself in life*. In short, he had been promised both science and wisdom. But he had been cheated, having been taught neither.

As a matter of fact, of all that he had been taught, nothing was indispensable. And, apart from mathematics, nothing was certain, nor even clearly useful. Thus, to read ancient literature, to learn fables, to study history, all this doubtless enriches the mind, but may also pervert it. This is so because 'fables make one imagine various events as possible when they are not'; as for histories, even the most truthful never present us with things as they really were. They cannot therefore 'form our judgment', that is teach us *to distinguish truth from falsehood.* On the contrary: they lead us to forget the distinction.

Eloquence and poetry are, undoubtedly, beautiful. But neither of them can be taught. They are natural endowments of the mind, not fruits of study. In order to convince people, one must speak to them clearly so as to enable them to understand easily; one must not heap upon them a mass of rhetorical figures. Plain speech is the best rhetoric.

Philosophy employs very subtle reasonings, and yet is it not true that there is 'nothing so strange and incredible that it has not been said by some philosopher'?

As for theology 'that teaches us how to attain heaven', is it not a completely superfluous science, since 'the way there is no less open to the most ignorant than to the most learned'? Is it not, also, a very dubious 'science'? For 'revealed truths . . . are above our intellect' and, therefore, 'to undertake an examination of them' obviously 'requires for its success some extraordinary aid from heaven; one would have to be superhuman'.

Mathematics alone found some recognition 'because of the certainty and self-evidence of its reasonings'; a very limited recognition, as a matter of fact, because not understanding its essence and true use (which is to nurture the soul in truth and to open the mind to the knowledge of the Universe), and believing that it was only the subservient means of the mechanical arts, the pre-Cartesian world did not succeed in building anything worth while on its firm and solid foundations.[1]

Thus nothing, or almost nothing, in scholastic science appeared to be of any value whatsoever. Small wonder ! Is it not true that all sciences receive their principles from philosophy ? And is not philosophy itself a realm of confusion, uncertainty, and doubt ? Small wonder therefore that from this first wave of scepticism which submerged Descartes and swept away the inherited certainties of his time, only two things emerged and were saved from disaster : belief in God, and belief in mathematics.

Let us note this. It is of great importance. As a matter of fact, Descartes will attempt in his metaphysics to link together these two certainties, and in such fashion as to make them support each other.

Nothing, now, is left over from the wisdom of humanism : wisdom without science is no more acceptable to Descartes than science without wisdom, for, as he tells us himself, he has ' *always had an extreme desire to learn to distinguish truth from falsehood in order to have clear insight into his actions and to proceed with assurance in this life* '.

III

The preceding pages describe the state of mind of the youthful Descartes when, in 1618, he set out for Holland. He did not go there to study, though we find his name inscribed on the register of the University of Franeker ; but dreaming of a military career, of adventures, of battles, of conquests, he went there, as did many a spirited youth of the seventeenth century, in order to take service in the

---

[1] Thus Descartes considers that his reform of mathematics has *not* the aim of making it *useful*, but, on the contrary, of giving it theoretical value.

army of Maurice of Nassau, the most famous captain of his time.

The military career of Descartes seems to have been a failure.[1] In any case it did not last long. He was not of the stuff that makes good soldiers. He probably could not bring himself to follow his own prescription for action—to abide by a decision *as if* it was the right one (though knowing that it was not). But believing, as he himself remarks elsewhere, that to act well we have to think well, he certainly could not abandon his concern for good, that is, for *true* thought. Thus the only battles Descartes ever fought were battles against confusion and error; his adventures were adventures of the spirit; his conquests the conquest of truth.

Did he ever regret having thus abandoned action for contemplation ? It seems not. He tells us that when he considers the ' various activities and pursuits of men at large, there is hardly one but seems to me vain and useless ' and, ' if there is any one among purely human occupations that has solid worth and importance, I venture to believe that it is the one I have chosen '. The way that he had taken when, in 1619, he asked himself: *Quod vitae sectabor iter ?* [2]—had brought him contentment. But how did he find this way? Everyone is familiar with the story of Descartes's *poêle*, the stove-heated chamber in which, alone, during the winter of 1619, he ' discoursed with himself about his thoughts '. His first thought was that the prevailing confusion in the sciences arose from the fact that they had been built up by many people over a long period of time. There is usually no order, no plan in houses or

---

[1] A happy failure for which we have to thank God. Yet Descartes's father, the old councillor, Pierre Descartes, was of another opinion when he said that his youngest son was not good for anything but to be bound in buckskin (*n'est bon qu'à être relié en veau*).

[2] [See below, *Private Thoughts*, p. 3.—ED.]

cities built by successive generations, in contradistinction to those that are the work of one man. Thus in order to bring clarity and system into the sciences the best thing to do was to make a clean sweep and begin anew.

Scarcely a modest enterprise. But modesty had never been the chief virtue of one who could doubt everything, but never had any doubt about his own ability.

But, continues Descartes, to achieve such clarity would be difficult, because ' as we were all children before we were men ', and as our minds in the process of education have become impaired and burdened by many confused ideas, ' it is impossible for our judgments to be as clear and as firm as they would be if we had had the full use of our reason from the moment of birth and had never had any other guide '.

Indeed, it would be marvellous if from our birth we *had* been in full possession of our powers of reason, not the reason that we have now, perverted as it is by tradition and cluttered up with all kinds of prejudices and errors, but of the *pure* and *essential* reason, such as we may assume Adam to have had on the day of his creation by God.

The idea is not new. It comes from Cicero, who probably had copied it from somebody. But among all those who had previously expressed it, none, not even Bacon (though he, too, mentions it), had taken it seriously; no-one had made it the basis of a plan of action. Nobody but Descartes, who, quite seriously, endeavours to restore to our reason its ' native ' purity, and thereby to bring human nature to its highest degree of perfection, and who, in order to do so, decides that ' as to the opinions that I had so far admitted to belief ' he must ' reject them bodily ', and put into his mind ' other, better opinions, or even the same ones *when once I had made them square with the norm of reason* '.

Or, as the first rule of the *Discourse on Method* enjoins us, he decides ' never to accept anything as true if I had not evident knowledge of its being so; that is, to accept only what presented itself to my mind so clearly and distinctly that I had no occasion to doubt it '.

IV

Let us pause here for a moment; we have reached an important, indeed a decisive point: the very point of decision, the starting point, at least according to Descartes, of all philosophical thinking. It is a deep intellectual, or even more a spiritual revolution, bringing with it a new science and a new metaphysics, that these prudent [1] and reticent phrases of the *Discourse* announce to us.

Every man needs, at least once in his life—and mankind, of course, needs it too, though not only once—to get rid of *all* his accustomed, accepted ideas, to destroy and to throw away *all* his beliefs and *all* his opinions, in order to submit them *all* to the judgment of reason, and the control of truth.

Now this is the method and, at the same time, the remedy that Descartes offers to us. The method, that is, the way, the only way that can lead us to truth; and the remedy, that is, the treatment, the only one that can cure indecision and doubt.

We have to get rid of *all* our ideas, to renounce *all* our opinions, to make ourselves free of *all* blindly accepted tradition, to reject *all* existing authorities: only thus can we hope to regain the native purity of our reason and to reach the certainty of truth. A formidable task? Alas ! there is no easy way to truth.[2]

[1] Descartes knows the virtue of prudence quite well; he does not want to share the fate of Galileo and so many others. Thus he sometimes wears a mask; *larvatus prodeo* are his words about himself (see below, *Private Thoughts*, p. 3); and if he says what he thinks, he does not always say all that he thinks, but only what he thinks fit to be said.

[2] The *Meditations* present it as a kind of spiritual exercise in which we have to train ourselves for a long time.

Let us not forget that we are in a maze. The sceptic Montaigne simply states what is the case. He doubts everything, and he is perfectly right. Is he not faced with a mass of conflicting opinions between which he has no means of choosing? Is he not pulled and pushed hither and thither, never finding firm ground upon which to rest? It is possible, indeed, that sometimes he goes too far, that among the things that he doubts there are some that are true. But he cannot know this; and nobody can, because in order to do so one must be able to *judge* them; to judge, that is *to distinguish between the true and the false*. And how could one do it without fear of erring once more, so long as there still remains in the mind some idea or opinion that, not having been tested and found true, could equally well be quite false and thus distort and vitiate our judgment?

No, there is only one way that can lead to success: that is to refuse to be drawn or pushed by any idea, impression, belief, whatsoever; and to try to make our minds an absolute void, a perfect *tabula rasa*; to efface and erase all inscriptions that have ever been made upon it.

As Descartes will say later (in a letter to Father Bourdin): ' If you have a basket of apples, some of which (as you know) are bad and will spoil and poison the rest, you have no other means than to empty your basket completely and then take and test the apples one by one, in order to put the good ones back in your basket and throw away those that are not '. Let us notice the sequence: we start by emptying our basket, but we will not (and we do not intend to) keep it empty: we will put back the good apples, having sorted them out of the mass.

Yet a problem arises. How shall we decide which of the apples are good, and which are not? In other words, these ideas, opinions, beliefs of which we have rid ourselves, which we refuse to accept and to which we deny our assent as long as we have not examined them and ' made them square with the norm of reason '—by what means shall we try them ? Surely by means of reason; for now that our reason has been stripped of all the false ideas that had 'obscured' its natural brightness, it has recovered its 'native perfection', so that it will now be capable of distinguishing between truth and falsehood. The fog of uncertainty has been blown away and the natural light can shine forth unclouded.

But how shall we proceed ? The sceptics have taught us that whatever is in the least obscure and confused is uncertain and doubtful: *we* shall stand this salutary teaching on its head, making it our principle that whatever is doubtful is so because it contains elements of confusion and darkness. Thus we shall assay and try our ideas *by doubt*. Doubt itself will be our touchstone: and any idea that the acid of doubt affects will thus be recognised as false metal, or at least as an alloy of poorish quality. As such it must be rejected, and we shall keep only those ideas which doubt is unable to touch; that is to say, those ideas that ' present themselves to our mind so clearly and so distinctly that we have no occasion to doubt them '.

Now if doubt is the acid which dissolves and destroys error, it is clear that we shall have to make it as strong as possible; only thus can we reach the assurance that its *aqua fortis* will yield us *in fine* the pure gold of truth.

The sceptic will be beaten by his own weapons. He doubts: let us, then, teach him to doubt. Our doubt will not be, like his, an unhappy and purely passive state of indecision and wavering; quite the contrary, it shall be an action, a free and voluntary action that we will pursue to its limit. Doubt, a passive state; and doubt, a willed activity: the difference between those two ' doubts ' is deep and far-reaching; as I have just pointed out, the sceptic, Montaigne, *submits* to doubt as its slave, through weakness, whereas Descartes employs doubt as his tool, or, if one prefers, as his weapon. Having used it freely he has, by his very act, freed himself from it and become its master.

Freedom, mastery—I should like to stress the importance of these concepts in the philosophy of Descartes. The fact of freedom is at the very basis of Cartesian thinking. Philosophy indeed is an exercise in freedom: and freedom alone makes it possible. It is only by a free act of our mind that we can decide to doubt, 'to suspend judgment', to 'withdraw the acceptance' of all the ideas that customarily present themselves to us. Our decision to review all our ideas in the light of a searching criticism was indeed a free decision; therefore our decision to say *no* to ourselves and to our own nature was similarly a free decision, as was also our decision to set ourselves—and our reasoning faculty—the task of re-ordering all our mental activities on a new plan. Thus we started with freedom, or better, *in* freedom, and it is through freedom that we shall reach truth, i.e. those clear and distinct ideas which our reason is unable to doubt. But what are 'these ideas in which the mind finds nothing obscure and confused'? What are the ideas that are, from the start, 'made to square with the norm of reason' and which therefore will form the pattern, the rule, by which we shall judge, the norm with which the mind will have to make all the others square? And what *is* reason, which is to apply the norm?

The obscure and confused ideas that engender doubt and are, in their turn, dismissed by doubt, are those that are given to us by the senses or are handed down by tradition. Whereas the clear and true ones, are, in the first place, mathematical ideas. And reason—genuine reason—will be, likewise, mathematical reason. This is so because, as we have already seen, Descartes believes that it is in mathematics alone that the human mind has reached self-evidence and certainty and has been able to build up a science, a body of knowledge in which it proceeds in a clear and orderly way, from the most simple things to the most complex constructions. Thus the Cartesian method, the method that Descartes tells us he formed by putting together the best of what he had found in the 'three arts or sciences' that he had 'studied a little when younger' (i.e., logic, the analysis of the ancients, and the algebra of the moderns) will be devised on the pattern of mathematics.

We will not, of course, be able simply to borrow from the mathematicians their modes of reasoning and to apply them, just as they stand, to other realms and other objects of knowledge. For, although ' among all those who have so far sought for truth in the sciences, only the mathematicians have been able to find some demonstrations, that is, some certain and self-evident reasonings ', we have to acknowledge, nevertheless, that their methods, or more exactly their techniques, remain strictly adapted to their subject-matter—' a subject-matter which is highly abstract and apparently useless '—and as for the Analysis of the ancients and the Algebra of our time '. . . the first is always so restricted to the considerations of figures that it cannot exercise the understanding without greatly wearying the imagination, and in the latter there is such complete slavery to certain rules and symbols that there results a confused and obscure art that embarrasses the mind instead of a science that develops it '. The first thing to do, therefore, will be to attempt a reform of mathematics itself. We shall have to generalise its methods, or, more exactly, to disentangle and firmly grasp the very essence of mathematical reasoning, the spirit that animates the unfolding of these long chains of perfectly ' simple and easy reasonings by means of which geometers are accustomed to carry out their most difficult demonstrations'.

This true essence of mathematical reasoning, a reasoning quite different from the purely syllogistic or logical one,

xxiv

consists in the fact that the mathematician, irrespective of the particular nature of the objects of his study, be it a geometrical construction or a numerical equation, strives to establish between them strict and precise proportions and to link them together by a series of well-ordered relations.

The finding out or establishing of relations, and of an order between the relations, is, according to Descartes, the very essence of mathematical thinking, a kind of thinking in which reason (*ratio*) implies, or even means, ratio or proportion; the ratio and proportion which determine an *order* and evolve into a *series*. The new science, which is at the same time a new logic which gives us the pattern of intelligibility and the true norm of reason, is the *mirabilis scientia* of relations and order.

These concepts of relation and order form the base of the Cartesian reform of algebra (as well as of the algebraisation of geometry and arithmetic). And it is the rules of this relational, algebraic thinking that form the basis of the apparently innocuous and even banal rules of the *Discourse*, at least the last three,[1] which enjoin us ' to divide every problem into as many parts as feasible and as requisite for its better solution ' (which means that we have to break up every complex relation or proportion into as many simple relations or proportions as possible); ' to direct our thoughts in an orderly way, beginning with the simplest objects, those most apt to be known, and ascending little by little in steps, as it were, to the knowledge of the most complex ' (which means that we have to start with the most simple relations or equations, those of the first degree, and build up, step by step, and in order, relations or equations of superior degrees), ' establishing an order in

---

[1] The first rule, that which instructs us not to receive anything as true so long as we do not clearly see it be so, expresses the general requirement of the *catharsis* of the mind by doubt.

thought even when the objects had no natural priority from one another ' (which means that we have to interpolate intermediate terms between the extreme ones on the assumption that they can all be linked together in a series). And finally, ' to make, throughout, such enumerations and such surveys that we can be sure of leaving nothing out ' (which means that we have to take care not to leave one of the terms, or unknown factors, of our problem without a relation to others, and that we must have as many equations as we have unknown factors).

It is perfectly clear that this *Method*, those rules which Descartes tells us he had conceived on that winter day of 1619, was devised only very much later, just because it does nothing else than formulate (in a rather cryptic manner) the modes of reasoning developed in the *Geometry*. It is obvious that Descartes, in his *Discourse* (in spite of his assertion to the contrary), shows us the way that we must follow, and not the winding and difficult path he had trodden himself. But neither the exact date of the great discoveries,[1] nor that of their formulation, really matter: it is certainly true that his first intuition of them, his dream of a science that would be genuine wisdom, dates from far back, from 1619, from the time when ' alone in his stove-heated chamber ', Descartes ' discoursed with himself about his own thoughts '.

V

I shall not attempt to retrace here, step by step, the history of the progressive development of Descartes's thought. I shall imitate his example and present it as it appears in its mature state. It is dominated by the idea of the unity of human knowledge and at the same time

---

[1] The most exact histories, as Descartes himself reminds us, never relate things as they really happened.

of its limits. The unity of mathematics follows from the fact that identical methods, the methods of the new algebra, can be applied as well in geometry as in arithmetic, to *number* as well as to *space*, that is to realms traditionally opposed to each other, *discrete* and *continuous* quantity.

The application of identical methods implies or means identical acts of the mind; which in turn reveals to us that it is not the objects—numbers, lines—that matter, but those acts or, rather, *operations* of our mind that link the objects together, compare them to each other, *measure* them by each other, and thus establish between them a serial order; an order of dynamic production (and not of classification, like the static order of genera and species in scholastic logic) in which each successive term depends on the preceding one and determines that which follows. Now if this is true, if it is the operational order that matters, the order which the algebraical formula discloses and presents to us in its intellectual unity, and not the objects that embody and exemplify it, then it is obvious that by means of these formulae every spatial relation can be transposed into a numerical one, and *vice versa*; or, at a deeper level, that every algebraic formula can be translated into the language of numbers and of lines. And it is obvious, too, that it is this science of order which supplies the foundation of rational knowledge, and this because it is reason in being, because in it our mind studies only its own acts, its own operations, its own diaphanous relations to itself.

Now, as science is nothing else than ' mind differently applied to objects ', it is clear that in order to build up the universe of truth, of knowledge, we have to find out the simplest and clearest ideas of these very objects, and ascend from these, step by step, and in an orderly way, to things ever more complex. This is so ' because everything that can fall under human knowledge, forms a sequence . . . and, so long as we avoid accepting as true what is not so, and always preserve the right order for deduction of one thing from another, there can be nothing too remote to be reached in the end, or too well hidden to be discovered '. It is by following this way, that is by starting with the intuition of ideas and not with the perception of things, and by following the order of composition inherent in our mind, that we shall be able to find out the true order of sciences, an order that is now perverted and hidden, and that we shall see grow and unfold itself into the magnificent ' tree of knowledge ', a tree of which philosophy is the root, physics the stem, and morals the fruit.

Descartes did not develop his ethics, though he gives us clear enough indications as to the kind of morals he would have built up : a morality of freedom, of generosity, of duty towards the general good of mankind. But he did develop his physics, a physics that is, at least in principle, nothing else than applied mathematics, or mechanics ; a physics based on the clear and distinct ideas of extension and motion, a physics that reduces all material being to an endless interplay of movements, governed by strict mathematical laws, in the uniform space of the infinite Universe.

It is probably because he has a glimpse of this ' tree ' that, as he tells us in his *Cogitationes privatae*, he was on 10 November 1619 filled with great enthusiasm: indeed, he began to ' understand the foundations of a marvellous science '.

But what were these foundations ? Descartes tells us, ' *Sunt in nobis semina scientiae*; the seeds of knowledge are in us '. This means that our mind is not a *tabula rasa* which has to receive everything from outside by the channel of sense-perceptions; on the contrary, we have *in ourselves* the foundations and the principles of science and knowledge, which is the reason why our thought, turning back upon itself, will be able to develop, in a luminous order and in perfect security, those long chains of reasons that the *Discourse* speaks to us about.

The seeds of knowledge are in us: that is the deep reason why the Cartesian endeavour is not a chimera, the reason why we can, and must, attempt to disencumber our reason of all the contents that it may have received from outside in the course of our life. These ' seeds of knowledge ' or, as Descartes will call them later, thus rediscovering the deep intuition of Plato, ' innate ideas ', ' eternal truths ', ' true and immutable natures ', purely intellectual essences that are utterly independent of the contents given to us by sense-perceptions, concepts that the rigorous catharsis of radical, methodical doubt does reveal in our soul: these are the firm and sure foundations—which Montaigne was not able to discover—upon which we can base our judgment.

Yet a question or two remains. The foundations and the method of science are firmly established. But it is *human* science and it is on *human* foundations that we are building it up. Human science, the science of a weak and, in any case, of a *finite* being, necessarily has limitations. Though the ' chain of reasonings ' extends *in infinitum, we* must stop somewhere. And even though extended beyond our reach in its indefinite progress, this chain cannot reach infinity. Infinity is beyond our grasp. Thus it is forever beyond our power—and this applies to any finite intellect— to comprehend, that is, distinctly to understand, either the infinitely great or the infinitely small. Our mind will never be able to embrace the infinity of space; nor the composition of even a finite line. And yet we perfectly well know that the space of the Universe is also infinite, just as the number of points present in the line is infinite. The idea of the infinite—this, by the way, is one of the greatest discoveries of Descartes—is a clear and positive and therefore a true idea. But it is—*for us*—an indistinct one.[1] The consequence is that all the questions that involve infinity are beyond our science. We cannot deal with an infinite number of factors nor with an infinite number of algebraic equations. Yet, unfortunately, there is certainly, even in the field of mathematics, an infinite number of objects that imply this infinity. Thus, for instance, there are all the lines that the ancients called 'mechanical' (and we 'transcendental'). We cannot deal with them algebraically and therefore, concludes Descartes, somewhat hastily identifying *his* science with *science*, they will for ever remain outwith the scope of truly scientific knowledge. From this it follows that in the realm of physics—physics is nothing else than mechanics, that is, in principle, applied geometry—there will be a number of objects, of motions, of mechanisms, which we will not be able to analyse completely into their constituent components. This is, perhaps, not so very important; for all physical objects are either motion or produced by motion, and motion is something that we understand perfectly well. But there is more: even if we do not take account of those patterns of motion that transcend our understanding, but consider only those that do not, we are bound to recognise that there are too many possibilities; many more, doubtless, than are realised in fact in the world. Deduction is not univocal; there are many ways of tracing

---

[1] Clearness and distinctness are not equivalent concepts. Distinctness implies clearness; the reverse, however, is not necessarily the case. An idea is *clear* when it is perfectly understood and distinguishable from all other ideas; but it is *distinct* only when its inner structure is perfectly clear to the mind. Thus, for instance, the idea of continuity is a clear idea but not a distinct one, since according to Descartes we do not understand the structure of the continuum and of its elements. An algebraic equation, on the other hand, is both clear and distinct. The idea of infinity is a clear idea and a positive one; nevertheless, it is not distinct as we do not understand how an infinity— be it multiplicity of pure number or of extension—can form a unity.

a line, and an infinite number of ways of reaching one point from another, and of producing the self-same effect. Now, of all the mechanical arrangements that are possible—and incompatible—which are the *real* ones ? We cannot say in advance; we must inquire, observe, experiment. Thus we are thrown back upon experience [1] and sense-perception, of whose value we are doubtful.

Further still, and on a deeper level, we have based our science on the ' seeds ' that are found in our minds, on the simple and primitive ideas that ' present themselves to our mind so clearly and distinctly that we have no occasion to doubt them '.

Yet, is this enough ? Have we the right to pass from the idea of the thing to the thing itself [2] as the Cartesian logic enjoins us to do ? Does the clearness and the distinctness of an idea guarantee, *eo ipso*, its *objective validity ?* It might, after all, have only a *subjective* validity, and the clear ideas, being clear to *us*, might indeed have only a very remote relation to the real world. It might even have no relations whatever with it.[3] Especially if, as Descartes asserts, it is in our own mind that we find them. After all, the clearness of an *idea* is one thing—and the real existence of the object of it quite another.[4]

[1] Cartesian science is by no means opposed to observation and experiment. On the contrary, it necessarily implies and requires it. We know that God uses a mechanism, but we do not know which one of all the possible mechanisms He has decided to use. As God is perfectly free in His choice, we have only one means to ascertain it—observation and experiment.

[2] Cartesian ideas are representations *in our mind* of objects that are *not* in the mind.

[3] Such is the case for ideas of sense-perception.

[4] We can have clear ideas of objects that do not exist *in rerum natura*, thus, for instance objects of geometry, squares, circles, straight lines; and even objects that *cannot exist*: as, for example, the idea of a rectilinear movement that is perfectly impossible in the real world.

The distinctness of an idea makes it valid *for our mind*. But how can we be certain that the real world conforms itself to the demands of *our reason?* Could it not happen that the real was, on the contrary, something obscure and irrational, something which reason cannot penetrate and make clear?

Now it is on the basis of the clear and distinct ideas of our mind that Descartes has banished from the real world— the world as it is in itself, independently of ourselves and of our reason—all sensible quality, all 'form', and all 'force', in short everything that is not mechanical, and has declared them 'mere appearance'. He has thus destroyed the well ordered, rich and colourful Cosmos of ancient and medieval science, substituting for it a new image or conception of the Universe, mere extension and motion, an image more strange and much more incredible than all the fables ever imagined by the philosophers. Has he really the right to do so?

Thus we see that the inner development of Cartesian science leads inevitably to the formulation of the epistemological question concerning the very foundations of this science; and the discovery that the clear and distinct ideas are found, or are, in ourselves, in our minds, brings with it the necessity of asking ourselves, 'what am I?' and, 'how is it to be explained that "I" am endowed with these ideas? Where do they come from? and, where do "I" come from?'—questions that clearly belong no longer to epistemology but to metaphysics;[1] questions that, for the seventeenth century, can only be formulated as questions about the soul and about God.

It is no more probable that Descartes ever seriously doubted the existence of God than that he ever doubted the

---

[1] The Cartesian question is by no means superfluous or obsolete. Most of the difficulties of contemporary science proceed from its neglect of a metaphysical foundation.

value of mathematics. Descartes is a deeply, and sincerely, religious mind.[1] But just as he could not accept uncritically the validity of mathematical concepts, so he was unable to accept on pure faith the traditional belief in God. He needed certainty and for him there is no certainty without proofs; and by proofs, he did not mean such proofs of God's existence as those that had been devised by medieval (and modern) scholastics; these are worthless, and the unbeliever (the sceptic) is perfectly right in refusing to accept them as valid. All of them are based upon a false philosophy, and even upon a false logic.[2] As a matter of fact, no-one is more convinced than Descartes is of the futility of all the traditional ' proofs of the existence of God ' or of the necessity of finding out better ones at least as clear and as demonstrative as the best demonstrations of geometry.

It is because Descartes demands proof that Pascal reproaches him. Pascal, of course, is perfectly right in one sense—and perfectly wrong in another. Absolutely right, for the reason that Descartes's God is not a God ' felt ' by the ' heart ', but a God demonstrated by reason, or grasped in an intellectual intuition. Descartes's God is not the God of ' Abraham, Isaac and Jacob ', the God of prayer and grace, the God of salvation from sin,[3] who, having created the world for man and man for Himself, follows and leads, with passionate interest, the destiny of mankind and especially of those human beings He has chosen and called to Him. The Cartesian God is an infinite Being that gives being to everything that is in His world. And His world is the infinite Universe where the Earth and Man play a very small part, and where every creature has just

[1] Cf. *supra*, p. xvii.

[2] The logic and the ontology of finiteness.

[3] The concept of ' sin ' is not a philosophical concept, and no more than that of the ' fall ' does it play any role in Descartes's thought.

as much right as man to consider itself the centre and aim of creation. He has given us being, reason and freedom. If we use them badly we fall into error. If we use them well, we shall reach the truth, and know God. We cannot and must not ask for more; we must not rely upon the common rhetoric of preachers. They are playing their part. But their part is not ours.

Once more Pascal is right. Descartes's God is a 'philosophical God'. Yet, what else can a philosopher's God possibly be? As a great philosopher said long after Descartes, philosophy must not be edifying, philosophy must be true.

Descartes's religion is certainly not that of Pascal, but why should we measure Descartes by Pascal's standards? We could, just as well, or even far better, do the opposite.[1] Yet it is a religion. And the God of Descartes is *God* and not a pale and lifeless abstraction. He is even the Christian God, as nobody can doubt who has read the texts Descartes left to us.

Here is the text of his youth. In his *Cogitationes privatae*, which I already have had occasion to quote, he notes: *Tria mirabilia fecit Dominus. Res ex nihilo ; liberum arbitrium ; Hominem Deum :* 'The Lord has made three marvels: things out of nothing; free will; and the Man who is God.'[2] It is rather curious and rather significant, this choice of the three marvels, that is, of irrational, or better to say supra-rational, things created by God. As a matter of fact, all three have something in common: in all three the infinite unites with the finite. Thus, God's act of creation, which places the world at an infinite distance from Himself, overcomes the infinite chasm that separates even finite Being from mere Nothingness. God's Incarnation unites His infinity to man's finitude; finally, freedom

---

[1] To Descartes, Pascal would appear as using the rhetoric of preachers.

[2] See below, p. 4.

of will, or of choice, is a realisation of the infinite in the finite. Freedom, indeed, even that of a finite being, is essentially, in itself, infinite.

Later on, in his mature years, in 1645, writing to Princess Elizabeth, his pupil, and probably the great love of his life, Descartes says: 'the first and principal intuitive truth . . . is that there is a God upon whom all things depend, whose perfections are infinite, whose power is immeasurable, whose decrees are unfailing'. Moreover, the idea of God is an *innate idea*, an idea that pertains to the very nature of man and is an essential possession of his mind. As a matter of fact, one could, according to Descartes, define man as the natural being that has an idea of God.

And in between, in the years when he was at work at the foundations of his science and his philosophy, in 1630, he writes to his friend Mersenne: 'I consider that all those to whom God has given the use of reason are bound to employ it principally in order to endeavour to know Him and to know themselves. It is thus that I have tried to begin my studies.'

It has often been pointed out—by others as well as by myself—how near this text is that of St. Augustine: *Deum et animam scire cupio;* 'I desire to know God and my soul'. And it is undoubtedly true that it was the teaching of St. Augustine with its Platonic tradition that inspired Descartes and nourished his opposition to the Aristotelian scholastics. Yet it would be wrong to present Descartes as a mere disciple of St. Augustine, and to minimise the difference, or even the opposition, between them. This because the text of St. Augustine that I have just quoted continues: *Nihilne plus? Nihil omnino*: 'Nothing more? Nothing whatever'; whereas Descartes goes on to say: 'and I will tell you that I could not find out the foundations of physics if I did not search for them in this way'.

It is enough for St. Augustine to know this God and his soul. But Descartes is not satisfied; he needs a *Physics*, a knowledge of the real world in order to be able to act and to direct himself in life, a knowledge that will make man master and possessor of nature and will give him the power to order and freely determine his very existence. And it is in order to put this science, whose ' foundations ' he has discovered, on a firm and secure basis that he develops his metaphysics and turns his steps towards God. Here as elsewhere the Cartesian search is the search for assurance of truth. Here as elsewhere the Cartesian way is the way of insight and freedom.

VI

Metaphysics is the science of that which is. And of our knowledge of that which is. In order to be able to build it, and thus give a firm basis to physics *as a science of the real world*, we have to find a point, at least one, where our knowledge grasps the real, or, better still, where our knowledge, our judgment coincides with the real. And, in order to reach that point, we have to make use once more of the method of doubt, and to make it even more radical and more exacting than the first time.

That first time, when we tried to make a general critical survey of all our ideas, we made a halt when confronted with the ' clear and distinct ' ones. Mathematics was accepted by us as indubitable. Now we shall go even further. Our doubt will encompass mathematics itself.

We shall proceed with the most extreme, the most pitiless rigour. The mere possibility of error shall be deemed good reason to condemn a whole realm of knowledge. Thus we shall condemn sense-perception and imagination, and, because of hallucinations and dreams, deny completely their claim to apprehend the real. We shall

condemn reasoning and even intellectual intuition because we err sometimes in performing the simplest
operations of arithmetic and geometry: that which
deceived us once could deceive us always. And we shall
reject the claim of clear and distinct ideas just because it
is this very claim that is in question.

We shall revive all the old arguments of the sceptics and
even devise new reasons to doubt. We shall adopt the
almost Manichean hypothesis of a powerful and malignant
spirit that deceives us always and everywhere ! [1] Which
means that always and everywhere we are immersed in
error.

Still, even if I err everywhere and always, even if all
my ideas and all my judgments are false, is it not necessary
that I myself, I who err or am deceived, should *be* or *exist*
just in order to be able to err, or to be deceived? And
moreover, even if all my ideas are false, it is certain,
nevertheless, that I have these ideas. It may be, of course,
that just now I am dreaming, that nothing of all that I see
and hear exists in *rerum natura*; it is possible even that
nothing exists at all, and there is no world, that I have no
body, that all that is, is illusion. Still I *have* this illusion, I
am conscious of it, and therefore I cannot doubt that I am.

The certainty of ' I am ', the clearness of ' I think ' [2]
(I am conscious) resist all the assaults of doubt. No
deception can creep into them. The judgment ' I am '

---

[1] Of course if we were *always* deceived by a malignant spirit, we
would not be able to *know* it.

[2] The term ' thought '—*pensée, cogitatio*—had, in Descartes's time, a
much wider meaning than it has now. It embraced not only ' thought '
as it is now understood, but all mental acts and data: will, feeling,
judgment, perception, and so on. The terms *cogitation* and *to cogitate*,
that are commonly used in the seventeenth and eighteenth centuries,
have, unfortunately, become obsolete; thus we have in most cases to
render ' thought ' by ' consciousness '. [See also below, Translators'
Note, p. xlv.—ED.]

is true every time that I make it; it is equally true every
time that I make any judgment whatever; every time that
I doubt or err. The ' I am ' is implied or, more exactly,
enveloped in all my judgments, in all my thoughts, in all
my acts or states of consciousness. Thought, consciousness,
implies and encloses being: ' I am ' is an immediate
consequence [1] of ' I think ' or ' I am conscious '.

Thus I think, I am conscious, and I am. But *what am I?*
The answer is clear; simply a being that thinks (i.e. is
conscious), that doubts, affirms, denies, and errs. Which,
of course, means a being imperfect and finite ; one, moreover, that *knows* it is imperfect and finite. Yet how could
it know that, that is, how could it have that clear intuition of its own essential finitude and imperfection if it
did not possess in itself an idea of something infinite and
perfect? In other words, how could it have an idea of
itself if it had not, at the same time, an idea of God?

Indeed, Cartesian logic has taught us that the prime and
positive idea, the idea that the mind conceives first of all
and by itself, is not, as is commonly held (and as is taught
by the scholastics) the idea of the finite but, on the contrary,
the idea of the infinite. It is not by negating the limitations
of the finite that the mind builds the negative idea of
infinitude; it is by introducing a limit, that is a negation,
into the idea of infinitude that we form the idea of finitude
(the non-infinite).

The traditional logic is misled by language that gives a
negative designation to a positive idea (and *vice-versa*).
But language, as often as not, and even more often than not,
is deceptive. It is made by and for common use; it is
based on images. It is not the embodiment of genuine
thought, of a thought clearly conscious of its own require-
ments. This thought, Cartesian thinking, starts with the

[1] A logical consequence, not an ontological one. ' I am ' follows
from ' I think ' because ' I think ' implies ' I am '.

infinite, the perfect. It conceives infinite space before it inscribes figures in it. It conceives God before proceeding to understand man.[1]

Thus, as Descartes told Princess Elizabeth, we *do* have an idea, and a clear one—of God. True, the vulgar, and the scholastic theologians, will deny it. As a matter of fact, they are not completely wrong; actually they do not have a clear idea of God but only a very confused one. Neither do they have a clear idea of themselves, that is, of the mind. Yet this is only because they do not know how to use their reason. They did not go through the strenuous catharsis of criticism and doubt that alone can restore the understanding to its pristine perfection; their ideas, therefore, are not clear and distinct intellectual intuitions but confused and obscure mixtures of imagination and abstract thought. Thus, though they have them *de facto* in the depth of their souls, they cannot actually grasp them because they are covered over by all the shadows that darken the natural light of their souls.

For us, for Descartes, it is different. We have cleansed our minds ; we enjoy, therefore, the actual possession of the idea of God: for us the relationship between being conscious of oneself and being conscious of God is self-evident.

I cannot analyse here the technical structure, nor the sources, of Descartes's proofs of the existence of God.[2] Yet I fear that their value, for the modern reader, may be obscured by the scholastic garb with which they are clothed. I will try, therefore, to hint at the deep intuition upon which they are based—the intuition that *my being, that is, the existence of a being conscious of himself, involves the being of God*—and to retrace the main steps of Descartes's demonstration.

[1] This implies the rejection of the traditional *via affirmationis* of scholastic theology and opens the way to Spinoza.

[2] *Cf.* my *L'Idée de Dieu et les preuves de son existence chez Descartes.* Paris, 1923.

We have already seen that ' I think ' (I am conscious), which implies ' I am ', involves ' I think God '; which means that the idea of God is an innate idea, an idea that belongs to our very essence. Moreover, it is a clear and simple idea; it is even the clearest and simplest of our ideas, though, of course, just because of its infinite perfection and richness, it is not a ' distinct ' one. Now, the idea of an infinite and infinitely perfect being, where does it come from? From myself? Of course not; it is much too perfect. How could a finite and imperfect mind produce an idea that so much surpasses its power that it cannot even comprehend it distinctly? The mind that produces an idea must be at least at the same level of perfection as the idea that it produces. It is clear, therefore, that *no* finite being, be it ever so much more perfect than ourselves, can produce this idea.[1] Only an infinite being, that is, God, can produce the idea of God. Only God could have given it to us. Accordingly we can conclude: *God is thought of ; therefore God exists.*

We could start with being instead of with consciousness, with the ' I am ' instead of the ' I think ' (I am conscious): our consciousness, indeed, is that of being, of our existence, of the existence of a finite and imperfect being. It is obvious that I am not even able to maintain myself in existence: if I could, I could prolong my existence at will. But I cannot extend it even to the next moment: from the fact that I am *now* I cannot infer that I shall still exist in ten minutes, in ten seconds and so on. My existence is given to me only now, in this instant. Moreover, my own essence, or nature, does not contain any ground, or reason, or cause, even for this instantaneous existence. Thus my being, so to say, is by no means my own.

It is clear that for Descartes ' being '—which implies reason, ground, cause of existence, power to maintain

[1] This rules out the powerful deceiver.

oneself in it—is not a passive enjoyment of a state, but an active, dynamic exertion of a power, of a potency to overcome the chasm of nothingness which, at every moment, is threatening to engulf us. To be, in the full meaning of the term, in its absolute meaning, is to be *causa sui*, the cause of oneself. This is not our case. Thus we must admit that our being is received from elsewhere, from another being. Yet no finite being could possibly give existence to, that is create, a being such as we are, a being possessing an idea of God, without himself having this idea. Therefore this finite being, which would be the source, or cause, of our existence, would be in the same situation as ourselves: he too would be obliged to receive his being from elsewhere, because, if he could give existence to himself and be *causa sui*, he would certainly give to himself all the perfections of which he has an idea, that is, he would make himself absolutely perfect. In other words, he would make himself God.

Thus it is only from God that a finite being can receive existence, and it is only God's continuous action—Descartes calls it continuous creation—that can maintain it in being.

We may, finally, proceed more directly. Our idea of God, a clear and true one, is that of an infinite, infinitely perfect being. As a matter of fact, we have only to analyse it and we shall see, as clearly as we see the truth of any geometrical proposition, that to its perfection pertains not only existence but this self-same absolute sovereignty of being which was implied in the descriptions ' cause of oneself' and ' giving existence to oneself'. God's essence implies *this* existence, and because of that, it is impossible to think of Him as non-existent. It would be to conceive of an imperfect perfection, a finite infinite—a contradiction in terms.

The absolute sovereignty of God's being implies and explains His absolute freedom and absolute omnipotence.

He created the world freely. He could, if He chose, abstain from creation. And He could, if He chose, have created quite another world. A world with a quite different geometry, and even a quite different arithmetic. But, of course, in that case, He would have given us—or rather those spiritual beings whom He would create instead of us—quite different clear and distinct innate ideas; for notwithstanding His omnipotence and His freedom, there are things that He cannot do; for instance, he cannot lie and deceive, and again He cannot change His freely given decrees for that would be utterly incompatible with His absolute and infinite perfection.

It is only now, having demonstrated the existence of God, that we are finally liberated from uncertainty and doubt. Knowing that God exists and that we are created by Him, we can both explain the presence in our souls of clear and distinct innate ideas, and justify our assurance of their validity: it is God, indeed, who endowed us with them; [1] it is God, therefore, who guarantees their truth, that is, their conformity with the real world created by Him. God's veracity [2] is thus the ultimate foundation of our reasoning, of the right that we have to conclude from the idea to the thing which it represents, to assert, for instance, the real existence of extension and motion, the validity of the mathematical sciences and of the physics based upon them. The reasoned-out confidence that we have in our reason is thus, for Descartes, justified only and alone by the reasoned-out confidence that we have in God. An atheist, denying the existence of God, must, therefore, necessarily be the prey of an absolute scepticism: he cannot have an assurance of anything whatever—not even

[1] The ' seeds of sciences ' that we find in us have been planted there by God.

[2] *Deus nec fallit nec fallitur*, God is neither deceiver nor is he deceived.

xlii

of mathematics—and, for him, to believe in his reason would be utterly unreasonable.

As for us, assured as we are of being created by a perfect God who cannot deceive us, nor wish us to be deceived, we can confidently proceed with the critical examination and evaluation of our mental faculties (such as memory, inference and so on) and of our ideas, and to ' measure ' their validity according to the standard of clearness and distinctness on the one hand, and the principle of divine veracity on the other. We shall find, indeed, that it is not only our clear and distinct ideas that have validity, but that even those that are not such have a certain relative validity, usually a pragmatic and not a speculative one, as, for instance, our sense-perceptions and passions. Yet there is one idea that, though essentially unclear and indistinct, can claim absolute truth: this is the idea of the union between body and soul, the idea of the unity of the human being.

The soul is a purely spiritual being. This we can prove (as a matter of fact we have already done so) by considering that the idea of the soul does not include the idea of the body and that we can (as we did) perfectly well deny the existence of our body without being in the least obliged to renounce, or even to modify, the exercise of our consciousness. Our soul is a being, the whole nature or essence of which is to think (to be conscious).

Conversely, the idea of matter, of body, does not and cannot include consciousness. Body is neither less nor more than extension; and extension can only be an object of thought, not its subject. Yet we know, or we feel, and are perfectly certain that we have a body, that we are united to it, that with it we form a real and intimate unity. We are not in the body as the pilot is in the ship. Besides, it is only this unity of body and soul that explains the existence in the soul itself of the ideas of the senses, of feelings, of bodily pleasures and pain, of passions. It is this unity, too which explains that our bodily faculties of imagination and sense are still, somehow, permeated with thought, and are able to perceive and to grasp, though imperfectly, things that are objects of pure understanding, such as space, geometrical form and so on, thus enabling us to give value to common experience and to devise scientific experiments.

Yet this unity is by no means understandable. How two utterly different substances, so different that they have nothing in common but existence,[1] can be united so as to make a compound one, can never be clearly seen by us.

We have reached the limit of clearness and distinctness. We have reached the region where some kind of mixed thinking must be applied, where we have to think about mind in terms of body, and of body in terms of mind. Along both ways, we must go as far as possible. Yet, they will never join. Incarnation of spirit, and not only of God, will forever remain a mystery.

We have to acknowledge this fact. At the same time, we have to go along both ways as far as we can, always bearing in mind that we must beware of hasty and premature judgment, and accept and assert as true only that which we clearly and distinctly perceive to be so. This Cartesian maxim has lost nothing of its urgency and actuality.

A. KOYRÉ

ECOLE PRATIQUE DES HAUTES ETUDES
PARIS, *April*, 1950

---

[1] This fact that there is nothing in common between thought (mind) and extension forms the basis of a purely mechanical physics.

TRANSLATORS' NOTE

As authority for the text we have used the edition of Adam and Tannery (1897-1913). Our translations have all been made directly from what Descartes himself wrote ; only occasional recourse has been had to the translations into French or Latin made in Descartes's lifetime, by way of a check on the rendering of difficult passages. Thus, the *Discourse* and *Dioptrics*, which form part of the same work, are translated from the French text of 1637. Our rendering of the *Meditations* follows the Latin text of 1642. The controversy between Hobbes and Descartes was originally printed along with the *Meditations* as the *Third Objections and Replies*, and again we have gone to the Latin text of 1642. The text of the *Rules for the Direction of the Mind* given by Adam and Tannery is based on collation of the Amsterdam edition of Descartes's *Opuscula Posthuma* (1701) and Leibniz's MS at Hanover, but mainly follows the former. Our selections from the *Principles of Philosophy* are based on the Latin text of 1644.

Our principle of selection has been : to include enough material to give an adequate general view of Descartes's system ; to exclude details of obsolete scientific theories and theological technicalities.

Accordingly, the *Meditations* and the controversy between Hobbes and Descartes have been translated in their entirety ;[1] and so has the *Discourse*, except for a few scientific passages, mostly in Part V.

Descartes's doctrine of method is further illustrated by our selections from the *Rules for the Direction of the Mind*.

Part I of the *Principles of Philosophy* mainly consists of

---

[1] Limitations of space unfortunately made it impossible to include the controversy between Gassendi and Descartes (the fifth set of the *Objections and Replies* printed with the *Meditations*). The reader who is interested in the argument between idealists and materialists is advised to make a particular study of this controversy—ED.

matter already found in another (and a more readable)
form in the *Meditations*. We have, however, selected certain passages that supply further exposition and development of the ideas of the *Meditations*. Since these passages
lack continuity, they are printed as separate pieces in the
original order, headed by the letters A to T for the sake
of reference.

Parts II, III and IV of the *Principles* contain much
obsolete scientific speculation, but along with this some
highly important statements of Descartes's views on the
fundamental concepts of physics, the laws of motion, the
nature and justification of scientific hypotheses, and the
relation of physics to sense-experience. The passages
containing these statements have here been grouped together. We have omitted all passages dealing with
theories of light, planetary motion, magnetism, and so on,
since their interest is merely historical. We have also
omitted the titles of sub-sections, which might distract the
modern reader's attention.

The *Dioptrics* contains passages of great importance,
especially in relation to Berkeley's *New Theory of Vision*,
which was in fact partly a polemic against Descartes's
views. (Descartes expressly argues against the view
Berkeley was later to take as axiomatic : viz, that in order
to know something by means of something else, we must
have immediate knowledge of the latter.[1]) Unfortunately,
since these important passages are scattered amongst
others dealing with obsolete optics and physiology and
with technical problems of lens manufacture, they have
been generally neglected. They are here presented in a
continuous form.

In translating, our general principle has been to produce
an English version intelligible as it stands, even if this
involves some departure from the original, rather than a
more literal version that is intelligible only when eked out
by footnotes or appendices. We have supplied words of
the original in parenthesis when some *nuance* might otherwise be lost. For example, the words *modus* and *percipere*

[1] See Berkeley, *New Theory of Vision*, Sections 9-10.

cannot always be well rendered by *mode* and *perceive*; but we judged that in many places where we have chosen another rendering, the original ought also to be indicated; thus, we thought it desirable to show whether *conceive* stands for *concipere* or *percipere*, especially as Descartes sometimes uses both words in the same passage.

The most important problem of a Descartes translation is the rendering of the verbs *cogitare* and *penser* and their derivatives. Since Locke, the traditional English renderings have been the verb *think* and the noun *thought*. We have decided to abandon this tradition, which seems to us to run the risk of seriously misrepresenting what Descartes says. In everyday XVIIth-century French, *pensée* had a rather wider application than in modern French; it was then natural, as it would not now be, to call an emotion *une pensée*. Similarly, *cogitare* and its derivatives had long been used in a very wide sense in philosophical Latin; for example, *cogitationes cordium* in Aquinas covers all internal states of mind. Descartes himself defines the words as applying not only to intellectual processes but also to acts of will, passions, mental images, and even sensations.[1] Now, as may be seen e.g. from the Oxford English Dictionary, *think* and *thought* in English have always had a predominantly intellectual reference; thought is naturally taken to be a cognitive process; and it would be most unnatural to call an act of will, and still more a fit of anger or a toothache, a " thought ". To use *think* and *thought* as the standard rendering for *cogitare* and *penser* and their derivatives gives Descartes's conception an intellectualistic cast that is not there in the original. Locke's polemic against the idea that the soul always " thinks " (*Essay concerning Human Understanding*, Book II, Chap. I) is pretty clearly *ignoratio elenchi* resulting from a misleading translation.

Our criticism of the traditional rendering would of course fall to the ground if Descartes were maintaining that all mental acts, in spite of their apparent differences, are " really " thoughts (in the way that McTaggart

[1] See e.g. below, *Principles of Philosophy*, Part 1, Section ix, p. 183.

maintains in *The Nature of Existence* that all mental states are " really " perceptions) and are only " misperceived " as being anything else. But Descartes expressly denies that the " evil genius " could make me " misperceive " the contents of my own mind.[1] Again, the view has been put forward that for Descartes even sensations and passions are " thoughts " *qua* objects of reflection ; but Descartes ascribes *cogitationes* of pleasure and pain, warmth and cold, to an unborn child, which he admits would be incapable of reflection.[2]

The words *think* and *thought* will sometimes do ; for example, in the *Discourse* we render *je pense donc je suis* by *I am thinking therefore I exist* because here the *pensée* involved, being an act of doubting, really is a thought, in the ordinary sense. We have, however, often found it advisable to use more general terms, such as the noun and verb *experience* and the adjective *conscious* ; we have fairly consistently used *conscious being* as a rendering of *res cogitans*. We have inserted the original words in parenthesis when it seemed needful—especially when different renderings of *cogitare* (etc.) occur in the same context.

Our translations of the *Discourse* and *Meditations* were very thoroughly revised by the General Editor and by Professor Guido Calogero, Visiting Professor of Philosophy at McGill University, now Professor of Philosophy at the University of Rome : we are extremely grateful to them for the care with which they carried out this heavy task, and for many helpful suggestions of theirs which we adopted as regards both these translations and other parts of the book. To the General Editor we wish also to express gratitude for compiling the Bibliography and for much valued assistance in selecting passages to be translated and in correcting the proofs. In particular we thank him for selecting the extracts from Descartes's correspondence given in this volume.

E. A.

November, 1952   P. T. G.

[1] See below, *Second Meditation*, pp. 69-75.   [2] See below, *Letters*, p. 266.

BIBLIOGRAPHY

A SELECTION

I. TEXTS

The standard edition of Descartes's works is:

Oeuvres de Descartes, publiées par Ch. Adam et P. Tannery, 12 vols., Paris 1897–1910; et Supplément: Index général, Paris 1913.

Apart from this, the following modern editions deserve particular mention:

Oeuvres et lettres. Textes présentés par A. Bridoux, Bibl. de la Pléiade, Paris 1937; repr. 1949. New, enlarged edn. 1966. (Handy edition in one volume.)

Oeuvres philosophiques. Textes établis, présentés et annotés par F. Alquié, 2 vols., Paris 1963–1967.

Discours de la méthode. Texte et commentaire, par É. Gilson. 2nd edn., Paris 1930; repr. 1939 and 1947; 4th edn., 1966.

Discours de la méthode. Précédé d'une introd. historique, suivi d'un commentaire critique, d'un glossaire et d'une chronologie, par G. Gadoffre. 2nd edn., Manchester 1961.

Les Méditations métaphysiques. Introd., notes et appendice par É. Thouverez, Paris 1932. (Reproduces the 1647 edn. of De Luynes's French translation, revised by Descartes; and the *Objections and Replies* transl. by Clerselier.)

Meditationes de prima philosophia. Texte latin et traduction du Duc de Luynes. Introd. et notes par G. Lewis. 2nd edn., Paris 1946; repr. 1960.

BIBLIOGRAPHY

Les Méditations métaphysiques. Texte, trad., *Objections et Réponses*, présentés par F. Khodoss. 5th edn., Paris 1968.

Regulae ad direçtionem ingenii: Règles pour la direction de l'esprit. Texte revu et traduit par G. Le Roy, Paris 1933. (Latin text and French translation on adjacent pages.)

Regulae ad directionem ingenii. Texte de l'édition Adam et Tannery; notice par H. Gouhier. 3rd edn., Paris 1959.

Les passions de l'âme. Introd. et notes par G. Rodis-Lewis, Paris 1955.

Traité des passions. Suivi de la correspondance avec la princesse Elisabeth. Présenté et annoté par F. Mizrachi, Paris 1965.

La naissance de la paix. Ballet dansé au Chasteau Royal de Stockholm (Dec. 1649). Publ. par A. Thibaudet et J. Nordstrom, 'Un ballet de Descartes', Revue de Genève I 163–185, Geneva 1920.

La naissance de la paix. Publ. also in: *Le Discours de la méthode . . . Lettres à Mersenne, à Balzac* . . . Postface par R. Campbell, Paris 1967.

Entretien avec Burman. Texte présenté, traduit et annoté par Ch. Adam, Paris 1937. (Concerning problematic passages in the *Meditations.*)

Correspondence of Descartes and Constantijn Huygens, 1635–1647, ed. L. Roth, Oxford 1926.

Correspondance, publiée avec introd. et notes par Ch. Adam et G. Milhaud, vols. I–VIII, Paris 1936–1963.

Lettres sur la morale: correspondance avec la princesse Elisabeth, Chanut et la reine Christine. Texte revu et présenté par J. Chevalier, Paris 1935; repr. 1955.

Correspondance avec Arnauld et Morus. Texte latin et traduction. Introd. et notes par G. Lewis, Paris 1953.

Lettres à Regius et remarques sur l'explication de l'esprit humain. Texte latin, traduction, introd. et notes par G. Rodis-Lewis, Paris 1959.

1

BIBLIOGRAPHY

II. ENGLISH TRANSLATIONS

The Philosophical Works of Descartes, rendered into English by E. S. Haldane and G. T. R. Ross, 2 vols., Cambridge 1911–12; repr. 1931–34; 1967. Paperback, New York 1955.

The Method, Meditations and Selections from the Principles of Descartes, transl. . . . by J. Veitch, fourteenth edn., Edinburgh and London 1907.

A Discourse on Method, transl. by J. Veitch, introd. by A. D. Lindsay. Everyman's Library, London and New York, n.d. (1912), repr. 1934 and 1949).

Discourse on Method; Meditations; Rules for the Direction of the Mind, transl. by L. J. Lafleur; New York and Indianapolis 1950; repr. 1961.

Discourse on Method; Optics, Geometry, and Meteorology, transl. by P. J. Olscamp, Indianapolis 1965.

The Geometry of René Descartes. Transl. from the French and Latin by D. E. Smith and M. L. Latham, Chicago 1925; repr. New York 1954.

The Living Thoughts of Descartes, with introd. essay by P. Valéry, London 1948.

Descartes' Philosophical Writings. Selected and translated by N. Kemp Smith, London 1952; New York 1952.

Philosophical Letters of Descartes, transl. and ed. by A. Kenny, Oxford, 1970.

III. BIOGRAPHIES

On Descartes's life, the following may be consulted:

A. BAILLET, *La Vie de Monsieur Des-Cartes*, Paris 1691.

CH. ADAM, *Vie et oeuvres de Descartes*, Paris 1910. (VOL. XII of the *Oeuvres de Descartes*, edd. Adam and Tannery, quoted above.)

E. S. HALDANE, *Descartes: his Life and Times*, London 1905.

CH. ADAM, *Descartes. Sa vie et son oeuvre*, Paris 1937.

li

J. Sirven, *Les années d'apprentissage de Descartes (1596–1628)*, Paris 1928.

C. de Rochemonteix, s.j., *Un collège de Jésuites aux XVIIe et XVIIIe siècles: le Collège Henri IV de La Flèche*, 4 vols., Le Mans 1899.

G. Cohen, *Écrivains français en Hollande dans la première moitié du XVIIe siècle*, Paris 1920.

IV. WORKS ON DESCARTES

The following is a list of selected works in English on Descartes's philosophy:

N. Kemp Smith, *Studies in Cartesian Philosophy*, London and New York 1902; repr. New York 1962.

É. Boutroux, 'Descartes and Cartesianism', in *The Cambridge Modern History*, vol. iv, ch. 27, Cambridge 1906; new issue 1934.

A. Boyce Gibson, *The Philosophy of Descartes*, London 1932; repr. New York 1967.

S. V. Keeling, *Descartes*, London 1934; 2nd edn., 1968.

——, 'Descartes'. Annual Lecture on a Master Mind. In *Proceedings of the British Academy*, vol. xxxiv, London 1948.

L. Roth, *Spinoza, Descartes and Maimonides*, Oxford 1924.

——, *Descartes' Discourse on Method*, Oxford 1937.

M. Versfeld, *An Essay on the Metaphysics of Descartes*, London 1940.

J. Maritain, *The Dream of Descartes, together with some other essays*, New York 1944; partly repeated in *Three Reformers: Luther—Descartes—Rousseau*, by the same, London 1947. (A criticism of Descartes from a neo-Thomist point of view.)

A. G. A. Balz, *Descartes and the Modern Mind*, New Haven and London 1952–7; repr. Hamden (Conn.) 1967.

——, *Cartesian Studies*, New York 1951. (On some followers of Descartes in the XVIIth century.)

H. H. JOACHIM, *Descartes's Rules for the Direction of the Mind*, reconstructed from notes taken by his pupils, ed. E. E. Harris, London 1957.

L. J. BECK, *The Method of Descartes. A study of the 'Regulae'*, Oxford 1952.

——, *The Metaphysics of Descartes. A Study of the Meditations*, Oxford 1965; New York 1965.

H. FRANKFURT, *Demons, Dreamers, and Madness. A Defense of Reason in Descartes' Meditations*, Indianapolis 1969.

F. BROADIE, *An Approach to Descartes' Meditations*, London 1970.

N. KEMP SMITH, *New Studies in the Philosophy of Descartes—Descartes as Pioneer*, London 1952.

A. KENNY, *Descartes. A Study of his Philosophy*, New York 1968.

Particular aspects are dealt with in the following books:

N. CHOMSKY, *Cartesian Linguistics*, New York 1966.

A. KOYRÉ, *Newtonian Studies*, Ch. III, 'Newton and Descartes', London 1965.

R. H. POPKIN, *The History of Scepticism from Erasmus to Descartes*, New York 1960.

L. D. C. ROSENFIELD, *From Beast-Machine to Man-Machine; Animal Soul in French Letters from Descartes to La Mettrie*; preface by P. Hazard, New York 1941; 2nd edn., 1968.

Studies on a variety of topics are to be found in the following two books:

A. SESONSKE and N. FLEMING, *Meta-'Meditations': Studies in Descartes*, Belmont, Calif., 1965. Contains, *inter alia;* N. MALCOLM, 'Dreaming and Skepticism'; O. K. BOUWSMA, 'Descartes' Evil Genius'; L. G. MILLER, 'Descartes, Mathematics, and God'; P. GASSENDI, 'Remarks concerning Meditation VI'; G. RYLE, 'Descartes' Myth'.

W. DONEY (ed.), *Descartes. A Collection of Critical Essays*, Garden City, N.Y., 1967; London and Melbourne 1968. Contains, *inter alia*, on the *Cogito*: A. J. AYER, 'I think, therefore I am'; B. WILLIAMS, 'The Certainty of the Cogito'; J. HINTIKKA,

'Cogito, Ergo Sum: Inference or Performance?'; N.
MALCOLM, 'Descartes' Proof that his Essence is Thinking'.—
On the *Meditations*: H. A. PRICHARD, 'Descartes' "Medita-
tions" '; A. K. STOUT, 'The Basis of Knowledge in Des-
cartes'; H. G. FRANKFURT, 'Descartes' Validation of Reason';
A. KENNY, 'Descartes on Ideas'.—Also: É. BRÉHIER, 'The
Creation of the Eternal Truths in Descartes's System';
A. GEWIRTH, 'Clearness and Distinctness in Descartes';
W. P. ALSTON, 'The Ontological Argument Revisited';
P. H. J. HOENEN, S.J., 'Descartes's Mechanicism'.

The following expositions in French and other languages are of
special interest:

(*a*) *General*

F. BOUILLIER, *Histoire de la philosophie cartésienne*, 2 vols., 3rd edn.,
Paris 1868.

L. LIARD, *Descartes*, Paris 1882; 2nd edn., 1903.

O. HAMELIN, *Le Système de Descartes*, Paris 1911; 2nd edn., 1921.

J. CHEVALIER, *Descartes*, Paris 1921.

ALAIN, *pseud.* (*i.e.* É. A. Chartier), *Idées: Platon, Descartes, Hegel*,
Paris 1932.

L. BRUNSCHVICG, *René Descartes*, Paris 1937.

L. LABERTHONNIÈRE, *Études sur Descartes*, 2 vols., Paris 1935.
——, *Études de Philosophie cartésienne*, Paris 1938.

J. BOORSCH, *État présent des études sur Descartes*, Paris 1937. (Contains a useful bibliography.)

H. GOUHIER, *Essais sur Descartes*, Paris 1937.

E. CASSIRER, *Descartes, Lehre-Persönlichkeit-Wirkung*, Stockholm
1939. Partly transl. in French by M. Francès and P.
Schrecker, in *Descartes, Corneille, Christine de Suède*, Paris 1942.

F. OLGIATI, *La filosofia di Descartes*, Milan 1937.

A. KOYRÉ, *Entretiens sur Descartes*, New York and Paris 1944.

C. SERRURIER, *Descartes, l'homme et le penseur*, Paris and Amsterdam
1951.

M. GUEROULT, *Descartes selon l'ordre des raisons*, vol. I: *L'âme et Dieu*, vol. II: *L'âme et le corps*, Paris 1953; 2nd edn., 1968.

F. ALQUIÉ, *Descartes. L'homme et l'œuvre*, Paris 1956.

G. RODIS-LEWIS, *Descartes. Initiation à la Philosophie*, Paris 1965.

Of special interest is the following volume which contains papers presented at a meeting of outstanding Descartes scholars, with a full report of the discussions revealing sharply conflicting points of view:

Descartes. Cahiers de Royaumont, Philosophie, No. II (Les Éditions de Minuit), Paris 1957.

(b) Particular aspects

H. GOUHIER, *La pensée religieuse de Descartes*, Paris 1924.

——, *La pensée métaphysique de Descartes*, Paris 1962.

——, *Les premières pensées de Descartes*, Paris 1958.

J. LAPORTE, *Le rationalisme de Descartes*, 2nd edn., Paris 1950.

G. RODIS-LEWIS, *Descartes et le Rationalisme*, Paris 1966.

É. GILSON, *La liberté chez Descartes et la théologie*, Paris 1913.

——, *Index scolastico-cartésien*, Paris 1913.

——, *Études sur le rôle de la pensée médiévale dans la formation du système cartésien*, Paris 1930; repr. 1951.

——, *Descartes und die Scholastik*, Bonn 1923.

A. KOYRÉ, *Essai sur l'idée de Dieu et les preuves de son existence chez Descartes*, Paris 1923.

L. BLANCHET, *Les antécédents historiques du 'Je pense, donc je suis'*, Paris 1920.

N. J. ABERCROMBIE, *Saint Augustine and French Classical Thought* (ch. III: 'Saint A. and the Cartesian Metaphysics'), Oxford 1938.

J. DE FINANCE, (S.J.), *Cogito cartésien et réflexion thomiste*, Paris 1946.

lv

É. Boutroux, *Des vérités éternelles chez Descartes*, Paris 1927. (French translation of B.'s Latin thesis of 1874, with preface by L. Brunschvicg.)

J. Wahl, *Du rôle de l'instant dans la philosophie de Descartes*, Paris 1920; 2nd edn., 1953.

G. Milhaud, *Descartes savant*, Paris 1921.

P. L. Boutroux, *L'imagination et les mathématiques selon Descartes*, Paris 1900.

J. Vuillemin, *Mathématiques et Métaphysique chez Descartes*, Paris 1960.

A. Koyré, *Études galiléennes*, Paris 1966.

P. Mouy, *Le développement de la physique cartésienne, 1646–1712*, Paris 1934.

Ch. Serrus, *La Méthode de Descartes et son application à la métaphysique*, Paris 1933.

A. Espinas, *Descartes et la morale*, 2 vols., Paris 1925; repr. 1937.

G. Lewis, *La morale de Descartes*, Paris 1957.

É. Krantz, *Essai sur l'esthétique de Descartes*, 2nd edn., Paris 1897.

A. Pirro, *Descartes et la musique*, Paris 1907.

W. M. Stewart, 'Descartes and Poetry' in *The Romanic Review*, Oct. 1938, pp. 212–42.

L. Lévy-Bruhl, 'The Cartesian Spirit and History', in *Philosophy and History* (eds. R. Klibansky and H. J. Paton), pp. 191–196, Oxford 1936; New York 1963.

G. Lanson, 'L'influence de la philosophie cartésienne sur la littérature française' in *Études d'histoire littéraire*, Paris 1929.

M. Leroy, *Descartes social*, Paris 1931.

G. Lewis, *L'individualité selon Descartes*, Paris 1950.

——, *Le problème de l'inconscient et le cartésianisme*, Paris 1950.

F. Alquié, *La découverte métaphysique de l'homme chez Descartes*, Paris 1950; 2nd edn., 1966.

M. Gueroult, *Nouvelles réflexions sur la preuve ontologique de Descartes*, Paris 1955.

J. Russier, *Sagesse cartésienne et religion; essai sur la connaissance de l'immortalité de l'âme*, Paris 1958.

L. Brunschvicg, *Descartes et Pascal, lecteurs de Montaigne*, Neuchâtel 1942; New York and Paris 1944.

Ch. Adam, *Descartes et ses amitiés féminines*, Paris 1932.

M. Néel, *Descartes et la princesse Élisabeth*, Paris 1946.

For Marx's and Engels' view of Descartes as the source of one of the two main trends of French materialism see:

F. Engels and K. Marx, *Die heilige Familie* (1845), ch. 6 (K. Marx, F. Engels, Werke, vol. II 132f., Berlin 1959). Engl. transl. (by R. Dixon), *The Holy Family, or Critique of critical critique*, Moscow 1956.

This is elaborated in many recent Marxist interpretations, e.g.

H. Lefebvre, *Descartes*, Paris 1947.

The following 'existentialist' interpretations may be mentioned:

K. Jaspers, *Descartes und die Philosophie*, Berlin and Leipzig 1937; repr. 1956. (French transl. by H. Pollnow, in *Revue Philosophique*, tom. LXII, Paris 1937, 'La pensée de Descartes et la philosophie'; and separately, Paris 1938.) Cp. the effective criticism of this book by E. Cassirer, *Die Philosophie im xvii. und xviii. Jahrhundert*, pp. 13–22 (*Philosophie: Chronique Annuelle*, publ. par l'Institut International de Collaboration Philosophique, fasc. V), Paris 1939.

J.-P. Sartre, *Descartes* (in the series, 'Les Classiques de la Liberté'), Paris 1946.

On the occasion of the tercentenary of the first appearance of the *Discours de la Méthode* collections of essays on Descartes were published in several periodicals. Of particular importance are the studies of various aspects of his thought in the following:

Revue Philosophique, tom. LXII, Paris 1937.

Revue de Métaphysique et de Morale, tom. XLIV, Paris 1937.

Revue de Synthèse, tom. XIV, Paris 1937.

Rivista di Filosofia Neo-Scolastica, Suppl. to tom. XIX, Milan 1937.

See also the following collections:

Travaux du IXe Congrès International de Philosophie (Congrès Descartes), publ. par R. Bayer, I: *Études Cartésiennes*, 3 vols., Paris 1937.

Descartes. Homenaje en el tercer centenario del 'Discurso del Método', Universidad de Buenos-Aires . . . 3 vols., Buenos-Aires 1937.

On the tercentenary of Descartes's death:

Revue Internationale de Philosophie, no 12, Brussels (April) 1950.

Descartes et le cartésianisme hollandais. Études et documents, Publications de l'Institut Français d'Amsterdam, Paris and Amsterdam 1951.

(c) Some Cartesian problems in later thought

R. A. WATSON, *The Downfall of Cartesianism, 1673–1712. A study of epistemological issues in late 17th century Cartesianism*, The Hague 1966.

G. W. LEIBNIZ, 'Notata quaedam circa vitam et doctrinam Cartesii'; 'Animadversiones in partem generalem Principiorum Cartesianorum'; and other critical writings, in *Die philosophischen Schriften*, TOM. IV, pp. 263–406, Berlin 1880.

Y. BELAVAL, *Leibniz, critique de Descartes*, Paris 1960.

C. S. PEIRCE, 'Questions Concerning Certain Faculties Claimed for Man'; 'Some consequences of four incapacities', in: *Collected Papers*, eds. C. Hartshorne and P. Weiss, vol. V, 135–189, Cambridge, Mass., 1934. (On 'The spirit of Cartesianism', 'in opposition to Cartesianism'.)

SIR E. WHITTAKER, *The Modern Approach to Descartes' Problem. The relation of the mathematical and physical sciences to philosophy* (The Herbert Spencer Lecture, Oxford 1948), Edinburgh 1948.

C. F. v. WEIZSÄCKER, *Descartes und die neuzeitliche Naturwissenschaft*, Hamburg 1958.

M. HAGMANN, *Descartes in der Auffassung durch die Historiker der Philosophie*, Winterthur 1955.

E. Husserl, *Cartesianische Meditationen und Pariser Vorträge* (= *Gesammelte Werke*, ed. Husserl-Archiv Louvain, TOM. 1), The Hague 1950. Appeared first in French transl., *Méditations cartésiennes. Introduction à la phénoménologie*, Paris 1931. Engl. transl. by D. Cairns, *Cartesian Meditations*, The Hague 1960.

M. Merleau-Ponty, *Phénoménologie de la perception*, Paris 1945; 4th edn., 1962. (Rejection of Descartes's 'Cogito', pp. 423–468.)

V. BIBLIOGRAPHIES AND SURVEYS

G. Sebba, *Bibliographia cartesiana. A critical guide to the Descartes literature 1880–1960*, The Hague 1964. (A comprehensive bibliography, with helpful comments.)

P. Mesnard, 'Descartes plus actuel que jamais', in: R. Klibansky (ed.), *Philosophy in the Mid-Century*, vol. IV, pp. 132–136, Florence 1959.

G. Rodis-Lewis, 'Descartes', in: R. Klibansky (ed.), *Contemporary Philosophy*, vol. III, pp. 73–81, Florence 1969.

W. Doney (ed.), *Descartes* (see p. liii above), pp. 369–386: 'Bibliography', lists a useful selection of articles in English, e.g. on: 1. Doubt concerning the senses and the argument from dreaming; 2. The *Cogito*; 3. The truth of clear and distinct perceptions and the charge of circularity (see also G. Nakhnikian, 'The Cartesian Circle revisited'. American Philosophical Quarterly, vol. IV, no. 3 (1967) pp. 251–255); 4. Arguments for the existence of God; 5. Substance, mind and body; 6. Clear and distinct ideas and method; 7. Extended substance and physics; 8. Comparisons with other thinkers.

McGill University, Montreal   Raymond Klibansky

CHRONOLOGICAL TABLE

1596   Descartes born at La Haye, in Touraine (March 31).

1606   Enters the Jesuit college of La Flèche.

1611   Hears of Galileo's having discovered the satellites of Jupiter.

1614   Leaves La Flèche.

1616   Takes his degree in law at Poitiers.

1618   Goes to Holland to serve in the army under Prince Maurice of Nassau.

Makes the acquaintance of Beeckman at Breda.

1619   Leaves Holland. Attends the Emperor Ferdinand's coronation.

Joins the Duke of Bavaria's forces.

There flashes upon him the idea of extending the method of analytical geometry to other studies (Nov. 10).

1622   Returns to France.

1623-25   Travels in Italy.

1625-28   After returning to France, stays sometimes in the country and sometimes in Paris.

1628   Composes the *Rules for the Guidance of the Mind.*

Leaves for Franeker, Holland, in the autumn.

1630   Moves to Amsterdam. Matriculates at Leyden University.

1632   Moves to Deventer.

1633   Returns to Amsterdam. Learns of Galileo's condemnation by the Inquisition.

1634   Suppresses his treatise on *The World.*

1635   His natural daughter is christened.

Moves to Utrecht.

1636   Moves to Leyden.

1637   The *Discourse on Method* is published (in June).
Moves to Santport.

1640 Returns to Leyden.

Bereaved of his father and his daughter.

1641 Moves to Endegeest.

The *Meditations* are published (in August).

1641-3 Quarrels between Descartes and Voëtius, Rector of Utrecht University.

1642 Utrecht University officially decides in favour of the old philosophy.

1643 Frequently visits Princess Elizabeth of Bohemia.

Moves to Egmond-op-den-Hoef.

Judgment is pronounced against him by the Utrecht magistrates.

1644 Visits France (May to November).

The *Principles of Philosophy* are published (in July).

On his return to Holland, takes up permanent residence at Egmond-Binnen near Alkmaar, till he leaves Holland in 1649.

1645 After receiving a letter from Descartes, the Utrecht magistrates forbid printed discussion of the new philosophy.

1647 Has trouble with Leyden University.

Visits France in the summer, and talks with Pascal.

Is awarded (but does not receive) a pension from the King of France.

1648 Again visits France, but leaves hurriedly upon the outbreak of the Fronde rebellion.

1649 Leaves Holland for Sweden at the invitation of Queen Christina.

Publishes the *Treatise on the Passions* (November).

1650 Dies at Stockholm on February 11.

PRIVATE THOUGHTS

from a Notebook begun 1 January 1619
and completed during the course
of the next few years

PRIVATE THOUGHTS [1]

Just as comedians are counselled not to let shame appear on their foreheads, and so put on a mask: so likewise, now that I am to mount the stage of the world, where I have so far been a spectator, I come forward in a mask.

When ingenious discoveries were presented to my notice as a young man, I used to try myself on my own account whether I could make the same discoveries even without reading the author; and from doing this I gradually came to notice that I was using certain rules.

The sciences now have masks on them; if the masks were taken off they would appear supremely beautiful. On surveying the chain of the sciences one will regard them as not being more difficult to retain in one's mind than the number-series is.

To all men's minds there are bounds set that they cannot pass. If people cannot use the principles for discovery, through lack of wit, nevertheless they can recognise the true value of the sciences; and this is enough to enable them to form correct judgments as to the estimate of things.

Vices I call diseases of the mind; they are not so easily diagnosed as diseases of the body; for we have often known true health of body, but never of mind.

In the year 1620 I began to understand the foundations of a wonderful discovery.

A dream, November 1619, about Ausonius Ode 7, beginning *Quod vitae sectabor iter ?* (Which road in life shall I follow ?)

---

[1] [For these Notes, known from a copy made by Leibniz, see above, Translators' Note.—Tr.]

3

It might seem strange that opinions of weight are found in the works of poets rather than philosophers. The reason is that poets wrote through enthusiasm and imagination; there are in us seeds of knowledge, as ⟨of fire⟩ in a flint; philosophers extract them by way of reason, but poets strike them out by imagination, and then they shine more bright.

The sayings of the sages can be reduced to a very few general rules.

There is in things one active power, love, charity, harmony.

The Lord has made three marvels: things out of nothingness; free will; and the Man who is God.

DISCOURSE ON THE METHOD

of rightly directing one's Reason
and of seeking Truth in the Sciences

*From the French text
published in 1637*

I

Good sense is the most fairly distributed thing in the world; for everyone thinks himself so well supplied with it, that even those who are hardest to satisfy in every other way do not usually desire more of it than they already have. In this matter it is not likely that everybody is mistaken; it rather goes to show that the power of judging well and distinguishing truth from falsehood, which is what we properly mean by good sense or reason, is naturally equal in all men; and furthermore, that the diversity of our opinions does not arise because some men are more rational than others, but only because we direct our thoughts along different ways, and do not consider the same things. For it is not enough to have a sound mind; the main thing is to apply it well. The greatest souls are capable of the greatest vices, as well as the greatest virtues; and those who walk only very slowly may make much more progress, if they always follow the straight road, than those who run and go astray from it.

For myself, I have never presumed to think my mind in any way more perfect than ordinary men's; indeed, I have often wished I had thoughts as quick, or an imagination as clear and distinct, or a memory as ample and as readily available, as some other people. And besides these I know of no other qualities that make for the perfection of the mind; for as regards reason or sense, inasmuch as it is the only thing that makes us men and distinguishes us from brutes, I should like to hold that it is to be found complete in each of us, and to follow here the common opinion of philosophers, who say that ' more ' and ' less ' apply only in the field of ' accidents ', and not

7

as between the 'forms' or natures of 'individuals' of the same 'species'.

But I venture to say that I think I have been very lucky; for certain paths that I have happened to follow ever since my youth have led me to considerations and maxims out of which I have formed a method; and this, I think, is a means to a gradual increase in my knowledge that will raise it little by little to the highest point allowed by the mediocrity of my mind and the brief duration of my life. For I have already reaped such fruits that although in my judgments of myself I try to lean towards diffidence rather than presumption; and although, when I regard with a philosophic eye the various activities and pursuits of men at large, there is hardly one but seems to me vain and useless; nevertheless, I do not fail to feel extreme satisfaction at the progress I think I have already made in the search for truth; and I conceive such hopes for the future that I venture to believe that, if there is any one among purely human occupations that has solid worth or importance, it is the one I have chosen.

All the same, it may be that I am wrong; what I take for gold and diamonds may be only a little copper and glass. I know how very liable we are to error in what relates to ourselves, and how much our friends' judgments are to be suspected when they are in our favour. But I shall be delighted to show in this Discourse what paths I have followed, and to represent my life as it were in a picture; in order that everybody may be able to judge of my methods for himself, and that my learning from common report what opinions are held of them may give me a new means of self-instruction, in addition to my usual means.

My design, then, is not to teach here the method everybody ought to follow in order to direct his reason rightly, but only to show how I have tried to direct my own. Those who set themselves to give precepts must regard themselves as more skilful than those to whom they give them; and if they fail in the smallest point, they must bear the blame. But I offer this work only as a history, or, if you like, a fable, in which there may perhaps be found, besides some examples that may be imitated, many others that it will be well not to follow. I thus hope that it will be useful to some people without being harmful to anybody, and that all will be grateful to me for my frankness.

I was brought up on letters from my childhood; and since it was urged on me that by means of them one could acquire clear and assured knowledge of all that is useful in life, I was extremely eager to learn them. But as soon as I had finished the whole course of studies at the end of which one is normally admitted among the ranks of the learned, I completely altered my opinion. For I found myself embarrassed by so many doubts and errors, that it seemed to me that the only profit I had had from my efforts to acquire knowledge was the progressive discovery of my own ignorance. And yet I was in one of the most celebrated schools in Europe; and I thought there must be learned men there, if there were such in any part of the globe. I had learned everything that the others were learning there; and, not content with the studies in which we were instructed, I had even perused all the books that came into my hands, treating of the studies considered most curious and recondite. At the same time I knew what judgment others made about me; I did not find myself considered inferior to my fellow-students, although there were some among them already marked out to fill the places of our masters. Moreover, our age seemed to me to be as flourishing, and as fertile in powerful minds, as any preceding one. This made me take the liberty of judging of all other men by myself, and of holding that there was no such learning in the world as I had been previously led to hope for.

I nevertheless did not fail to esteem the exercises with which people busy themselves in the schools. I realised that the languages we learn are necessary for the under-standing of ancient literature; that the gracefulness of the fables stimulates the mind; that the memorable deeds related in historical works elevate it, and help to form one's judgment if they are read with discretion; that the reading of good books is like a conversation with the best men of past centuries—in fact like a prepared conversation, in which they reveal only the best of their thought; that eloquence has points of incomparable strength and beauty; that poetry contains passages of entrancing delicacy and sweetness; that mathematics contains very subtle devices that can greatly help to gratify our curiosity, as well as to further all the arts and lessen human toil; that moral treatises comprise various lessons and exhortations to virtue that are highly useful; that theology teaches how to attain heaven; that philosophy enables one to talk plausibly on all subjects and win the admiration of people less learned than oneself; that jurisprudence, medicine, and the other sciences bring honours and wealth to those who cultivate them; and finally that it is well to have examined them all, however much superstition and error they contain, so as to know their true value and avoid being deceived.

But I thought I had already given enough time to languages, and likewise to reading the works of the ancients and their histories and fables. For it is almost the same thing to hold converse with men of other centuries as to travel. It is well to know something about the manners of different peoples, in order to form a sounder judgment of our own, and not think everything contrary to our own ways absurd and irrational, as people usually do when they have never seen anything else. But a man who spends too much time travelling becomes a foreigner in his own country; and too much curiosity about the customs of past centuries goes as a rule with great ignorance of present customs. Besides, fables make one imagine various events as possible when they are not; and the most faithful historians, even if they do not alter or exaggerate the importance of matters to make them more readable, at any rate almost always leave out the meaner and less striking circumstances of the events; consequently, the remainder has a false appearance, and those who govern their conduct by examples drawn from history are liable to fall into the extravagances of the paladins of romance and conceive designs beyond their powers.

I esteemed eloquence highly, and I was in love with poetry; but I thought both were natural gifts of the mind rather than fruits of study. Those who reason most powerfully, and whose thoughts are best digested so as to be made clear and intelligible, are still the best able to urge their proposals, even though they speak only *bas breton* and have never learnt rhetoric. And those whose fancies are most pleasing and who can express them with the greatest embellishment and sweetness would not fail to be the best poets, though unacquainted with the *Ars Poetica*.

I especially delighted in mathematics, because of the certainty and self-evidence of its reasonings; but I did not yet discern its real use; thinking that it only subserved the mechanical arts, I was surprised that on such firm and solid foundations nothing more exalted had been built. The moral treatises of the ancient pagans, on the other hand, I compared to proud and magnificent palaces built only on sand and mud. They highly exalt the virtues, and make them appear more worthy of esteem than anything in the world; but they do not teach us well how to recognise the virtues; often what they call by so fair a name is really insensibility, or pride, or despair, or parricide.

11

I revered our theology, and aspired as much as anyone else to attain heaven; but having learnt as an assured fact that the way is not less open to the most ignorant than to the most learned, and that the revealed truths that lead us there are above our intellect, I should not have dared to subject them to my weak reasonings ; and I thought that to undertake an examination of them required for its success some extraordinary aid from heaven; that one would have to be superhuman.

I will say nothing of philosophy but this: seeing that it has been cultivated by the most outstanding minds of several centuries, and that nevertheless up to now there is no point but is disputed and consequently doubtful, I had not enough presumption to hope to fare better there than others had; and considering how many different opinions on a given matter may be upheld by instructed persons, whereas there can at most be only one that is true, I almost regarded as false whatever was no more than plausible.

As for the other sciences, inasmuch as they borrow their first principles from philosophy, I judged that no solid building could have been made on such shaky foundations; and neither the honour nor the profit that they promised was enough to induce me to learn them. For I did not feel myself obliged, thank heaven, to mend my fortune by making science my profession; and though I made no pretence of a Cynic contempt for fame, I yet made very slight account of fame that I could only hope to win by false pretences. Finally, as regards pseudo-sciences, I thought I knew their worth well enough already so as not to be liable to be taken in by the promises of an alchemist, the predictions of an astrologer, the imposture of a magician, or the artifices and boasts of those who profess to know more than they do.

That was why, as soon as my age allowed me to pass from under the control of my instructors, I entirely abandoned the study of letters, and resolved not to seek after any science but what might be found within myself or in the great book of the world. So I spent the rest of my youth in travel, in frequenting courts and armies, in mixing with people of various dispositions and ranks, in collecting a variety of experiences, in proving myself in the circumstances where fortune placed me, and in reflecting always on things as they came up, in a way that might enable me to derive some profit from them. It appeared to me that I could find much more truth in such reasonings as every man makes about the affairs that concern himself, and whose issue will very soon make him suffer if he has made a miscalculation, than in the reasonings of a man of letters in his study, about speculations that produce no effect and have no importance for him—except that perhaps he will feel the more conceited about them, the more remote they are from common sense, since he will have had to use the greater amount of ingenuity and skill in order to make them plausible. And I always had an extreme desire to learn to distinguish truth from falsehood in order to have clear insight into my actions and proceed in this life with assurance.

It is true that, so long as I merely considered the ways of other men, I found little ground for assurance; here also I observed as much diversity as I had previously in the field of philosophical opinions. Thus the greatest profit I derived here was this: from noticing many things that seem to us extravagant and ridiculous, but are none the less commonly accepted and approved in other great nations, I learnt not to believe too firmly anything that I had been convinced of only by example and custom. I thus gradually freed myself from many errors that may obscure the light of nature in us and make us less capable of hearing reason. But after spending some years thus in study of the book of the world, and in trying to gain experience, there came a day when I resolved to make my studies within myself, and use all my powers of mind to choose the paths I must follow. This undertaking, I think, succeeded much better than it would have if I had never left my country or my books.

II

I was in Germany at the time; the fortune of war (the war that is still going on) had called me there. While I was returning to the army from the Emperor's coronation, the onset of the winter held me up in quarters in which I found no conversation to interest me; and since, fortunately, I was not troubled by any cares or passions, I spent the whole day shut up alone in a stove-heated room, and was at full liberty to discourse with myself about my own thoughts. One of the first things I thought it well to consider was that as a rule there is not such great perfection in works composed of several parts, and proceeding from the hands of various artists, as in those on which one man has worked alone. Thus we see that buildings undertaken and carried out by a single architect are generally more seemly and better arranged than those that several hands have sought to adapt, making use of old walls that were built for other purposes. Again, those ancient cities which were originally mere boroughs, and have become large towns in process of time, are as a rule badly laid out, as compared with those towns of regular pattern that are laid out by a designer on an open plain to suit his fancy; while the buildings severally considered are often equal or superior artistically to those in planned towns, yet, in view of their arrangement—here a large one, there a small—and the way they make the streets twisted and irregular, one would say that it was chance that placed them so, not the will of men who had the use of reason. And yet all along there have been officials whose task it was to see that private buildings subserved public amenity. This shows the difficulty of great accomplishments when one

15

must needs work on the basis of other men's labours. Similarly, I conceived, peoples that were once half-savage and grew civilised only by degrees, and therefore made their laws only in so far as they were forced to by the inconvenience of crimes and disputes, could not have such good public order as those that have observed, ever since they first assembled, the decrees of some wise legislator. Likewise, it is quite certain that the constitution of the true religion, whose ordinances were made by God alone, must be incomparably better ordered than any others. And to speak of human affairs, I believe that the great prosperity of Sparta was due, not to the goodness of each of its laws in particular (for many were very strange, and even immoral), but to their having been devised by a single man, and thus tending to a single end. It thus seemed to me that since book-learning, at least in so far as its reasonings are only probable, not demonstrative, has been made up, and has developed gradually, from the opinions of many different men, it is therefore not so close to the truth as the simple reasonings that a man of good sense may perform as regards things that come up. Again, I reflected, we were all children before we were men; we must have been governed a long time by our own appetites on the one hand and our preceptors on the other; these two sides must frequently have been opposed, and very likely there have been times when neither side urged us to the best course. Thus it is practically impossible for our judgments to be so clear or so firm as they would have been if we had had the full use of our reason from the moment of birth, and had never had any other guide.

True, we do not observe that all the houses of a city are pulled down merely with the design of rebuilding them in a different style and thus making the streets more seemly; but we do see that many men have theirs pulled down in order to rebuild them, and that they are even sometimes

16

obliged to, when the houses are in danger of falling in any case, and the foundations are insecure. By this parallel I became convinced that it would not be sensible for a private citizen to plan the reform of a state by altering all its foundations and turning it upside down in order to set it on its own feet again, or again for him to reform the body of the sciences or the established order of teaching them in the schools;- but that as to the opinions I had so far admitted to belief, I could not do better than to set about rejecting them bodily, so that later on I might admit to belief either other, better opinions, or even the same ones, when once I made them square with the norm of reason. I firmly believed that in this way I should much better succeed in the conduct of my life than if I built only upon old foundations, and leant upon principles which in my youth I had taken on trust without ever examining whether they were true. For although I recognised various difficulties in this undertaking, nevertheless they were not irremediable, nor were they comparable to those attending the slightest reform in public affairs. Such large bodies are very hard to raise up when once they fall, or even to keep up when once they are shaken; and their fall cannot but be a heavy one. Again, any imperfections they may possess (and the very differences among States make it certain that many do possess them) have no doubt been much softened by custom; custom has even avoided or imperceptibly corrected many faults that prudence could not so well provide against. Finally, they are almost always more tolerable than any change would be; just as high roads that wind about between the hills become gradually so well beaten and convenient through being much used that it is far better to follow them than to try to take a short cut by climbing rocks and going down to the bottom of precipices.

That is why I could in no way approve of those turbulent and restless characters who, although not summoned by birth or fortune to the control of public affairs, are yet constantly effecting some new reform—in their own heads. And if I thought there was the least ground in this work for my being suspected of this madness, I should be very loth to let it be published. My plan has never gone further than an attempt to reform my own thoughts and rebuild them on ground that is altogether my own. Although my work has given me much pleasure, so that I am now showing you the draft, it is not that I want anyone to imitate it. Those whom God has favoured more highly will very likely have loftier designs; but I am afraid that for many people even my own design may be too bold. The mere resolution to get rid of all opinions one has so far admitted to belief is in itself not an example for everybody to follow; the world is mostly made up of two types of mind to which it is wholly unsuitable. First, there are those who think they are cleverer than they are, and cannot help forming precipitate judgments, and are not patient enough to direct all their thoughts in an orderly way; consequently, if they once took the liberty of doubting the principles they had accepted, and leaving the common track, they would never be able to keep to the path that one must take as a short cut, and would remain lost all their life long. Secondly, there are those who have enough sense or modesty to judge that they are not so well able to distinguish truth from falsehood as some other men are who could instruct them; such people must content themselves with following the opinions of those others, rather than look for better opinions on their own account.

For myself, I should doubtless have belonged to the latter class, if I had only had one teacher, or had never known the differences that have always existed between the opinions of those best qualified. But from college days I had learnt that one can imagine nothing so strange and incredible but has been said by some philosopher; and

since then, while travelling, I have realised that those
whose opinions are quite opposed to ours are not, for all
that, without exception barbarians and savages; many of
them enjoy as good a share of reason as we do, or better.
Again, I considered how a given man with a given mind
develops otherwise when he is brought up from infancy
among Frenchmen or Germans than he would if he
had always lived among Chinese or cannibals; how, again,
even in the fashion of dress, the very thing that we liked
ten years ago, and may like again ten years hence, seems
to us at present extravagant and ridiculous. Thus it is by
custom and example that we are persuaded, much more than
by any certain knowledge; at the same time, a majority
of votes is worthless as a proof, in regard to truths that are
even a little difficult of discovery; for it is much more
likely that one man should have hit upon them for himself
than that a whole nation should. Accordingly I could
choose nobody whose opinions I thought preferable to other
men's; and I was as it were forced to become my own guide.

But, like a man walking alone in the dark, I resolved to
go so slowly, and use so much circumspection in all matters,
as to be secured against falling, even if I made very little
progress. In fact, I would not begin rejecting out of hand
any of the opinions that might have previously crept into
my belief without being introduced by reason, until I
had first taken enough time to plan the work I was undertaking, and to look for the true method of attaining
knowledge of everything that my mind could grasp.

The subjects I had studied a little when I was younger
included, among the branches of philosophy, logic, and
in mathematics, geometrical analysis and algebra. These
three arts or sciences, it appeared, ought to make some
contribution towards my design. But on examination I
found that so far as logic is concerned, syllogisms and most
of the other techniques serve for explaining to others what

one knows; or even, like the art of Lully,[1] for talking without judgment about matters one is ignorant of; rather than for learning anything. And although logic comprises many correct and excellent rules, there are mixed up with these so many others that are harmful or superfluous, that sorting them out is almost as difficult as extracting a Diana or Minerva from a block of rough marble. As for the analysis of the ancients, and the algebra of our time, besides their covering only a highly abstract and apparently useless range of subjects, the former is always so restricted to the consideration of figures, that it cannot exercise the understanding without greatly wearying the imagination; and in the latter, there is such a complete slavery to certain rules and symbols that there results a confused and obscure art that embarrasses the mind, instead of a science that develops it. That was why I thought I must seek for some other method, which would comprise the advantages of these three and be exempt from their defects. And as a multitude of laws often gives occasion for vices, so that a State is much better ruled when it has only a very few laws which are very strictly observed; in the same way, instead of the great number of rules that make up logic, I thought the following four would be enough, provided that I made a firm and constant resolution not to fail even once in the observance of them.

The first was never to accept anything as true if I had not evident knowledge of its being so; that is, carefully to avoid precipitancy and prejudice, and to embrace in my judgment only what presented itself to my mind so clearly and distinctly that I had no occasion to doubt it.

The second, to divide each problem I examined into as many parts as was feasible, and as was requisite for its better solution.

[1 A kind of logical symbolism invented by the Catalan philosopher, Raymond Lully (1235-1315).—Tr.]

The third, to direct my thoughts in an orderly way; beginning with the simplest objects, those most apt to be known, and ascending little by little, in steps as it were, to the knowledge of the most complex; and establishing an order in thought even when the objects had no natural priority one to another.

And the last, to make throughout such complete enumerations and such general surveys that I might be sure of leaving nothing out.

Those long chains of perfectly simple and easy reasonings by means of which geometers are accustomed to carry out their most difficult demonstrations had led me to fancy that everything that can fall under human knowledge forms a similar sequence; and that so long as we avoid accepting as true what is not so, and always preserve the right order for deduction of one thing from another, there can be nothing too remote to be reached in the end, or too well hidden to be discovered. I had no great difficulty over looking for a starting-point. I knew already that I must start with the simplest objects, those most apt to be known; and seeing that, among all those who have so far sought for truth in the sciences, only mathematicians have been able to find some demonstrations, that is to say, some certain and self-evident reasonings, I had no doubt that I must start from the objects that they treated of. The only advantage I hoped for here was that I should habituate my mind to nourish itself on truths and not acquiesce in bad arguments. But for all that, I had no idea of learning all the special sciences commonly called mathematics. While these treat of different objects, they yet all agree in merely considering relations or proportions that hold between these objects. I thought it best, therefore, to treat only of such proportions generally; to consider as terms between which they held only such objects as would facilitate the knowledge of them; and at the same time not to restrict them in any way to such terms, since I wanted to improve their application wherever else it might be suitable. I took it into account that for such knowledge I should sometimes have to consider each of the relations severally, and sometimes merely to remember them or again to treat of several simultaneously. I decided therefore that relations taken severally were best regarded as holding between straight lines; for I could find no simpler objects—none more distinctly representable in imagination and sensation; but that for purposes of record or of dealing with several simultaneous relations, I had best use certain symbols, as compact as possible; in this way I aimed at borrowing all that is best in geometrical analysis and in algebra, and correcting all the defects of one by means of the other.

And in fact I venture to say that the exact observance of the few rules I had chosen gave me such powers of unravelling all the problems covered by these two sciences that in the two or three months I spent in examining them I not only solved some that I had formerly considered very difficult, but was also in the end apparently able to determine by what means, and to what extent, a solution was possible, even in fields where I was still ignorant of one. To this end, I began with the simplest and most general problems; and every truth I discovered was a rule applicable towards further discoveries. My claim will not appear too conceited if you consider that, since there is only one truth in any matter, whoever discovers it knows as much about it as can be known. For instance, a child who has been taught arithmetic and does an addition according to the rules may be assured that he has discovered all that the human mind can discover as regards the sum he is considering. Indeed, my method of following the proper order and exactly enumerating all conditions of the problem comprises everything that gives the rules of arithmetic their certainty.

But my special pleasure in this method was that it ensured my using my reason in all fields, if not perfectly, at least as best I could; and besides, with practice I found my mind becoming habituated to conceive its objects more clearly and distinctly; and since my method was not bound up with any special subject-matter, I hoped to apply it to the problems of other sciences as usefully as I had in algebra. Not that I should have ventured off-hand to examine all that might arise; that would in itself have been contrary to the prescribed order. But observing that the principles of those sciences must all be derived from philosophy, in which so far I could discover nothing certain, I thought my first task must be to establish such certainty; and since this is the most important matter of all, and the field where precipitation and prejudice are most to be feared, I thought I must not try to accomplish this till I had reached a more mature age than twenty-three (my age at the time), and had first spent a long time in preparation; I must eradicate from my mind all the errors I had so far accepted, and amass a variety of experiences to afford materials for my reasonings; and I must constantly practise my chosen method, in order to become steadily better and better grounded in it.

III

Before beginning to rebuild the house in which one lives, one must not merely pull it down, and make provision for materials, and for architects (unless one does one's own architecture), and besides have ready a carefully drawn plan; one must also have provided oneself with another house where one may conveniently stay while the work goes on. In the same way, in order not to be in a state of indecision in action at a time when reason would oblige me to be so in thought, and not to fail to live thereafter as happily as I could, I formed a provisional code of morals, consisting just of three or four maxims; I will tell you what they are.

The first was to obey the laws and customs of my country; faithfully keeping to the religion in which by God's favour I was brought up from childhood, and ruling my life in all other matters by the most moderate and least extravagant opinions commonly accepted in practice by the most judicious men among those with whom I should have to live. For since I had begun from that time to count my own opinions worth nothing, because I wished to submit them all to examination, I was sure I could do no better than to follow those of judicious men. There may indeed be men as judicious among the Persians or Chinese as among ourselves; but it seemed to me most useful to rule my life according to the views of those with whom I should have to live. And in order to have real knowledge of their opinions, I thought I must attend to what they practised rather than what they preached; not only because, in the corruption of our manners, few people will say what they really believe, but also because many people do not

24

know this themselves. For the mental act of believing a thing is different from the act of knowing that one believes it; and the one act often occurs without the other. Among many opinions equally well accepted I chose only the most moderate; both because these are always the most convenient in practice, and are probably superior (extremes being as a rule bad); and also in order that I might not depart from the right path, in case of being mistaken, as widely as I should if I chose one extreme when I ought to have pursued the other. In particular I placed in the class of extremes all promises by which one renounces some of one's freedom. Not that I disapprove of the laws allowing people to make vows or contracts that oblige them to be faithful to some good end (or even, for the security of commerce, to some indifferent end), as a remedy against the inconstancy of weak characters. Observing, however, that there was nothing in the world that remained always in the same condition, and that my own special aim was to perfect my judgments more and more, not to let them deteriorate, I should have thought I was grossly sinning against good sense if, on account of approving of something at the moment, I were to bind myself to regard it as good later on, when it might have ceased to be so, or when I might have ceased to regard it as such.

My second maxim was to be as firm and resolute in action as I could, and to follow out my most doubtful opinions, when once I had settled upon them, no less steadily than if they had been thoroughly assured. In this I would imitate travellers lost in a wood; they must not wander about turning now to this side, now to that, and still less must they stop in one place; they must keep walking as straight as they can in one direction, and not change course for slight reasons, even if at the beginning their choice was determined perhaps by mere chance; for in

this way, even if they do not arrive just where they wish, they will at least finally get somewhere where they will probably be better off than in the middle of a wood. Similarly, it often happens in life that action brooks no delay; and it is a sure truth that, when we cannot discern the most correct opinion, we must follow the most probable. And even if we can observe no more likelihood in one than another, we must settle upon some opinion, and consider it afterwards in practice not as doubtful but as perfectly true and certain; for our ground for settling upon it really is of this sort. This maxim could henceforth set me free from all the regrets and remorse that usually trouble the consciences of those weak and stumbling characters who let themselves set out on some course of action as a good one and then in their inconstancy decide afterwards that it is bad.

My third maxim was to try always to conquer myself rather than fortune; to change my desires rather than the order of the world; and in general to form the habit of thinking that only our thoughts are completely within our own power; so that, after we have done our best, everything in the field of external things that we do not succeed in getting is an absolute impossibility so far as we are concerned. This, I thought, would be sufficient to prevent my wanting in future what I could not obtain, and thus to make me content. For our will naturally pursues only what our understanding represents to it as somehow possible; so assuredly, if we consider all external goods as equally remote from our power, we shall not repine at the lack of those which seem our birthright when we are deprived of them by no fault of our own, any more than we do at not possessing the kingdoms of China and Mexico. And making a virtue of necessity, as the phrase is, we shall not desire health when we are ill, or freedom when we are in prison, any more than we now wish to have bodies of a material as incorruptible as diamond, or wings to fly like birds. But I admit it needs long practice and repeated meditation to get used to regarding everything in this light. This, I think, was the secret of those philosophers of old who could withdraw from the dominion of fortune, and, amid suffering and poverty, could debate whether their Gods were as happy as they. For they continually busied themselves with considering the limits laid down by nature, and so thoroughly convinced themselves that only their thoughts were in their own power, that this was enough to restrain them from any desire for other objects; and their command of their thoughts was so absolute that they had some reason for thinking themselves richer, more powerful, freer, and happier than all other men; for without this philosophy, however favoured men may be by nature and fortune, they never command what they want to such an extent.

Finally, to conclude this moral code, I decided to review the various occupations of human life so as to try to choose the best; and without wishing to say anything about other people's occupations, I thought I could do no better than to go on with the one I was then engaged in; namely, to spend all my life in cultivating my reason, and to advance as far as I could in the knowledge of truth, following my self-imposed method. Since beginning to use this method, I had had such extreme pleasures that I thought one could not get greater or purer ones in this life; every day I discovered by means of it some truths that appeared to me quite important and that were commonly not known to other men; and my delight in them so filled my mind that nothing else could affect it. Besides, the only basis of the three preceding maxims was my aim to continue to gain knowledge. For God has given each of us some light to distinguish truth and falsehood; and I should have thought myself obliged not to rest content, even for a moment, with other men's opinions, if I had not resolved in due course to use my own judgment in examining them; nor could I have avoided scruples about following them, if I had not hoped, all the same, to lose no chance of discovering better opinions if possible. Finally, I could not have limited my desires, or been content, if I had not been following a path by which I thought I could acquire all the knowledge, and therewith all the true good, that was within my reach. For our will does not choose to pursue or avoid anything unless that be represented by our understanding as good or bad; so right judgment suffices for right action; and the best possible judgment suffices for one's doing the very best that one can, that is, for one's acquiring all virtues and in general all other attainable goods; and with this certainty, one cannot fail to be happy.

Having assured myself of these maxims, I set them on one side, along with the truths of faith, which have always come first in my belief; and as regards all my other opinions, I was free to undertake getting rid of them. I hoped for better success in this if I mixed with men than if I stayed any longer in the stove-heated room, where I had had all these ideas; so I set out again on my return journey, before the winter was well ended. I spent the whole of the following nine years in roaming about in the world, aiming to be a spectator rather than an actor in all the comedies of life; and while reflecting especially on those points of every subject that might make it suspect and give us occasion to make mistakes, I kept on all the time eradicating from my mind any errors that might have slipped into it so far. Not that I imitated the sceptics, who doubt just for the sake of doubting and affect to be always undecided; on the contrary, my whole aim was to reach security, and cast aside loose earth and sand so as to reach rock or clay. I had fair success, I think; I tried to discover the falsity or uncertainty of the propositions

I was examining not by weak conjectures, but by clear and certain reasoning; I thus never met with propositions so doubtful but that I drew from them some pretty certain conclusion—if it was only the conclusion that no certainty was to be found here. And, just as when one pulls down an old house, one ordinarily keeps the demolished materials for building a new one; so, in the process of destroying those of my opinions which I judged to be ill-founded, I made several observations, and acquired a variety of experience, of which I have since made use in establishing more certain opinions. Moreover, I continued practising my self-imposed method; besides being generally careful to direct my thoughts according to the rules, I reserved some hours from time to time to be used specially in practising it in problems of mathematics, or perhaps also in some others that I could reduce as it were to a semi-mathematical form, abstracting from any principles of other sciences, which I found insufficiently secure. . . . And so, while in appearance my life was just like that of anybody who has no care but to lead a pleasant and innocent life, who is careful to keep his pleasures free from vice, and who goes in for all reputable pastimes to enjoy leisure without boredom, I was steadily pursuing my design, and profiting by the knowledge of truth; all the more, perhaps, than I should have if I had only read books or mixed with educated men.

However, these nine years passed without my taking any side as regards the commonly disputed problems of the schools, or beginning to look for the basis of any philosophy more certain than the popular one. The example of many fine intellects that had previously had this plan, and had not, I thought, met with any success, made me imagine the difficulties to be great; perhaps I should not have ventured to undertake it so soon, if I had not noticed that some people were spreading a rumour of my having already succeeded. I cannot say what was the foundation for this idea; if my conversation contributed towards it to some extent, it must have been because I admitted ignorance more frankly than is usual with people who have made some study; and perhaps also because I showed my reasons for doubting much that other people regard as certain; rather than because I boasted of some positive doctrine. But being unwilling to be taken for what I was not, I thought I must try by every means to live up to my reputation; and just eight years ago this wish made me resolve to leave all places where I might have acquaintances and withdraw to this country [Holland]. Here the long course of the war led to the establishment of such discipline that the armies that are kept up seem to be used only in order to make the enjoyment of the fruits of peace all the more secure; and amidst a great and populous nation, extremely industrious and more concerned with their own business than curious about other people's, while I do not lack any conveniences of the most frequented cities, I have been able to live a life as solitary and retired as though I were in the most remote deserts.

I do not know whether I need tell you of my first meditations; for they are perhaps too metaphysical and uncommon
for the general taste. At the same time I am in a way
obliged to speak of them so as to make it possible to judge
whether the foundation I have chosen is secure enough.
I had noticed long before, as I said just now, that in conduct
one sometimes has to follow opinions that one knows
to be most uncertain just as if they were indubitable; but
since my present aim was to give myself up to the pursuit
of truth alone, I thought I must do the very opposite, and
reject as if absolutely false anything as to which I could
imagine the least doubt, in order to see if I should not be
left at the end believing something that was absolutely
indubitable. So, because our senses sometimes deceive
us, I chose to suppose that nothing was such as they lead us
to imagine. Because there are men who make mistakes
in reasoning even as regards the simplest points of geometry
and perpetrate fallacies, and seeing that I was as liable to
error as anyone else, I rejected as false all the arguments
I had so far taken for demonstrations. Finally, considering
that the very same experiences (*pensées*) as we have in
waking life may occur also while we sleep, without there
being at that time any truth in them, I decided to feign
that everything that had entered my mind hitherto was
no more true than the illusions of dreams. But immediately upon this I noticed that while I was trying to think
everything false, it must needs be that I, who was thinking
this (*qui le pensais*), was something. And observing that this
truth ' I am thinking (*je pense*), therefore I exist ' was so solid
and secure that the most extravagant suppositions of the

sceptics could not overthrow it, I judged that I need not scruple to accept it as the first principle of philosophy that I was seeking.

I then considered attentively what I was; and I saw that while I could feign that I had no body, that there was no world, and no place existed for me to be in, I could not feign that I was not; on the contrary, from the mere fact that I thought of doubting (*je pensais à douter*) about other truths it evidently and certainly followed that I existed. On the other hand, if I had merely ceased to be conscious (*de penser*), even if everything else that I had ever imagined had been true, I had no reason to believe that I should still have existed. From this I recognised that I was a substance whose whole essence or nature is to be conscious (*de penser*) and whose being requires no place and depends on no material thing. Thus this self (*moi*), that is to say the soul, by which I am what I am, is entirely distinct from the body, and is even more easily known; and even if the body were not there at all, the soul would be just what it is.

After this I considered in general what is requisite to the truth and certainty of a proposition; for since I had just found one that I knew to have this nature, I thought I must also know what this certainty consists in. Observing that there is nothing at all in the statement ' I am thinking, therefore I exist ' which assures me that I speak the truth, except that I see very clearly that in order to think I must exist, I judged that I could take it as a general rule that whatever we conceive very clearly and very distinctly is true; only there is some difficulty in discerning what conceptions really are distinct.

Next, I reflected on the fact that I was doubting, and that consequently my being was not wholly perfect (for I saw clearly that knowledge was a greater perfection than doubt). I decided to enquire whence I had learnt to think of something more perfect than myself, and I recognised it as

32

evident that this idea must come from some nature that was really more perfect. As regards my ideas of many other external things—the sky, the earth, light, heat, and innumerable other objects—I was not so much concerned to know their source; for I discovered nothing in them that appeared to make them higher than myself. If they were true, they might depend on my own nature, in so far as it had some degree of perfection; if not, I might have got them from nothingness—they might be in me because I had some defect. But this could not hold good for the idea of an existence more perfect than my own; it was manifestly impossible to have got this from nothingness; and since it is no less contradictory that the more perfect should follow from and depend on the less perfect, than that something should proceed from nothing, likewise I could not have got it from myself. So the only possibility left was to hold that the idea had been put in me by a nature really more perfect than myself, and in fact possessing all the perfections of which I could have any idea; that is to say, to explain myself in one word, by God. And to this I added that since I knew of some perfections that I did not possess, I was not the only being in existence (here, by your leave, I will freely use scholastic terms), but that there must needs be some other more perfect being on whom I depended, and from whom I had received all that I had. For if I had been alone and independent of everything else, so that my slight participation in perfect being were from myself, I could by parity of reasoning have had from myself all the remainder of perfection that I knew I lacked; I could myself have been infinite, eternal, immutable, omniscient, almighty—in short, have had all the perfections I discovered in God. For, according to the arguments I have just used, all that I had to do in order to know God's nature, as far as my own allowed, was to consider, as regards every property of which I found any idea in myself,

33

whether the possession of it was a perfection or not; and I was certain that no property that indicated any imperfection was in God, but that all others were. Thus, I saw that doubt, inconstancy, sorrow, and so on could not be in God; for I myself should have liked to be rid of them. Further, I had ideas of a plurality of sensible and corporeal things; for even if I were to suppose that I was dreaming and that all I saw or imagined was a sham, I yet could not deny that these ideas were really in my consciousness. But I had already recognised quite clearly in my own case that the intelligent and the corporeal nature are distinct; so, considering that all composition is a sign of dependence and dependence is manifestly a defect, I concluded that it could not be a perfection in God to be composed of these two natures, and consequently that he was not; but that if there were any bodies in the world, or again any intelligences or other natures that were not entirely perfect, then their being must depend on his power, so that without him they could not subsist for a single moment.

After this I wished to seek for other truths; I took the subject-matter of geometry, which I conceived to be a continuous body or a space indefinitely extended in length, breadth, and height or depth, divisible into distinct parts, which may have distinct shapes and sizes and may be moved or transposed in all sorts of ways; for the geometers assume all this in their subject-matter. I went through some of the simpler proofs, and observed that their high degree of certainty is founded merely on our conceiving them distinctly (according to the principle mentioned above). I also observed that there was nothing in them to assure me of the existence of the subject-matter. For instance, I saw quite well that, assuming a triangle, its three angles must be equal to two right angles; but for all that I saw nothing that assured me that there was any triangle in the real world. On the other hand, going back

34

to an examination of my idea of a perfect Being, I found that this included the existence of such a Being; in the same way as the idea of a triangle includes the equality of its three angles to two right angles, or the idea of a sphere includes the equidistance of all parts (of its surface) from the centre; or indeed, in an even more evident way. Consequently it is at least as certain that God, the perfect Being in question, is or exists, as any proof in geometry can be.

The reason why many people are convinced that there is difficulty in knowing God, and even in knowing what their soul is, is that they never raise their mind above sensible objects, and are so used to think of things only by way of imagining them (a mode of thought specially adapted to material things) that whatever is unimaginable appears to them unintelligible. This is clear from the maxim held even by scholastic philosophers, ' there is nothing in the intellect but has previously been in sense '; and yet the ideas of God and the soul have certainly never been in sense. And it seems to me that those who try to use their imagination to understand them are acting just as though they tried to use their eyes to hear sounds or smell odours. There is, however, also this difference: the sense of sight gives us no less assurance of the reality of its objects than the senses of smell or hearing; whereas neither our imagination nor our senses can ever assure us of anything at all, except with the aid of our understanding.

Finally, if there are still men not sufficiently convinced of the existence of God and of their soul by the reasons I have brought forward, I would have them know that everything else that seems to them more sure—that they have a body, that there are stars and an earth, and so on— is really less certain. For while we are morally certain of these things, so that it seems we cannot doubt them without being extravagant; at the same time, if it is a question of metaphysical certainty, one cannot reasonably deny that there is good reason for not being entirely certain of them. One need only consider that in sleep one may imagine in just the same way that one has a different body, and that one sees different stars and a different earth, while none of this is so. How do we know that the experiences (*pensées*) occurring in our dreams are any more illusory than the others? They are often no less lively and distinct And if the best minds study the question as much as they like, I think they will find no adequate grounds for removing this doubt, if they do not presuppose the existence of God. For in the first place, what I took just now as a principle, viz. that whatever we conceive very clearly and distinctly is true, is assured only because God is or exists, and is a perfect being, and everything in us comes from him. It follows that, since our ideas or notions have positive reality and proceed from God, in so far as they are clear and distinct, they must to this extent be true. If we often have ideas with some error in them, these must be among those that contain some confusion or obscurity; for in this regard they participate in nothingness; that is, they occur in us in this confused form only because we are not wholly perfect. And clearly there is no less contradiction in God's originating error or imperfection as such, than in the origin of truth or perfection from nothingness. But if we did not know that all truth and reality in us proceeds from a perfect and infinite being, then, however clear and distinct our ideas might be, we should have no reason to be certain that they had the perfection of truth.

Now when once the knowledge of God and the soul has made us certain of this rule, it is quite easy to see that the fancies we create in sleep should not make us doubt in any way the truth of the experiences (*pensées*) we have when awake. For if it happened even in sleep that one had some specially distinct idea; if, for instance, a geometer devised some new proof; then sleep would be no bar to its being true. The commonest delusion of dreams is that they represent various objects in the same manner as our external senses; but it does not matter that this gives us reason to doubt the truth of such ideas; for they are often capable of deceiving us even when we are not asleep; for instance, when men with jaundice see everything as yellow, or when the stars or other very remote bodies appear much smaller than they are. For, in conclusion, waking or sleeping, we should never let ourselves be convinced except by the evidence of our reason. Note that I say our reason, not our imagination or our senses. Although we see the sun ' very clearly ', we must not therefore judge that it has only the size we see; and we can ' distinctly ' imagine a lion's head on a goat's body, but we need not therefore conclude that a chimera exists in the world; for reason does not insist to us that what we thus see or imagine is real. But reason does insist that all our ideas or notions must have some basis of truth; for otherwise it would be impossible that God, who is all-perfect and all-truthful, should have placed them in us. And since our reasonings are never so evident nor so complete in sleep as in waking life, although sometimes our imagination then attains an equal or higher degree of force and detail, reason also insists that while our thoughts cannot all be true, because we are not wholly perfect, what truth they have must assuredly occur in those we have when awake rather than in our dreams.

V

I should very much like to go on and show further here the entire chain of truths that I have derived from these principles. But to do this I should have to discuss several questions disputed among the learned, and I have no wish to be embroiled in dispute with them. So I think I had better refrain, and merely state them in general terms, leaving it to wiser heads to decide whether it would be useful for the public to have more detailed information. I always adhered to my former resolution not to assume any principle, except the one I have just used to prove the existence of God and the soul; and to accept nothing as true that did not appear clearer and more certain than the demonstrations of geometers formerly did. Nevertheless I venture to say that I not only soon found a way to satisfy myself about the principal problems that are usually dealt with in philosophy, but also discerned certain laws that God has established in nature, and of which he has implanted ideas in our minds, such that on sufficient reflection we cannot doubt that they are exactly observed by all objects and events in the world. By considering these laws in consecutive order I have come, I think, to discover various truths more useful and important than I had ever before learnt or even hoped to learn.

Since I endeavoured to explain these principles in a treatise that certain considerations prevent me from publishing,[1] I cannot do better towards making them known than by summarising its contents. My aim was to include all the knowledge I thought I possessed, before I began

[1] [The treatise, *Le Monde*, not published during Descartes's life because of his reaction to the condemnation of Galileo (1633).—Tr.]

38

writing, as to the nature of material things. . . . (But)
so that I could express my judgment with more freedom
without being obliged to follow or to refute the accepted
opinions of the learned, I decided to leave them the real
world as their debating-ground, and merely talk about
what would happen in a new world, supposing that God
were now to create, somewhere in ' imaginary' space,
enough matter to form it; [1] and gave the various parts of
this matter a various and disorderly agitation, so as to
form a chaos as confused as poets could feign; and
thereafter only lent his ordinary co-operation to Nature, and
allowed her to act according to the laws he established.
So I first of all described this matter, and tried to give a
representation of it such that nothing in the world, I think,
is clearer or more intelligible, except what I said just now
about God and the soul. For in fact I expressly supposed
it to have none of those forms or qualities of which the
Schoolmen dispute; and, in general, to have only properties which it was so natural to the mind to know that
nobody could even pretend not to. Moreover, I showed
what the laws of nature were; and resting my arguments
on no other principle than God's infinite perfection, I tried
to prove all the laws that might have been doubted, and
to show that they are of such a kind that, even if God
created several worlds, there could be none in which they
were not observed. Then I showed how the great part
of the matter of this chaos must, in consequence of these
laws, dispose and arrange itself in such a way as to resemble
the heavens in our world; and how accordingly some of its

[1] [Descartes here refers with polite irony to the scholastic idea that the
universe is a finite sphere with ' imaginary' space outside it; it was
much debated in the schools whether God could create something in
the ' imaginary' space. Cf. Aquinas, *Summa Theologica*, I[a], q.xlvi, art.
i ad viii[um]: ' When it is said that *above the heavens there is nothing, above*
indicates a merely imaginary place—the possibility of imagining further
dimensions superadded to the dimensions of the heavenly body '.—Tr.]

parts must form an earth; and others, planets and comets, a sun and fixed stars. Here I developed the subject of light; I explained at length the nature of the light that must be found in the sun and stars, and how it instantaneously travelled across the immense distances of the heavens, and how it was reflected from the planets and comets to the earth. I added several points about the substance, situation, movement, and all the various qualities of these heavens and stars; and I thought I had thus said enough to show that nothing is observed in the heavens and stars of the real world but must—or at least could—present a similar appearance in the world I was describing. From that I proceeded to a special discussion of the earth; how, although I had expressly supposed that God had given no gravity to the matter of which it was composed, yet none the less all its parts would tend exactly towards its centre; and how, there being water and air on its surface, the arrangement of the heavens and the heavenly bodies, in particular the moon, must cause a flux and reflux similar in all regards to what is observed in our seas. . . .

At the same time I did not wish to infer from all this that our world was created in the way I suggested; for it is much more likely that from the beginning God made it in the form it was intended to have. But it is certain, and is an opinion commonly accepted among theologians, that the act by which he now preserves it is identical with the act of creation; so that, if in the beginning God had given the world only the form of a chaos, then, so long as he established the laws of Nature, and then lent her his aid to act in her normal way, one may believe, without prejudice to the miracle of creation, that merely on this account the purely material world might have become just what we now observe. And its nature is much more easily conceived if one thus watches its gradual origin than if one considers it as ready made. . . .

I went on to describe animals and in particular men. But since I had not yet enough knowledge to speak of them in the same style as other objects, namely by demonstrating effects from their causes and showing from what seeds and in what manner Nature must produce them, I confined myself to imagining that God should form a human body just like our own both in the outward shape of its limbs and in the interior arrangement of its organs, without using any matter but what I had described, and without placing in it, to begin with, any rational soul, or anything to serve as a vegetative or sensitive soul. . . . Examining the functions that might result in such a body, what I found were precisely those that may occur in us unconsciously, without any co-operation of the soul, that is to say of the element distinct from the body of which I said above that its nature is merely to be conscious; the very operations in which irrational animals resemble us; but I could find none of the operations that depend on consciousness and are alone proper to us as men; whereas I could find a place for these on the further supposition that God created a rational soul, and joined it to the body in a way that I described.[1]

* * *

I specially dwelt on showing that if there were machines with the organs and appearance of a monkey, or some other irrational animal, we should have no means of telling that they were not altogether of the same nature as those animals; whereas if there were machines resembling our bodies, and imitating our actions as far as is morally possible, we should still have two means of telling that, all the same, they were not real men. First, they could never use words or other constructed signs, as we do to declare our thoughts to others. It is quite conceivable that a

---

[1] [There follows a long passage on physiology, in particular the circulation of the blood, which is now of merely historical interest.—Tr.]

machine should be so made as to utter words, and even utter them in connexion with physical events that cause a change in one of its organs; so that e.g. if it is touched in one part, it asks what you want to say to it, and if touched in another, it cries out that it is hurt; but not that it should be so made as to arrange words variously in response to the meaning of what is said in its presence, as even the dullest men can do. Secondly, while they might do many things as well as any of us or better, they would infallibly fail in others, revealing that they acted not from knowledge but only from the disposition of their organs. For while reason is a universal tool that may serve in all kinds of circumstances, these organs need a special arrangement for each special action; so it is morally impossible that a machine should contain so many varied arrangements as to act in all the events of life in the way reason enables us to act.

Now in just these two ways we can also recognise the difference between men and brutes. For it is a very remarkable thing that there are no men so dull and stupid, not even lunatics, that they cannot arrange various words and form a sentence to make their thoughts (*pensées*) understood; but no other animal, however perfect or well bred, can do the like. This does not come from their lacking the organs; for magpies and parrots can utter words like ourselves, and yet they cannot talk like us, that is, with any sign of being aware of (*qu'ils pensent*) what they say. Whereas men born deaf-mutes, and thus devoid of the organs that others use for speech, as much as brutes are or more so, usually invent for themselves signs by which they make themselves understood to those who are normally with them, and who thus have a chance to learn their language. This is evidence that brutes not only have a smaller degree of reason than men, but are wholly lacking in it. For it may be seen that a very small degree of reason

42

is needed in order to be able to talk; and in view of the inequality that occurs among animals of the same species, as among men, and of the fact that some are easier to train than others, it is incredible that a monkey or parrot who was one of the most perfect members of his species should not be comparable in this regard to one of the stupidest children or at least to a child with a diseased brain, if their souls were not wholly different in nature from ours. And we must not confuse words with natural movements, the expressions of emotion, which can be imitated by machines as well as by animals. Nor must we think, like some of the ancients, that brutes talk but we cannot understand their language; for if that were true, since many of their organs are analogous to ours, they could make themselves understood to us, as well as to their fellows. It is another very remarkable thing that although several brutes exhibit more skill than we in some of their actions, they show none at all in many other circumstances; so their excelling us is no proof that they have a mind (*de l'esprit*), for in that case they would have a better one than any of us and would excel us all round; it rather shows that they have none, and that it is nature that acts in them according to the arrangements of their organs; just as we see how a clock, composed merely of wheels and springs, can reckon the hours and measure time more correctly than we can with all our wisdom.

I went on to describe the rational soul, and showed that, unlike the other things I had spoken of, it cannot be extracted from the potentiality of matter, but must be specially created; and how it is not enough for it to dwell in the human body like a pilot in his ship, which would only account for its moving the limbs of the body; in order to have in addition feelings and appetites like ours, and so make up a true man, it must be joined and united to the body more closely. Here I dwelt a little on the subject of the soul, as among the most important; for,

43

after the error of denying God, (of which I think I have
already given a sufficient refutation), there is none more
likely to turn weak characters from the strait way of virtue
than the supposition that the soul of brutes must be of the
same nature as ours, so that after this life we have no more
to hope or fear than flies or ants. Whereas, when we realise
how much they really differ from us, we understand much
better the arguments proving that our soul is of a nature
entirely independent of the body, and thus not liable to
die with it; and since we can discern no other causes
that should destroy it, we are naturally led to decide that
it is immortal.

VI

It is three years now since I finished the treatise comprising all these matters; and I was beginning to revise it so as to put it into the hands of a printer, when I learnt that certain persons to whom I defer, and who have hardly less authority over my actions than my own reason has over my thoughts, had disapproved of a physical theory published a little while before by somebody else.[1] I will not say I held this, but I had certainly noticed nothing in it, before their condemnation, that I could imagine prejudicial to either religion or society; nothing, therefore, that would have stopped my putting it in writing if reason had convinced me of it. This made me fear that there might be some mistake in my own theories, in spite of the great pains I have always been at not to admit to belief any new ones of which I had not very certain demonstrations, and not to write anything that could turn out to the disadvantage of anybody; and it was enough to alter my previous decision to publish. For while my previous reasons for the decision were very strong, my inclination, which has always made me hate the occupation of writing books, promptly made me find excuses enough for not doing it. The reasons on either side are such as I should like to state here; not only that, but the public may be interested to know them.

I have never made much of the products of my own mind; and so long as the only fruits I gathered from the method I use were just that I satisfied my own mind about some problems in the speculative sciences, or tried to govern my conduct by the rules I had learnt from the method, I did

[1] [Descartes refers to the condemnation of Galileo.—Tr.]

not think myself obliged to write anything about it. For as regards conduct, everyone is so full of his own wisdom that there might be found as many reformers as heads if anybody were allowed to undertake to make any change other than those whom God has set up as sovereigns over the nations, or has endowed with sufficient grace and zeal to be prophets; and although I very much liked my speculative ideas, I thought other people had their own, and perhaps liked these even better. But when once I had arrived at some general notions in physics, and begun to test them in various special problems, and had seen how far-reaching they were, and how different they were from the principles that have been used up to now, I thought I could not keep them hid without gravely sinning against the law that obliges us to procure the general good of mankind so far as in us lies. For I thus saw that one may reach conclusions of great usefulness in life, and discover a practical philosophy in the place of the speculative philosophy taught by the Schoolmen; one which would show us the energy and action of fire, air, and stars, the heavens, and all other bodies in our environment, as distinctly as we know the various crafts of our artisans, and could apply them in the same way to all appropriate uses and thus make ourselves masters and owners of nature. . . . I designed to spend all my life in seeking after a science so much required; and since I had found a road by which I thought one must infallibly discover it, if not prevented by the shortness of life or the lack of experiments, I judged that there was no better remedy against these two obstacles than to communicate faithfully to the public what small discoveries I had made. Thus the best minds would be led to contribute to further progress, each one according to his bent and ability, in the necessary experiments, and would communicate to the public whatever they learnt, so that one man might begin where another left off; and thus, in the combined lifetimes and labours of many, much more progress would be made by all together than any one could make by himself.

I further observed, as regards experiments, that the progress of knowledge makes them more and more necessary. At the beginning it is best to make use only of what presents itself to our senses in any case, and cannot but be noticed if we reflect even a little, rather than to seek after rarer and more recondite observations ; for the latter often deceive us, so long as the causes of the more common are still unknown; and the conditions on which they depend are almost always so special and so minute that it is very hard to discern them. My general order of procedure on the other hand has been this. First, I have tried to discover in general the principles or first causes of all that exists or could exist in the world. To this end I consider only God, who created them, and I derive them merely from certain root-truths that occur naturally to our minds. Then I considered the first and most ordinary effects deducible from these causes, . . . and then I tried to descend to more special cases. But in view of the wide variety of these, I thought it impossible for the human mind to distinguish the forms or species of bodies actually found on earth from an infinity of others that could be found there if it had been God's will to put them there; and, consequently, impossible to make them of use to mankind; except by reaching the causes through the effects, and using many special experiments. So, reviewing in mind all the objects that have ever been present to my senses, I venture to say that I have never observed anything that I could not readily explain on the principles I discovered; but I have to admit that the potentialities of nature are so ample and vast, and my principles so simple and general, that, as regards almost any particular effect that I observe, I begin by knowing only there are various ways that it can be deduced from the principles; and my greatest problem, as a rule, is to find out in which of these ways it results from them. Here I know of no other resource than to look out once more for experiments that would give different results according as one or the other explanation is right. I have reached a point where I think I can see the general line of experiments that would be useful to this end; but I also see that the kind and number that would be needed are such as could not possibly all be carried out with my own hands and at my own cost, even if my income were a thousand times greater. So my future progress in the knowledge of nature will be greater or less according to my opportunities of making experiments. I resolved to make this known in my treatise; and to show clearly the possible usefulness to the public of such experiments, so as to oblige all who desire the general good of mankind—all who are really virtuous, not merely in pretence or in the opinion of others—to inform me of their previous results, and to help me in future research.

I have, however, since had grounds for changing my view. I decided indeed that I must still write down any of my discoveries that I judged to be of some importance, and to use the same care as though I were meaning to have them printed. I wanted the opportunity for a thorough examination; for one looks more closely at what one thinks is to be seen by others than at what one does merely on one's own account; and often what seemed true when I first got the idea turned out false when I tried to put it on paper. Moreover, I wanted to lose no chance of benefiting the public if I could; and I desired that, if my writings were worth anything, those who had them after my death might use them as might be most suitable. On the other hand, I decided absolutely against agreeing to their being published during my life; so that neither the opposition and controversy they might meet with, nor any reputation

they might win me, should occasion my losing the time that
I aim to spend in self-instruction. For while every man
is bound to procure, so far as in him lies, the good of other
men, and a man who is no help to anyone else is really
worthless; at the same time our concern must extend further
than the present, and it is right to neglect what might be
profitable to the living when one's aim is to do something
else that will benefit posterity even more. I want to make
it clear that the little I have learnt so far is hardly anything
in comparison with what I do not know and still have hopes
of finding out. The gradual discovery of truth in science is
like making money; when once a man becomes rich, he has
less difficulty in making a great profit than he previously
had in making much smaller profit when he was poorer.
Or, again, to make another comparison: a commander's
strength normally grows in proportion to his victories;
and he needs more skill just to hold on after losing a battle
than he does to conquer whole cities and provinces after
winning one. For the endeavour to overcome all the
difficulties and errors that prevent our arriving at the
knowledge of truth is really a series of engagements; and
it is a defeat to accept some false opinion on a matter of
some generality and importance; one needs afterwards
much more skill to restore one's former position than one
does to make great advances when once one has secure
principles. For my own part, any scientific discoveries
I may have made . . . are, I may say, merely the necessary
consequences of five or six main problems that I have
surmounted—which I reckon as so many engagements
in which luck was on my side. I even venture to say that,
with two or three more such victories, I should completely
accomplish my aims; and my age is not so advanced but
that I may, in the ordinary course of nature, still have the
leisure to do this. But I think I am the more bound to
make good use of the time left to me, the more hope I have

that I can use it well; and I should undoubtedly have many occasions to lose it, if I published the foundations of my physics. For while they are almost all so evident that one need only understand them in order to believe them, and there is none for which I think myself unable to give a demonstration; at the same time, since it is impossible that they should accord with all the various opinions of other men, I foresee that I should often be distracted by the opposition they would arouse.

You may say that this opposition would be useful to me; both in showing me my blunders, and also because, if I had done anything worth while, other people would thus learn more about it; and (since many heads are better than one) they might begin to use my results, and help me in turn with their own discoveries. But although I know I am extremely liable to go wrong, and hardly ever trust the first ideas that come to me, at the same time my experience of possible objections prevents my hoping for any advantage from them. I have often made trial of the judgments both of those I held for friends, and of others to whom I thought myself indifferent, and even of certain people whose spite and envy would, I knew, be eager enough to discover things that affection would hide from my friends; but it has hardly ever happened that an objection has been raised that I had not wholly foreseen, unless indeed it were quite wide of the mark; so that I have hardly ever met with any critic of my views but seemed either less severe or less fair than myself. And I have never observed that by means of the usual scholastic disputes any truth previously unknown has been discovered; each side is out for victory, and so the aim is to make plausibility count rather than to weigh the opposing arguments; and those who have been good advocates for a long time are not afterwards better judges on that account.

As for the usefulness to other people of my publishing my

ideas, it might not be very great, seeing that so far I have not made so much progress but that much would have to be added before practical applications were made. I think I may say without vanity that if anyone can do this it must be myself rather than anyone else; not that there may not be in the world many minds incomparably excelling my own; but one cannot get such a good idea of a thing, or make it one's own so well, when one learns it from someone else, as when it is one's own discovery. This is so true here that I have often noticed that highly intelligent persons to whom I have explained some of my views and who seemed to understand them distinctly at the time, have almost completely transformed them when reporting them, so that I could no longer acknowledge them as my own. Here I would beg posterity never to believe what is ascribed to me if I have not published it myself. I am not surprised at the absurdities attributed to ancient philosophers, whose own writings we lack; I do not judge on that account that their ideas were so very unreasonable (seeing that they were the first minds of their times) but only that they have been badly reported. Likewise, we see that there has hardly ever been one of their followers who surpassed them; I am convinced that Aristotle's most passionate disciples of today would think themselves lucky to have as great a knowledge of nature as he had, even if that meant never having a greater. They are like ivy, which does not tend to climb higher than the trees that support it, and indeed often grows downwards after reaching the tree-top. For it seems to me that they take a downward step—become in a way worse informed than if they had kept away from studies —when they are not satisfied with an understanding of what is intelligibly explained by their author, but wish, besides that, to find in him the solution of problems about which he says nothing and perhaps never thought. At the same time their way of philosophising is very convenient for men of very mediocre minds: for the distinctions and principles they use are so obscure that they can talk about everything as confidently as if they had knowledge, and can maintain what they say against the subtlest and cleverest men, and there is no convincing them. They are, it seems to me, like a blind man who, so as to fight without disadvantage against one who can see, should make him come down to the bottom of some dark cellar. I may say that it is their concern that I should not publish the principles I employ in philosophy; for since these are very simple and evident, my publishing them would be like opening some windows and letting in the daylight to the cellar where they have gone down to fight.

But even the better minds have no cause to wish to know my views; for if they wish to be able to talk about everything, and to get the reputation of learning, they will achieve this more easily by being content with plausibility, which is not hard to attain on all kinds of questions, than in seeking for truth, which is discovered only gradually on some points, and which obliges one to admit ignorance frankly when it is a matter of discussing other points. If they do prefer the knowledge of some few truths to the vanity of apparent omniscience (and in truth it is far preferable), and wish to carry out a design like my own, then I need say nothing more for their benefit than I have already said in this Discourse. For if they can make more progress than I, they will *a fortiori* be able to find out for themselves all that I think I have found out. Again, as I have examined nothing but in an orderly way, it is certain that what still remains to be discovered is intrinsically harder and more hidden than what I have been able to hit on so far; and they would have less pleasure by far in learning it of me than by themselves; besides, the practice they will get by first looking for easy points and advancing by gradual degrees to the more difficult will be more useful than any instruction of mine could be. For my own part, I am convinced that, if from my youth up I had been taught all the truths I have since sought to demonstrate, and had had no difficulty about learning them, I should perhaps never have known any more, or at least should never have got the practice and the skill I think I have in steadily finding new truths as I set myself to look for them. In a word, if there is any work that could not be better carried out than by him who began it, it is the work I am engaged in.

True, as regards possibly useful experiments, one man alone could not manage to do them all; but also he could not usefully employ any hand but his own; except for artisans or other such people, whom he could pay, and whom the hope of making money (a very powerful motive) would lead to carry out exactly all his instructions. Voluntary helpers who might offer themselves from curiosity or desire of learning something, are as a rule more ready with promise than with performance, and make fine proposals none of which comes to anything; moreover, they would infallibly want to be paid by the explanation of some problems, or at least by useless compliments and conversation, which could not but cost so much time that it would mean a loss. And as for other people's experiments, even if they were willing to inform one about them (as those who call them ' secrets ' would never do), they are mostly bound up with so many superfluous conditions or ingredients that it would be very hard to decipher the true element in them. Besides, one would find the explanations of them to be almost always so bad, or even so untrue (because they were carried out by men who tried to show their agreement with their own principles), that even if some might be useful, they just would not be worth the time needed to single them out. So if there were in the world a man assuredly known to be able to make discoveries of the greatest possible importance and public utility, and whom on this account other men were trying in every way to help achieve his aims, I think all they could do for him would be to contribute to the necessary costs of experiments, and further, to ensure against his having his leisure taken away by anybody's importunities. But I am not so presumptuous as to wish to make any extraordinary promises; nor do I feed on any vain idea that the public must have a great interest in my designs; besides, I am not so mean-spirited as to wish to accept from anyone's hand a favour I might be thought not to have deserved.

All these considerations together led to my deciding three years ago not to publish the treatise I had on hand; and even resolving not to publish during my lifetime any other work so general in scope, nor yet one making it possible to understand the foundation of my physics. But I have since had two grounds for feeling bound to include with this Discourse some special treatises, and to give the public some account of my actions and my aims. First, if I did not, many who know of my former intention of having some writings printed might imagine my reasons for not doing so were more discreditable to me than they are. I have no excessive love for glory—I might even venture to say I dislike it, thinking it opposed to tranquility which I prize above everything; at the same time, I have never tried to hide my actions as if they were crimes, nor have I taken much care to remain unknown, both because I should have thought I was doing myself an injustice, and because this very care would have caused me some worry that would have been opposed to the perfect peace of mind that I seek. So, while I myself was indifferent about becoming known or not, I could not avoid getting some sort of reputation; and I thought I must do my best in order at least to escape a bad one. My other reason for writing was that I saw daily how my design of self-instruction was held up, because there are an infinity of experiments needed that I cannot possibly carry out without the help of others. I do not flatter myself so much as to hope the public will share my interests much; at the same time, I do not wish to do myself the injustice of giving those who survive me an occasion to reproach me some day because I could have bequeathed to them far greater achievements than I did, if only I had not been too neglectful of showing them how they could contribute towards my designs.

I thought it convenient to choose certain subjects which, without being too controversial, or obliging me to explain my principles more than I wish, would none the less show pretty clearly my scientific ability, or my lack of it. I cannot say whether I have succeeded, and I would not anticipate anybody's judgment by talking about my writings myself; but I should be very glad of their being examined, and to further this end I would request all who have some objections to make to be so good as to send them to my publisher, so that he may let me know of them, and I will try to add my reply at the same time; thus the reader will see both sides together and be a better judge of the truth. For I cannot undertake that I shall ever make long replies; if I recognise mistakes, I will admit them frankly; if I detect none, I shall simply say what I think is needed to defend what I have written; I shall not add the explanations of any new point, otherwise I should be continually passing from one point to another.

Some of my remarks at the beginning of the *Dioptrics* and the *Meteors* may be shocking at first because I call them 'suppositions', and appear to have no wish to prove them. If my reader has the patience to read the whole book attentively, I hope he may be satisfied. For it is my view as to the connexion of my conclusions that, just as the last are proved by the first, which are their causes, so the first may in turn be proved from the last, which are their effects. It must not be thought that here I am committing the fallacy called by logicians a vicious circle; for the effects are for the most part known with certainty by experience, so that the causes from which I have deduced them serve not to prove but to explain them— must, indeed, be themselves proved by means of them. I used the term ' suppositions ' merely with this meaning, that while I think I can derive them from the primary truths explained just now, I particularly wished not to do so; for otherwise certain people, who fancy they understand in a day all that somebody else has thought about for twenty years, and whose penetration and liveliness of mind makes them more liable to go wrong and less capable of getting at truth, might take occasion to construct on what they conceive to be my principles some extravagant philosophy for which I should be blamed. For, as regards what are entirely my own views, I make no excuse for their novelty; besides, if the grounds for them are well considered, I am sure that they will be found so simple and so much in agreement with common sense that they will seem less strange and extraordinary than any other possible views on the same subject. Moreover I make no boast of being the first discoverer of any of them; I rather boast that I have never accepted them either because they have, or because they have not, been said by others, but only because reason has convinced me of them.

. . . I am writing in French, my native language, rather than in Latin, the language of my teachers, because I hope for a better judgment of my opinions from those who use only their natural reason in its purity than from those who only trust old books. And as for those who combine good sense with learning—the only judges I wish to have—I am sure they will not be so partial to Latin as to refuse to listen to my arguments because I explain them in the vulgar tongue.

For the rest, I will not speak here in detail of my hopes for further progress in science, nor yet bind myself in the sight of the public by any promise I am not sure of fulfilling; I will only say that I have resolved to spend the rest of my life in trying to obtain such knowledge of nature that one could derive from it rules in medicine more certain than have been reached so far; and my inclination is so far removed from all other aims, especially such as could help some people only by harming others, that, even if circumstances obliged me to follow them, I think I could not succeed. Of this I make here a public declaration. I know it cannot serve to make me a person of standing in the world, but then I do not in the least want to be; and I shall always hold myself more obliged to those by whose favour I may enjoy unimpeded leisure, than I should be for offers of the most honourable employments in the world.

MEDITATIONS
ON FIRST PHILOSOPHY

Wherein are demonstrated the Existence of God
and the Distinction of Soul
from Body

*From the Latin text
of the second edition
published in 1642*

FIRST MEDITATION

What can be called in Question

Some years ago now I observed the multitude of errors that I had accepted as true in my earliest years, and the dubiousness of the whole superstructure I had since then reared on them; and the consequent need of making a clean sweep for once in my life, and beginning again from the very foundations, if I would establish some secure and lasting result in science. But the task appeared enormous, and I put it off till I should reach such a mature age that no increased aptitude for learning anything was likely to follow. Thus I delayed so long that now it would be blameworthy to spend in deliberation what time I have left for action. Today is my chance; I have banished all care from my mind, I have secured myself peace, I have retired by myself; at length I shall be at leisure to make a clean sweep, in all seriousness and with full freedom, of all my opinions.

To this end I shall not have to show they are all false, which very likely I could never manage; but reason already convinces me that I must withhold assent no less carefully from what is not plainly certain and indubitable than from what is obviously false; so the discovery of some reason for doubt as regards each opinion will justify the rejection of all. This will not mean going over each of them—an unending task; when the foundation is undermined, the superstructure will collapse of itself; so I will proceed at once to attack the very principles on which all my former beliefs rested.

What I have so far accepted as true *par excellence*, I have got either from the senses or by means of the senses. Now I have sometimes caught the senses deceiving me; and a wise man never entirely trusts those who have once cheated him.

'But although the senses may sometimes deceive us about some minute or remote objects, yet there are many other facts as to which doubt is plainly impossible, although these are gathered from the same source: e.g. that I am here, sitting by the fire, wearing a winter cloak, holding this paper in my hands, and so on. Again, these hands, and my whole body—how can their existence be denied? Unless indeed I likened myself to some lunatics, whose brains are so upset by persistent melancholy vapours that they firmly assert they are kings, when really they are miserably poor; or that they are clad in purple, when really they are naked; or that they have a head of pottery, or are pumpkins, or are made of glass; but then they are madmen, and I should appear no less mad if I took them as a precedent for my own case.'

A fine argument! As though I were not a man who habitually sleeps at night and has the same impressions (or even wilder ones) in sleep as these men do when awake! How often, in the still of the night, I have the familiar conviction that I am here, wearing a cloak, sitting by the fire—when really I am undressed and lying in bed! 'But now at any rate I am looking at this paper with wide-awake eyes; the head I am now shaking is not asleep; I put out this hand deliberately and consciously; nothing so distinct would happen to one asleep.' As if I did not recall having been deceived before by just such thoughts in sleep! When I think more carefully about this, I see so plainly that sleep and waking can never be distinguished by any certain signs, that I am bewildered; and this itself confirms the idea of my being asleep.

'Well, suppose I am dreaming, and these particulars, that I open my eyes, shake my head, put out my hand, are incorrect, suppose even that I have no such hand, no

62

such body; at any rate it has to be admitted that the things that appear in sleep are like painted representations, which cannot have been formed except in the likeness of real objects. So at least these general kinds of things, eyes, head, hands, body, must be not imaginary but real objects. Painters themselves, even when they are striving to create sirens and satyrs with the most extraordinary forms, cannot give them wholly new natures, but only mix up the limbs of different animals; or even if they did devise something so novel that nothing at all like it had ever been seen, something wholly fictitious and unreal, at least they must use real colours in its make-up. Similarly, even if these general kinds of things, eyes, head, hands and so on, could be imaginary, at least it must be admitted that some simple and more universal kinds of things are real, and are as it were the real colours out of which there are formed in our consciousness (*cogitatione*) all our pictures of real and unreal things. To this class there seem to belong: corporeal nature in general, and its extension; the shape of extended objects; quantity, or the size and number of these objects; place for them to exist in, and time for them to endure through; and so on.

'At this rate we might be justified in concluding that whereas physics, astronomy, medicine, and all other sciences depending on the consideration of composite objects, are doubtful; yet arithmetic, geometry, and so on, which treat only of the simplest and most general subject-matter, and are indifferent whether it exists in nature or not, have an element of indubitable certainty. Whether I am awake or asleep, two and three add up to five, and a square has only four sides; and it seems impossible for such obvious truths to fall under a suspicion of being false.'

But there has been implanted in my mind the old opinion that there is a God who can do everything, and who made me such as I am. How do I know he has not brought it about that, while in fact there is no earth, no sky, no extended objects, no shape, no size, no place, yet all these things should appear to exist as they do now? Moreover, I judge that other men sometimes go wrong over what they think they know perfectly well; may not God likewise make me go wrong, whenever I add two and three, or count the sides of a square, or do any simpler thing that might be imagined? 'But perhaps it was not God's will to deceive me so; he is after all called supremely good.' But if it goes against his goodness to have so created me that I am always deceived, it seems no less foreign to it to allow me to be deceived sometimes; and this result cannot be asserted.

Perhaps some people would deny that there is a God powerful enough to do this, rather than believe everything else is uncertain. Let us not quarrel with them, and allow that all I have said about God is a fiction. But whether they ascribe my attaining my present condition to fate, or to chance, or to a continuous series of events, or to any other cause, delusion and error certainly seem to be imperfections, and so this ascription of less power to the source of my being will mean that I am more likely to be so imperfect that I always go wrong. I have no answer to these arguments; I am obliged in the end to admit that none of my former ideas are beyond legitimate doubt; and this, not from inconsideration or frivolity, but for strong and well-thought-out reasons. So I must carefully withhold assent from them just as if they were plainly false, if I want to find any certainty.

But it is not enough to have observed this; I must take care to bear it in mind. My ordinary opinions keep on coming back; and they take possession of my belief, on which they have a lien by long use and the right of custom, even against my will. I shall never get out of the habit of assenting to and trusting them, so long as I have a view of them answering to their real nature; namely, that they are doubtful in a way, as has been shown, but are yet highly probable, and far more reasonably believed than denied. So I think it will be well to turn my will in the opposite direction; deceive myself, and pretend they are wholly false and imaginary; until in the end the influence of prejudice on either side is counterbalanced, and no bad habit can any longer deflect my judgment from a true perception of facts. For I am sure no danger or mistake can happen in the process, and I cannot be indulging my scepticism more than I ought; because I am now engaged, not in action, but only in thought.

I will suppose, then, not that there is a supremely good God, the source of truth; but that there is an evil spirit, who is supremely powerful and intelligent, and does his utmost to deceive me. I will suppose that sky, air, earth, colours, shapes, sounds and all external objects are mere delusive dreams, by means of which he lays snares for my credulity. I will consider myself as having no hands, no eyes, no flesh, no blood, no senses, but just having a false belief that I have all these things. I will remain firmly fixed in this meditation, and resolutely take care that, so far as in me lies, even if it is not in my power to know some truth, I may not assent to falsehood nor let myself be imposed upon by that deceiver, however powerful and intelligent he may be.[1] But this plan is irksome, and sloth brings me back to ordinary life. I am like a prisoner who happens to enjoy an imaginary freedom during sleep, and then begins to suspect he is asleep; he is afraid to wake up, and connives at the agreeable illusion. So I willingly slip back into my old opinions, and dread waking up, in case peaceful rest should be followed by the toil of waking life, and I should henceforth have to live, not in the light, but amid the inextricable darkness of the problems I raised just now.

[1] [Cp. *Princ.*, i. xxxix; below, pp 188-9, §j.—Tr.]

SECOND MEDITATION

The Nature of the Human Mind : it is better known than the Body

Yesterday's meditation plunged me into doubts of such gravity that I cannot forget them, and yet do not see how to resolve them. I am bewildered, as though I had suddenly fallen into a deep sea, and could neither plant my foot on the bottom nor swim up to the top. But I will make an effort, and try once more the same path as I entered upon yesterday; I will reject, that is, whatever admits of the least doubt, just as if I had found it was wholly false; and I will go on until I know something for certain— if it is only this, that there is nothing certain. Archimedes asked only for one fixed and immovable point so as to move the whole earth from its place; so I may have great hopes if I find even the least thing that is unshakably certain.

I suppose, therefore, that whatever things I see are illusions; I believe that none of the things my lying memory represents to have happened really did so; I have no senses; body, shape, extension, motion, place are chimeras. What then is true? Perhaps only this one thing, that nothing is certain.

How do I know, however, that there is not something different from all the things I have mentioned, as to which there is not the least occasion of doubt?—Is there a God (or whatever I call him) who gives me these very thoughts? But why, on the other hand, should I think so? Perhaps I myself may be the author of them.—Well, am *I*, at any rate, something?—' But I have already said I have no senses and no body—' At this point I stick; what follows from

66

this? Am I so bound to a body and its senses that without them I cannot exist?—' But I have convinced myself that nothing in the world exists—no sky, no earth, no minds, no bodies; so am not I likewise non-existent?' But if I did convince myself of anything, I must have existed. ' But there is some deceiver, supremely powerful, supremely intelligent, who purposely always deceives me.' If he deceives me, then again I undoubtedly exist; let him deceive me as much as he may, he will never bring it about that, at the time of thinking (*quamdiu cogitabo*) that I am something, I am in fact nothing. Thus I have now weighed all considerations enough and more than enough; and must at length conclude that this proposition ' I am ', ' I exist ', whenever I utter it or conceive it in my mind, is necessarily true.

But I do not yet sufficiently understand what is this ' I ' that necessarily exists. I must take care, then, that I do not rashly take something else for the ' I ', and thus go wrong even in the knowledge that I am maintaining to be the most certain and evident of all.[1] So I will consider afresh what I believe myself to be before I happened upon my present way of thinking; from this conception I will subtract whatever can be in the least shaken by the arguments adduced, so that what at last remains shall be precisely the unshakably certain element.

What, then, did I formerly think I was? A man. But what is a man? Shall I say ' a rational animal '? No; in that case I should have to go on to ask what an animal is and what ' rational ' is, and so from a single question I should fall into several of greater difficulty; and I have not now the leisure to waste on such subtleties. I will rather consider what used to occur to me spontaneously and naturally whenever I was considering the question ' what am I? ' First came the thought that I had

[1] [Cp. *Princ.*, I. x; below, pp. 183-4, § B.—TR.]

a face, hands, arms—in fact the whole structure of limbs that is observable also in a corpse, and that I called ' the body '. Further, that I am nourished, that I move, that I have sensations (*sentire*), that I am conscious (*cogitare*) ; [1] these acts I assigned to the soul. But as to the nature of this soul, either it did not attract my attention, or else I fancied something subtle like air or fire or aether mingled among the grosser parts of my body. As regards ' body ' I had no doubt, and I thought I distinctly understood its nature; if I had tried to describe my conception, I might have given this explanation: ' By *body* I mean whatever is capable of being bounded by some shape, and comprehended by some place, and of occupying space in such a way that all other bodies are excluded; moreover of being perceived by touch, sight, hearing, taste, or smell; and further, of being moved in various ways, not of itself but by some other body that touches it.' [2] For the power of self-movement, and the further powers of sensation and consciousness (*sentiendi, vel cogitandi*), I judged not to belong in any way to the essence of body (*naturam corporis*); indeed, I marvelled even that there were some bodies in which such faculties were found.

What am I to say now, when I am supposing that there is some all-powerful and (if it be lawful to say this) malignant deceiver, who has taken care to delude me about everything as much as he can ? Can I, in the first place, say I have the least part of the characteristics that I said belonged to the essence of body ? I concentrate, I think, I consider; nothing comes to mind; it would be wearisome

[1] [Sensation is not as yet counted as a species of *cogitatio*, because it is conceived as something dependent on the body, whose existence may therefore be doubted along with that of the body; it is regarded, in the *prima facie* view Descartes is here expounding, as an activity of sense-organs.—Tr.]

[2] [Cp. *Princ.*, i. liii; below, pp. 192-3, § o.—Tr.]

and futile to repeat the reasons. Well, what of the properties I ascribed to the soul? Nutrition and locomotion?
Since I have no body, these are mere delusions. Sensation? This cannot happen apart from a body; and in
sleep I have seemed to have sensations that I have since
realised never happened.[1] Consciousness (*cogitare*)? At
this point I come to the fact that there is consciousness
(*or* experience: *cogitatio*); of this and this only I cannot be deprived. *I* am, *I* exist; that is certain. For
how long? For as long as I am experiencing (*cogito*),
maybe, if I wholly ceased from experiencing (*ab omni
cogitatione*), I should at once wholly cease to be.[2] For the
present I am admitting only what is necessarily true;
so 'I am' precisely taken refers only to a conscious being;
that is a mind, a soul (*animus*), an intellect, a reason—words
whose meaning I did not previously know. I am a real
being, and really exist; but what sort of being? As I
said, a conscious being (*cogitans*).

What now? I will use my imagination. I am not that
set of limbs called the human body; I am not some rarefied
gas infused into those limbs—air or fire or vapour or
exhalation or whatever I may picture to myself; all these
things I am supposing to be nonentities. But I still have
the assertion 'nevertheless *I* am something'. 'But
perhaps it is the case that these very things which I suppose
to be nonentities, and which are not properly known to me,
are yet in reality not different from the " I " of which I
am aware?' I do not know, and will not dispute the
point; I can judge only about the things I am aware of.

[1] [The concept of sensation used here, as on p. 68, does not treat
sensation as a mere species of consciousness, but as an event that can
occur only if sense-organs are really affected.—Tr.]

[2] [The verb and noun 'experience' here have to be used to supplement 'conscious(ness)', because this refers primarily to a power or
condition, and it is important to have words here that refer rather to an
activity.—Tr.]

I am aware of my own existence; I want to know what is this ' I ' of which I am aware. Assuredly, the conception of this ' I ', precisely as such, does not depend on things of whose existence I am not yet aware; nor, therefore, on what I feign in my imagination. And this very word ' feign ' shows me my mistake; it would indeed be a fiction to *imagine* myself to be anything, for imagination consists in contemplating the likeness or picture of a body. Now I know for certain that I am, and that at the same time it is possible that all these images, and in general everything of the nature of body, are mere dreams. When I consider this, it seems as absurd to say ' I will use my imagination, so as to recognise more distinctly who I am ', as though I were to say ' I am awake now, and discern some truth; but I do not yet see it clearly enough; so I will set about going to sleep, so that my dreams may give me a truer and clearer picture of the fact '. So I know that nothing I can comprehend by the help of imagination belongs to my conception of myself; the mind's attention must be carefully diverted from these things, so that she may discern her own nature as distinctly as possible.[1]

What then am I ? A conscious being (*res cogitans*). What is that ? A being that doubts, understands, asserts, denies, is willing, is unwilling; further, that has sense and imagination.[2] These are a good many properties—if only they all belong to me. But how can they fail to ? Am *I* not the very person who is now ' doubting ' almost everything; who ' understands ' something and ' asserts ' this one thing to be true, and ' denies ' other things; who ' is willing ' to know more, and ' is unwilling ' to be deceived; who ' imagines ' many things, even involuntarily, and perceives many things coming as it were from the ' senses ' ? Even if I am all the while asleep; even if my

[1] [Cp. *Princ.*, I. lxxiii; below, pp. 197-8, § s.—TR.]
[2] [Cp. *Princ.*, I. liii; below, pp. 192-3, § o.—TR.]

creator does all he can to deceive me; how can any of these things be less of a fact than my existence? Is any of these something distinct from my consciousness (*cogitatione*)? Can any of them be called a separate thing from myself? It is so clear that it is I who doubt, understand, will, that I cannot think how to explain it more clearly. Further, it is I who imagine; for even if, as I supposed, no imagined object is real, yet the power of imagination really exists and goes to make up my experience (*cogitationis*). Finally, it is I who have sensations, or who perceive corporeal objects as it were by the senses. Thus, I am now seeing light, hearing a noise, feeling heat. These objects are unreal, for I am asleep; but at least I seem to see, to hear, to be warmed. This cannot be unreal; and this is what is properly called my sensation; further, sensation, precisely so regarded, is nothing but an act of consciousness (*cogitare*).[1]

From these considerations I begin to be a little better acquainted with myself. But it still appears, and I cannot help thinking, that corporeal objects, whose images are formed in consciousness (*cogitatione*), and which the senses actually examine, are known far more distinctly than this ' I ', this ' something I know not what ', which does not fall under imagination. It is indeed surprising that I should comprehend more distinctly things that I can tell are doubtful, unknown, foreign to me, than what is real, what I am aware of—my very self. But I can see how it is; my mind takes pleasure in wandering, and is not yet willing to be restrained within the bounds of truth. So be it, then; just this once I will ride her on a loose rein, so that in good time I may pull her up and that thereafter she may more readily let me control her.

[1] [Notice the difference between this concept of sensation and the one provisionally used on pp. 68-9. See also *Princ.*, I. ix; below, p. 183, § A.—Tr.]

Consider the objects commonly thought to be the most distinctly known, the bodies we touch and see. I will take, not body in general, for these generic concepts (*perceptiones*) are often the more confused, but one particular body; say, this wax. It has just been extracted from the honeycomb; it has not completely lost the taste of the honey; it retains some of the smell of the flowers from which it was gathered; its colour, shape, size are manifest; it is hard, cold, and easily handled, and gives out a sound if you rap it with your knuckle; in fact it has all the properties that seem to be needed for our knowing a body with the utmost distinctness. But while I say this, the wax is put by the fire. It loses the remains of its flavour, the fragrance evaporates, the colour changes, the shape is lost, the size increases; it becomes fluid and hot, it can hardly be handled, and it will no longer give out a sound if you rap it. Is the same wax, then, still there? 'Of course it is; nobody denies it, nobody thinks otherwise.' Well, what was in this wax that was so distinctly known? Nothing that I got through the senses; for whatever fell under taste, smell, sight, touch, or hearing has now changed; yet the wax is still there.

'Perhaps what I distinctly knew was what I am now thinking of: namely, that the wax was not the sweetness, nor the fragrance of the flowers, nor the whiteness, nor the shape, nor the sound, but body; manifested to me previously in those aspects, and now in others.' But what exactly am I thus imagining? Let us consider; let us remove what is not proper to the wax and see what is left: simply, something extended, flexible, and changeable. But what is its being 'flexible' and 'changeable'? Does it consist in my imagining the wax to be capable of changing from a round shape to a square one and from that again to a triangular one? By no means; for I comprehend its potentiality for an infinity of such changes, but I cannot run through an infinite number of them in imagination; so I do not comprehend them by my imaginative power. What again is its being 'extended'? Is this likewise unknown? For extension grows greater when the wax melts, greater still when it boils, and greater still again with increase of heat; and I should mistake the nature of wax if I did not think this piece capable also of more changes, as regards extension, than my imagination has ever grasped. It remains then for me to admit that I know the nature even of this piece of wax not by imagination, but by purely mental perception. (I say this as regards a particular piece of wax; it is even clearer as regards wax in general.) What then is this wax, perceived only by the mind? It is the very same wax as I see, touch, and imagine —that whose existence I believed in originally. But it must be observed that perception of the wax is not sight, not touch, not imagination; nor was it ever so, though it formerly seemed to be; it is a purely mental contemplation (*inspectio*); which may be either imperfect or confused, as it originally was, or clear and distinct, as it now is, according to my degree of attention to what it consists in.

But it is surprising how prone my mind is to errors. Although I am considering these points within myself silently and without speaking, yet I stumble over words and am almost deceived by ordinary language.[1] We say we see the wax itself, if it is there; not that we judge from its colour or shape that it is there. I might at once infer: I see the wax by ocular vision, not by merely mental contemplation. I chanced, however, to look out of the window, and see men walking in the street; now I say in ordinary language that I 'see' them, just as I 'see' the wax; but what can I 'see' besides hats and coats, which may cover automata? I judge that they are men; and

[1] [Cp. *Princ.*, I. lxxiv; below, p. 198, § T.—TR.]

73

similarly, the objects that I thought I saw with my eyes, I really comprehend only by my mental power of judgment.

It is disgraceful that a man seeking to know more than the mass of mankind should have sought occasions for doubt in popular modes of speech! Let us go on, and consider when I perceived the wax more perfectly and manifestly; was it when I first looked at it, and thought I was aware of it by my external senses, or at least by the so-called ' common ' sense, i.e. the imaginative faculty ? or is it rather now, after careful investigation of its nature and of the way that I am aware of it ? It would be silly to doubt as to the matter; for what was there distinct in my original perception? Surely any animal could have one just as good. But when I distinguish the wax from its outward form, and as it were unclothe it and consider it in its naked self, I get something which, mistaken as my judgment may still be, I need a human mind to perceive.

What then am I to say about this mind, that is, about myself? (So far, I allow of no other element in myself except mind.) What is the ' I ' that seems to perceive this wax so distinctly ? Surely I am aware of myself not only much more truly and certainly, but also much more distinctly and manifestly. For if I judge that wax exists from the fact that I see this wax, it is much clearer that I myself exist because of this same fact that I see it. Possibly what I see is not wax; possibly I have no eyes to see anything; but it is just not possible, when I see or (I make no distinction here) I think I see (*cogitem me videre*), that my conscious self (*ego ipse cogitans*) should not be something. Similarly, if I judge that wax exists from the fact that I touch this wax, the same result follows: I exist. If I judge this from the fact that I imagine it, or for some other reason, it is just the same. These observations about the wax apply to all external objects. Further, if the perception of the wax is more distinct when it has become

74

known to me not merely by sight or by touch, but from a plurality of sources; how much more distinct than this must I admit my knowledge of myself to be! No considerations can help towards my perception of the wax or any other body, without at the same time all going towards establishing the nature of my mind. And the mind has such further resources within itself from which its self-knowledge may be made more distinct, that the information thus derived from the body appears negligible.

I have thus got back to where I wanted; I now know that even bodies are not really perceived by the senses or the imaginative faculty, but only by intellect; that they are perceived, not by being touched or seen, but by being understood; I thus clearly recognise that nothing is more easily or manifestly perceptible to me than my own mind. But because the habit of old opinion is not to be laid aside so quickly, I will stop here, so that by long meditation I may imprint this new knowledge deep in my memory.

THIRD MEDITATION

Concerning God : that He exists

I will now shut my eyes, stop my ears, withdraw all my senses; I will even blot out the images of corporeal objects from my consciousness; or at least (since that is barely possible) I will ignore them as vain illusions. I will discourse with myself alone and look more deeply into myself; I will try to grow by degrees better acquainted and more familiar with myself. *I* am a conscious being; that is, a being that doubts, asserts, denies, understands a few things, is ignorant of many, is willing or unwilling; and that has also imagination and sense; for as I observed before, even if the external objects of sense and imagination should be nonentities, yet the modes of consciousness that I call sensations and images (in so far as they are merely modes of consciousness) do, I am certain, exist in me.

In these few words I have given a list of all the things I really know, or at least have so far observed that I know. Now I will consider more carefully whether there may be other things in me that I have not yet discovered. I am certain that I am a conscious being. Surely then I also know what is required for my being certain about anything? In this primary knowledge there is only a clear and distinct perception of what I assert; now this would not be enough to make me certain as to the truth of the matter if it could ever happen that something clearly and distinctly perceived in this way should be false; so it looks as though I could lay down the general rule: whatever I perceive very clearly and distinctly is true.[1]

[1] [Cp. *Princ.*, i. xlv-xlvi; below, p. 190, § L.—Tr.]

'But I previously accepted many things as altogether certain and obvious which I have since found to be doubtful.' What were these things? Earth, sky, stars, and the rest of what I got from the senses. Now what did I clearly perceive about them? Only that the ideas or thoughts (*cogitationes*) of such things occurred in my mind. But even now I do not deny that such ideas occur in me. But it was something different that I used to assert, and that habitual belief made me think I clearly perceived what nevertheless I did not perceive: viz. that there were external objects which these ideas proceeded from, and exactly resembled. Here I went wrong; or at least, if I did judge truly, it was not on the strength of my perception.

Well, when I was considering some very simple and easy point in arithmetic or geometry, e.g. that two and three together make five, did I perceive this clearly enough to assert its truth? My only reason for afterwards doubting such things was that it occurred to me that perhaps some God might have given me such a nature that I was deceived even about what seemed most obvious. Now whenever the preconceived view that there is a supremely powerful God occurs to me, I must admit that He could, if He wished, make me go wrong even about what I think I see most clearly in my mind's eye. But whenever I turn to the things themselves which I think I perceive very clearly, I am quite convinced by them so that I spontaneously exclaim: 'Let who will deceive me, he can never bring it about that I should be a nonentity at the time of thinking I am something; nor that it should ever be true that I have never existed, since it is now true that I exist; nor even that two and three together should be more or less than five; or other such things in which I see a manifest contradiction.' And at any rate, since I have no occasion to think there is a Divine deceiver, nor have I yet any sufficient certainty that there is any God,

77

the argument depending on that supposition is a very slight—so to say, a metaphysical—reason for doubting. Still, to remove it as soon as possible, I must examine whether there is a God, and if so, whether He can be a deceiver; without knowing this, I seem unable to be quite certain of anything else.[1]

At this point, logical order seems to require, first a classification of all my experiences (*cogitationes*), and then an inquiry which of them it is that truth and falsehood properly inhere in. Some of these experiences are as it were pictures of objects, and these alone are properly called ideas; e.g. when I think of (*cogito*) a man, a chimera, the sky, an angel, or God. Others have additional properties; when I will, am afraid, assert, or deny, there is always something that I take as the object of my experience (*cogitationis*), but my experience comprises (*cogitatione complector*) more than the likeness of the thing in question; of these experiences, some are termed volitions or emotions, others are termed judgments.[2]

Now ideas considered in themselves, and not referred to something else, cannot strictly speaking be false; whether I imagine a she-goat or a chimera, it is not less true that I imagine one than the other. Again, falsehood is not to be feared in the will or the emotions; I may desire what is evil, or what does not exist anywhere, but it is none the less true that I desire it. Only judgments remain; it is here that I must take precaution against falsehood. Now the chief and commonest error that is to be found in this field consists in my taking ideas within myself to have similarity or conformity to some external object; for if I were to consider them as mere modes of my own consciousness, and did not refer them to anything else, they could give me hardly any occasion of error.

[1] [Cp. *Princ.*, I. xiii; below, p. 184, § G.—TR.]
[2] [Cp. *Princ.*, I. xxxii; below, p. 187, § F.—TR.]

Of these ideas some seem to be innate, some acquired, and some devised by myself. My concepts 'thing', 'truth', 'consciousness' (*cogitatio*) seem to come merely from my own nature; my hearing a noise, seeing the sun, feeling the fire, I have up to now held to proceed from external objects; and finally sirens, hippogriffs, etc. are my own invention. (But perhaps I could regard my ideas as all acquired, all innate, or all devised by myself; I have as yet no clear view of their real origin.)

The chief problem is about the ideas that I regard as taken from external objects. What is my motive for thinking them similar to those objects? Nature seems to have taught me. Moreover, I find they do not depend on my will, or upon myself; I often get them even if I do not wish; for instance, I now feel heat willy-nilly, and so think this sensation or idea of heat comes to me from an object other than myself—from the heat of the fire I am sitting over. And nothing appears more obvious than the judgment that what the object implants in me is its own likeness rather than something else.

I will now see if these reasons are valid. When I say 'Nature taught me this', I mean I have a spontaneous impulse to believe it; not, that some natural light shows me its truth. There is a big difference: whatever the light of nature shows me (e.g. that if I am doubting it follows that I exist, and so on) is absolutely beyond doubt; for there can be no faculty, equally trustworthy with this light, to show me that such things are not true; but as for my natural impulses, I have often judged that they have urged me in the wrong direction, when it was a question of choosing the good; so I do not see why I should trust them any more in other respects.

Again, although these ideas do not depend on my will, it does not necessarily follow that they proceed from external objects. The impulses I spoke of just now occur in me, and yet they appear alien to my will; so perhaps there exists in me some other faculty, as yet imperfectly known to me, that generates such ideas; just as I have always so far thought such ideas are formed in me in dreams without the help of any external objects.

Finally, even if they did proceed from objects other than myself, it does not follow that they must resemble them. Indeed, I seem to have often observed a vast difference, in many respects. For example, I find within myself two different ideas of the sun. One is derived, so to say, from the senses, and is a typical example of the ideas I regard as acquired; by this the sun appears very small. The other I get from astronomical reasoning; that is, it is derived from my innate notions, or at least is somehow my own work; by this the sun is represented as many times bigger than the earth. Both ideas cannot resemble the sun that exists outside me; and reason convinces me that the idea most unlike the sun is the very one that seems to be derived most directly from the sun.

All this is enough to prove that up to now it has not been by any certain judgment, but only by some blind impulse that I have believed in objects other than myself which implant in me ideas or pictures of themselves, through the sense-organs or in some other way.

At this point, however, there occurs to me a way of investigating whether any of the objects of which there are ideas within me also exist outside me. I can see no inequality among ideas taken merely as certain states of consciousness (*cogitandi quidam modi*); all of them seem to originate from myself in the same way; but in so far as one represents one object, and another another, there are obviously great differences. For indubitably the ideas that manifest substances to me are something more, have, so to say, a greater amount of representative reality, than those which merely represent states or accidents; and again, my conception of a supreme God, eternal, infinite, omniscient, almighty, and Creator of all that exists besides himself, certainly has a greater amount of representative reality than the ideas by which finite substances are manifested.

Now it is already clear by the light of nature that the complete efficient cause must contain at least as much as the effect of that cause. For where, pray, could the effect get its reality if not from the cause? And how could the cause supply it, without possessing it itself? So it follows both that something cannot be made by nothing, and that what is more perfect, or contains in itself a greater amount of reality, cannot be made by what is, or has, less. This is obvious not only as regards those effects that have actual or inherent reality; but also as regards ideas, in which only representative reality is to be considered. That is: not merely is it impossible that a previously non-existent stone, say, should now begin to exist without being produced by something containing all that is inherent in the stone, either as it inheres in the stone (*vel formaliter*) or in some higher form (*vel eminenter*); [1] or again, that heat should be induced in a subject previously not hot, except by something of at least the same grade of perfection as heat; but further I cannot have the idea of heat, or of a stone, without its being put into me by a cause in which there is in fact as much reality as I conceive to exist in the heat or the stone. For though this cause can transfer none of its actual or inherent reality to my idea, it must not be thought on that account that the cause must be less real; rather I must consider that the idea itself is of such a nature

[1] [Here as elsewhere I have not tried to translate the scholastic terms literally; they had degenerated to mere jargon by Descartes's time, and literal translation would be nonsense to most modern readers. I have, however, supplied the original words in parenthesis where it seemed desirable.—TR.]

as to require for its own part no inherent reality except what it borrows from my consciousness, of which it is a state. But the specific representative reality comprised in my idea must be got from a cause possessing at least the same degree of inherent reality as the idea has of representative reality.[1] For if we suppose something to be found in an idea that was not in its cause, it will have it from nothing; and however imperfect a mode of existence it is for something to exist in the intellect representatively, by way of an idea, it is certainly not nothing, and so cannot come from nothing.

Moreover, I must not suspect that, because the reality I consider in my ideas is merely representative, this degree of reality need not occur actually in the cause of the ideas— that it is enough for it to occur representatively. For the representative mode of existence belongs to ideas, from their very nature; and in the same way actual existence belongs to the causes of ideas, from *their* very nature—at least this is true of the first and principal causes. And though one idea may originate from another, an infinite regress here is impossible; we must at last get back to some primary idea whose cause is as it were an archetype, containing actually any reality whatever that occurs in the idea representatively. So it is clear to me by the light of nature that the ideas in me are like pictures; they may fall short of the perfection of the things from which they are taken, but cannot contain anything greater or more perfect.

The longer and more carefully I examine these points, the more clearly and distinctly I am aware of their truth. What then am I to conclude? Suppose some one of my ideas has so high a degree of representative reality that I am sure the perfection so represented does not inhere in myself, either in its own proper form or in some higher

[1] [Cp. *Princ.*, I. xvii; below, pp. 184-5, § D.—Tr.]

form; and that therefore I myself cannot be the cause of that idea. From this, I must conclude, it necessarily follows that I am not alone in the world; there is something else—the cause of the idea in question. If on the other hand no such idea is to be found in me, I shall have no argument to demonstrate the existence of something other than myself; for after careful examination of all the arguments, I have not been able to find any other up to now.

Now my ideas include, besides my idea of myself (as to which there can be no problem just now), various ideas representing God, inanimate corporeal objects, angels, animals, and finally other men like myself.

As regards ideas standing for other men, or animals, or angels, I can easily see that they could be formed from my ideas of myself, corporeal objects and God; even if there were in the world no men but me, no animals, and no angels.

As for my ideas of corporeal objects, they contain nothing so great that it seems it could not originate from myself. For if I look more clearly and examine them one by one, as I yesterday examined the idea of the wax, I observe that it is only of a very few properties that they give me clear and distinct perception: viz. magnitude or extension in length, breadth, and depth; shape, which arises from this extension's having boundaries; position, a relation between objects possessing shape; and motion, or change of position; to these may be added substance, duration, and number. Other properties—light and colours, sounds, odours, flavours, heat and cold, and other tactile qualities—are experienced (*cogitantur*) by me only in a very obscure and confused way, so that I do not even know whether they are real or illusory, that is, whether the ideas I have of them are ideas of positive reality or not. I observed indeed a little while ago that falsehood strictly so called, intrinsic (*formalem*) falsehood, can occur only in judgments; but in ideas there does occur another sort of falsehood, relative to their subject-matter (*materialis*)—viz. when they represent what is not a positive thing as if it were one. Thus, my ideas of cold and heat are so far from being clear and distinct that I cannot learn from them whether cold is merely absence of heat, or heat merely absence of cold; whether both are real qualities or neither is. Now there can be no ideas that are not as it were ideas of realities; so if in truth cold is merely absence of heat, the idea that represents it to me as something real and positive is fairly called false; and so for other such ideas.

To such ideas I need assign no author other than myself. If they are false, that is, do not represent any objects, I know by the light of nature that they proceed from nonentity—they occur in me simply because my nature is lacking in something, not being fully perfect; and if they are true, yet the degree of reality that they exhibit is so low that I cannot distinguish it from nonentity, and I do not see why they cannot originate from myself.

As for the clear and distinct elements in my ideas of corporeal objects, it should seem I may have borrowed some of them from my idea of myself; viz. substance, duration, number, and so on. I think (*cogito*) that a stone is a substance, or an entity that is capable of existing in its own right; I also think I am a substance. Of course I conceive of myself as a thinking (*cogitantem*), not an extended being, and of the stone as an extended, not a thinking, being; and these conceptions are utterly different; but they seem to agree as regards the definition of substance. Again, I perceive that I exist now, and I remember that I existed previously; again, I have various experiences (*cogitationes*) and apprehend their number; I thus get ideas of duration and number, which I can afterwards transfer to any other objects. The other constituents of my ideas of corporeal objects—extension, shape, position, and motion—cannot indeed exist as such in me, since I am nothing but a conscious being; but because they are only certain aspects (*modi*) of a substance, and I am a substance, it seems possible for them to be contained in me in a higher form.[1]

It only remains to be considered whether there is some element in the idea of God that could not have originated from myself. By the word ' God ' I mean a substance that is infinite, independent, supremely intelligent, supremely powerful, and the Creator of myself and anything else that may exist. The more I consider all these attributes, the less it seems possible for them to have originated from myself. So, by what I said above, it must be inferred that God exists.

I have indeed the idea of a substance just from the fact of being a substance; but I could not on that account have the idea of an infinite substance, for I myself am finite; unless, indeed, that idea proceeded from some substance that was really infinite.

I must not think that my conception of the infinite has come about, not through a proper idea, but by a denial of the finite—as I conceive of rest and darkness by way of the denial of motion and light; on the contrary, I clearly understand that there is more reality in an infinite than a finite substance, and that therefore in a way my primary concept (*perceptionem*) is rather of the infinite than of the finite—rather of God, than of myself. How could I understand my doubting and desiring—that is, my lacking something and not being altogether perfect—if I had no idea of a more perfect being as a standard by which to recognise my own defects ?[2]

---

[1] [Cp. *Princ.*, I. lii-liii; below, pp. 192-3, § o.—TR.]
[2] [Cp. *Princ.*, I. xxiii; below, pp. 185-6, § E.—TR.]

Nor can it be said that this idea of God may be false in relation to its subject-matter, and thus come from nothingness —as I observed just now about the ideas of heat and cold and so on. On the contrary, it is supremely clear and distinct and representatively more real than any other; none is in itself truer, or less open to the suspicion of falsehood. This idea, I say, of being supremely perfect and infinite is true in a special degree; for even if it may be imagined that no such being exists, yet it cannot be imagined that, as I said about the idea of cold, the idea does not manifest to me any [positive] reality. Moreover, it is supremely clear and distinct; for all my clear and distinct conceptions (*quidquid . . . percipio*) of any genuine reality that involves some perfection are wholly comprised in it. It is nothing against this that I do not comprehend the infinite, or that there are in God countless things that I not only cannot comprehend, but perhaps cannot in any way reach with my mind (*cogitatione*); for it belongs to the definition of the infinite that I who am finite cannot comprehend it. It is enough for me to understand and believe just this: whatever I clearly conceive (*percipio*), and know to involve some perfection, and perhaps countless other things as well that I do not know, must exist in God, either as such or in a higher form; so that my idea of God has the highest degree of truth, and is the most clear and distinct, of all my ideas.[1]

'But perhaps I am something greater than I myself understand. Perhaps all the perfections I attribute to God are somehow in me potentially, though they do not emerge yet and are not yet brought into actuality. For I experience already a gradual increase of my knowledge; I do not see what is to prevent its being thus increased more and more indefinitely; nor why, when my knowledge has thus grown, I may not use it to acquire all the other

[1] [Cp. *Princ.*, I. xxiii-iv, liv; below, pp. 185, 192, §§ E, O.—TR.]

perfections of God; nor, finally, why the potentiality of such perfections, if it exists in me already, is not enough to produce the idea of them.'

All these things are impossible. First, it is true that my knowledge gradually increases, and I have many potentialities as yet unactualised; but this is alien to the idea of God, which implies absolutely no potentiality; for the mere fact of gradual growth is a sure proof of imperfection. Again, even if my knowledge always grow more and more, yet I see that it will never be actually infinite; for it will never reach a point where it is not capable of still further increase. God, on the contrary, I judge to be actually infinite, so that nothing can be added to his perfection. Finally, I can see that the representative existence of an idea cannot be produced by mere potential existence, which strictly speaking is nothingness, but only by actual or objective (*formali*) existence.

There is none of these points that is not obvious on careful reflection, by the light of nature; but when I reflect less, and the images of sensible objects blind my mind's eye, I cannot so easily remember why the idea of a more perfect being than myself must proceed from some being that really is more perfect. This makes me want to inquire further whether I myself, who have the idea, could exist, if no such being existed. Now from what source could I have my being? Either from myself, or from my parents, or from some things, whatever they may be, less perfect than God; for there cannot be thought or imagined anything more perfect than he, nor even equally perfect.

Now if I had existence from myself, I should have no doubts or wants, and in general nothing would be lacking in me; I should have endowed myself with all the perfections of which I have any idea—in fact I should myself be a God. I must not think it would perhaps be harder to get what I lack than what I already have; on the contrary, it is manifestly far more difficult that I should have come to exist (*fuisse*)—that a conscious being or substance should come out of nothing—than that I should acquire knowledge of many things I am now ignorant of—knowledge that is a mere accident of this substance. At any rate, if I got that greater attribute from myself, I should not have denied myself this knowledge which it is easier to get; nor, for that matter, have denied myself any of the qualities that I conceive (*percipio*) as involved in the idea of God. For they do not seem to me any harder to get; and if it were harder, it would also seem harder to me, if indeed I had got my other qualities from myself; for then I should know by experience that my power was limited to the latter.

I cannot evade the force of these arguments by supposing that I always have existed as I do now; as though it followed that there was no need to look for any author of my being. For the whole duration of life is divisible into countless parts, all mutually independent; so from my having existed a little while ago it does not follow that I need exist now, unless some cause creates me anew at this very moment, in other words preserves me. For it is clear, when one considers the nature of time, that just the same power and agency is needed to preserve any object at the various moments of its duration, as would be needed to create it anew if it did not yet exist; there is thus only a conceptual distinction between preservation and creation, and this is one of the things that are obvious by the light of nature. So what I must now ask myself is whether I have any power of bringing it about that I, who now exist, shall also exist a little while from now; for since I am merely a conscious being (*res cogitans*) or at least am now dealing with that precise part of me which is a conscious being, I should undoubtedly be conscious (*conscius essem*)[1] of any such power if I had it. Now I actually find I have none; and from this very fact I realise most clearly that I depend on some being other than myself.

'Maybe this being is not God; maybe I was produced by my parents, or by some causes less perfect than God.' But, as I said before, it is clear the cause must comprise at least as much as the effect; and I am a conscious being and have an idea of God within myself; so whatever may be alleged to be my cause must also be acknowledged to be a conscious being and to possess the idea of all the perfections I attribute to God. About this cause the question may again be raised: Is it from itself that it has existence, or from some further cause? If it has existence from itself, it is clear by the foregoing that it is itself God; for since it has the power of existing in its own right (*per se*), it undoubtedly has also the power of possessing all the perfections of which it has an idea, that is, all that I conceive to exist in God. If on the other hand it has existence from another cause, the question will similarly arise again for this cause; does it exist of itself or from a further cause? And finally we shall reach the ultimate cause, namely God. It is obvious that an infinite regress is here impossible; especially as I am here dealing not merely with the cause that once upon a time produced me, but also in particular with the cause that preserves me in the present.

Again, it cannot be imagined that perhaps several part-causes concurred in my making, and I got the idea of one of the perfections I attribute to God from one, and the idea of another from another; so that each of those perfections is to be found somewhere in the universe, but not all joined together in some one being, God. On the contrary, unity, simplicity, or the inseparability of all God's attributes,

1 [For *conscius*, see *Princ.*, I. ix; below, p. 183, § A.—Tr.]

89

is itself one of the chief perfections I conceive him to have. And at any rate the idea of this one among all God's perfections, his unity, could not have been put in me by any cause, without my getting from that cause the ideas of other perfections as well; for the cause could not make me understand all the perfections as combined and inseparable, without at the same time making me perceive what these perfections were.

As for my parents, even if all the beliefs I have ever had about them were true, they certainly do not preserve me; nor did they in any way even make me, in so far as I am a conscious being; they merely induced certain dispositions in the matter in which I have hitherto held that I inhere— that is, that my mind inheres (for I mean here by 'I' only the mind). So no problem arises here about them. On all counts, the conclusion must be: from the mere fact that I exist, and have in me some idea of a most perfect being, that is, God, it is clearly demonstrated that God also exists.

It only remains for me to examine how I got this idea from God. I did not derive it from the senses; it did not at any time come to me unexpectedly, as normally happens with the ideas of sensible objects when those objects affect (or seem to affect) the external sense-organs; and it is not my own invention, for I can neither add anything to it nor subtract anything from it. So it can only be innate in me, just as the idea of myself is.

And certainly it is not surprising that God, when he created me, should have implanted this idea in me, to be as it were an artist's mark impressed on his work. This mark need not be anything distinct from the work itself. From the mere fact of my creation by God, it is highly worthy of belief that I am made somehow to his image and likeness, and that I perceive this likeness, which comprises the idea of God, by the same faculty as enables me to

perceive myself. That is to say: when I turn my mind's
eye on myself, I understand, not only that I am an incomplete being dependent on another, and indefinitely
craving for greater and greater, better and better things;
but also, at the same time, that he on whom I depend
comprises all these greater things, not merely in an indefinite potentiality, but actually and infinitely, and
therefore that he is God. The whole force of the argument
lies in this: I realise that I could not possibly exist with the
nature I actually have, that is, one endowed with the idea
of God, unless there really is a God; the very God, I mean,
of whom I have an idea; and he must possess all the
perfections of which I can attain any notion (*cogitatione*),
although I cannot comprehend them; and he must be
liable to no defects. From this it is clear enough that he
cannot be deceitful; for it is obvious by the light of nature
that any fraud or deceit depends on some defect.

But before examining this more carefully, and at the
same time seeking for other truths inferable from this,
I wish to stay a little in the contemplation of God; to
meditate within myself on his attributes; to behold,
wonder at, adore the beauty of this immeasurable Light,
so far as the eye of my darkened understanding can bear it.
For just as we believe that the supreme happiness of another
life consists merely in this contemplation of the Divine
Majesty; so even now the same contemplation, though
much less perfect, makes us aware that we can get from it
the greatest joy of which we are capable in this life.

FOURTH MEDITATION

Truth and Falsehood

In the last few days I have accustomed myself to withdraw my mind from the senses; I have been careful to observe how little truth there is in our perceptions of corporeal objects; how much more is known about the human mind, and how much more again about God. I thus have now no difficulty at all in turning my thoughts (*cogitationem*) from imaginable objects to objects that are purely intelligible and wholly separate from matter. And certainly my idea of the human mind in so far as it is a conscious being, not extended in length, breadth, and depth nor owing any other characteristic to the body, is much more distinct than the ideas I have of any corporeal object. And when I observe that I am doubting, or am an incomplete and dependent being, there comes to me a clear and distinct idea of an independent and complete being, namely God; and from the mere fact that such an idea occurs in me, or that I who have it exist, the conclusion is manifest to me that God exists likewise, and that my whole existence depends on him from moment to moment; so much so, that I am confident that the human mind can know nothing more certainly or more evidently. At this point I think I see a way of passing from this contemplation of the true God, ' in whom are hidden all the treasures of knowledge and wisdom ', to the knowledge of other things.

First, I can see the impossibility of God's ever deceiving me. Any fraud or deception involves imperfection; the ability to deceive may to some degree argue skill or power, but the will to deceive is a sign of malice or weakness, and so cannot occur in God.

Next, I am aware of having the faculty of judging. This, like everything else that is in me, I have received from God; and since God would not deceive me, he cannot have given me a faculty whose right employment could ever lead me astray.

The only doubtful point that remains here is that it seems to follow that therefore I can *never* go wrong. If I owe whatever is in me to God, and he has given me no faculty of going wrong, it seems that I never can go wrong. Certainly, so long as I think only of God, and turn my attention wholly to him, I can discern no cause of error or falsehood. But when I turn back to myself, I am aware of my liability to innumerable errors. When I look for a cause of these, I observe that I possess not only a real and positive idea of God, the supremely perfect being, but also what I may call a sort of negative idea of nothingness— of that which is furthest removed from all perfection. I am a kind of intermediate between God and nothingness, between the Supreme Being and non-being (*non ens*); my nature is such that, in so far as I am a creature of the Supreme Being, I have nothing in me to deceive me or lead me astray; nevertheless, in so far as I also participate some-how in nothingness, non-being—that is, in so far as I am not myself the Supreme Being, and am lacking in no end of things—it is not surprising that I am deceived. Thus I know at any rate that error as such is not a positive reality dependent on God, but merely a deficiency; and in order to go wrong I need no faculty expressly given me by God; I happen to go wrong because the faculty of right judgment that he has given me does not exist in me in an infinite degree.

This, however, is not yet wholly satisfactory. Error is not a pure negation; it is a privation—the lack of some

93

knowledge that in some way ought to be in me. And considering the nature of God, it seems impossible for him to have put in me a faculty not perfect of its kind, or lacking in some perfection it ought to have. For, the more skilled the artisan, the more perfect are the works that proceed from him; if so, how can anything made by the sovereign Maker of all things fail to be beyond all comparison? God could undoubtedly have created me incapable of being deceived; again, he undoubtedly always wills what is best; then is it better for me to be deceived than not to be deceived?

On more careful reflection I observe in the first place that it is not to be wondered that God does some things whose reasons I do not understand; and I must not doubt his existence on account of coming across other things about which I do not grasp why or how he made them. For I know already that my nature is very weak and limited, whereas the Divine Nature is immeasurable, incomprehensible, infinite; this is enough to show me that innumerable things whose causes are unknown to me lie in God's power. For this very reason, I consider the usual enquiries about final causes to be wholly useless in physics; it could not but be rash, I think, for me to investigate the aims of God.

Further, whenever we are enquiring whether God's works are perfect we must have regard, not to any creature by itself, but to the whole universe. What might well seem extremely imperfect, if it existed alone, is most perfect when conceived as part of a world. It is true that, since I have resolved to doubt everything, I have not so far any certain knowledge that anything beyond myself and God; but on the other hand, considering God's infinite power, I cannot deny that he has made, or at least could make, many other things, so that I must be conceived as a part of a universe.

Turning now specially to my own case and considering the nature of my errors—for they alone argue imperfection in me—I observe that they depend on two concurrent causes: on my faculty of cognition, and my faculty of choice or free will; that is, on the intellect and at the same time on the will. By the mere intellect I do no more than perceive the ideas that are matter for judgment; and precisely so regarded the intellect contains, properly speaking, no error. There may be innumerable things of which I have no idea; but this is not properly to be called a privation, but a merely negative lack, of the ideas. I can bring forward no reason to show that God ought to have given me a greater power of knowledge than he did; however skilled I understand an artisan to be, I do not think he ought to have put into every one of his works all the perfections he is able to put into any.

Again, I cannot complain that I received from God a restricted or imperfect will or freedom; for I am aware of no bounds upon its scope. Indeed, the following seems to me very remarkable. Nothing else in me is so perfect or so great but that I understand the possibility of something still more perfect, still greater. For instance, if I consider the faculty of understanding, I discern at once that in me it is very slight and greatly restricted. I thereupon form the idea of a far greater faculty; indeed, of the greatest possible, an infinite one; and I perceive, from the mere fact that I can form the idea of this, that it belongs to the nature of God. Similarly, if I examine my faculty of memory, or imagination, or any other, I find none that I do not see to be slight and circumscribed in me, but immeasurable in God. It is only will, or freedom of choice, that I experience in myself in such a degree that I do not grasp the idea of any greater; so that it is in this regard above all, I take it, that I bear the image and likeness of God. For although God's will is incomparably greater

95

than mine, both by reason of the knowledge and power that accompany it and make it more firm and efficacious, and by reason of its object—of its greater scope—yet it does not seem to be greater when considered precisely as will.[1] Will consists simply in the fact that we are able alike to do and not to do a given thing (that is, can either assert or deny, either seek or shun); or rather, simply in the fact that our impulse towards what the intellect presents to us as worthy of assertion or denial, as a thing to be sought or shunned, is such that we feel ourselves not to be determined by any external force. There is no need for me to be impelled both ways in order to be free; on the contrary, the more I am inclined one way—either because I clearly understand it under the aspect of truth and goodness, or because God has so disposed my inmost consciousness (*intima cogitationis meae*)—the more freely do I choose that way. Divine grace and natural knowledge certainly do not diminish liberty; they rather increase and strengthen it.[2] Indeed, the indifference that I am aware of when there is no reason urging me one way rather than the other, is the lowest grade of liberty; it argues no perfection of free will, but only some defect or absence of knowledge; for if I always saw clearly what is good and true, I should never deliberate as to what I ought to judge or choose; and thus, although entirely free, I could never be indifferent.

From this I see that the cause of my errors is not the power of willing that I have from God, considered in itself; for that is most ample, and perfect of its kind; nor yet is it the power of understanding; for there is no doubt that whatever I understand, since my understanding it comes from God, I understand correctly, and cannot possibly be deceived about. Whence then do my errors originate? Surely, just from this: my will extends more

[1] [Cp. *Princ.*, I. xxxv; below, pp. 187-8, § H.—TR.]
[2] [Cp. *Princ.*, I. xl-xli; below, pp. 188-9, § J.—TR.]

widely than my understanding, and yet I do not restrain
it within the same bounds, but apply it to what I do not
understand. Since it is here indifferent, it easily turns
aside from truth and goodness; and so I fall into both
error and sin.[1]

For instance, during these last few days I have been
considering whether anything in the world exists, and have
observed that, from the very fact that I am examining
the question, it necessarily follows that I do exist. I could
not but judge to be true what I understood so clearly; not
because I was compelled to do so by any external cause,
but because the great illumination of my understanding
was followed by a great inclination of the will; and my
belief was the more free and spontaneous for my not
being indifferent in the matter. But at this moment I
am not merely knowing that I exist, in so far as I am a
conscious being; there occurs to me also an idea of
a corporeal nature, and it so happens that I am doubtful
whether the consciousness (*natura cogitans*) that is in me—
or rather, that is myself—is different from this corporeal
nature, or whether both are the same thing; and, let us
suppose, so far there is no convincing reason that occurs
to my mind in favour of either view. Surely just on this
account I am indifferent whether I assert or deny either,
or even abstain from judgment on the matter altogether.

This indifference, moreover, extends not only to things
that the understanding knows absolutely nothing about,
but in general to everything that the understanding does
not know clearly enough at the time when the will
deliberates. However much I may be drawn one way by
probable conjectures, the mere knowledge that they are
only conjectures and not certain and indubitable reasons,
is enough to incline my assent the other way. I have had
proof enough of this in the last few days; all the things

[1] [Cp. *Princ.*, I. xxxv; below, pp. 187-8, § H.—Tr.]

in whose truth I had previously had the greatest possible belief, I now supposed to be quite false, simply because I had observed the possibility of having some sort of doubt about them.

Now when I do not perceive clearly and distinctly enough what the truth is, it is clear that if I abstain from judgment I do right and am not deceived. But if I assert or deny, I am using my free will wrongly; if the side I take is falsehood, then clearly I shall be in error; if I embrace the other side, I shall by chance fall upon the truth, but nevertheless this decision will be blameworthy; for it is obvious by the light of nature that perception by the understanding should always come before the determination of the will. There is inherent in this wrong use of free will [1] the privation in which the nature (*forma*) of error consists; this privation, I say, is inherent in the actual operation in so far as it proceeds from me; not in the faculty I received from God, nor even in the operation, in so far as it depends on him.

I have no reason, either, for complaining that God did not give me a greater power of understanding, or a greater measure of the light of nature, than he did in fact; for it belongs to the notion of a finite understanding that there should be many things it does not understand; and it belongs to the notion of a created understanding that it should be finite. Indeed, I have reason to thank God, who never owed anything to me, for what he has bestowed; it is not for me to think that, if he has not given me something, I am deprived of it, or he has robbed me of it. [2]

Again, I have no reason for complaining that God gave me a will extending more widely than my understanding; for what constitutes will is just a single thing, so to speak indivisible; it seems incompatible with its nature that

[1] [Cp. *Princ.*, I. xlii; below, pp. 189–90, § K.—Tr.]
[2] [Cp. *Princ.* I. xxxvii; below, p. 188, § I.—Tr.]

anything should be subtracted from it; moreover, the wider its extent is, the more grateful I should be to its Giver.

Finally, I must not complain that God co-operates with me when I perform those acts of will, or those judgments, in which I go wrong. In so far as those acts depend on God, they are wholly true and good; and in a way it is a greater perfection in me to be able to perform those acts than if I were not able. And the privation that constitutes the proper essence (*ratio formalis*) of error and guilt requires no divine co-operation; for it is not a thing, and, in its relation to God as cause, it must be called not a privation, but a mere negation. For it is surely no imperfection in God that he gave me freedom to assent or not to assent to certain things of which he put no clear and distinct perception in my understanding;[1] but it undoubtedly is an imperfection in me not to use this freedom well, and to make decisions about what I do not properly understand. I can see indeed that God could easily have brought it about that, while remaining a free agent, and limited in knowledge, I should never in fact go wrong; he might either have implanted in my understanding clear and distinct perceptions of everything that I was ever going to deliberate about; or else have impressed it on my memory, so firmly that I could never forget it, that I must never decide about anything that I did not clearly and distinctly understand. And I readily understand that if God had so made me, then I myself, considered as a complete whole, should have been more perfect than I am now. But I cannot on that account deny that in some way the perfection of the universe is greater, because some parts of it are not exempt from going wrong and others are, that it would be if all parts were exactly alike. And I have no right to complain that the part God has wished me to play in the world is not the greatest and most perfect of all.

[1] [Cp. *Princ.*, I. xxxiv; below, p. 187, § G.—Tr.]

99

Moreover, although I cannot avoid going wrong in the first way—viz. by manifest perception of everything I have to deliberate about—I can do so in the second way—viz. by simply remembering that I must avoid making a decision, whenever the truth of the matter is not clear. I am indeed conscious of my weakness; I cannot adhere constantly to one and the same idea at all times; but by careful and reiterated meditation I may bring it about that this idea comes to mind whenever necessary, and thus get into the habit of not going wrong.

This is the chief and greatest perfection of man; so I think today's meditation has been of no small service, since I have been investigating the cause of error and falsehood. And surely no other cause is possible than the one I have explained. For whenever I restrain my will in making decisions, so that its range is confined to what the understanding shows it clearly and distinctly, I just cannot go wrong. For every clear and distinct perception is something; so it cannot come from nothingness, but must have God for its author; God, I say, the supremely Perfect, who it is absurd should be deceitful; therefore, it is indubitably true. Thus today I have learnt, not only what to avoid, so as not to be deceived, but also what to do, so as to attain the truth; I shall certainly attain it if only I take enough notice of all that I perfectly understand, and distinguish this from everything else, which I apprehend more obscurely and confusedly. For the future I will take good care of this.

FIFTH MEDITATION

The Nature of Material Things: God's Existence again considered

There are many matters still to be investigated as regards the attributes of God and the nature of myself, or my mind; perhaps I shall take them up again elsewhere. For the moment—since I have now observed what I must do and avoid so as to attain truth—the most urgent task seems to be to try to get out of the difficulties I fell into on previous days, and see if any certainty is to be had as regards material objects.

Before enquiring whether any such objects exist outside me, I must consider the ideas of them, precisely as occurring in my consciousness, and see which of them are distinct and which are confused. I distinctly imagine quantity, the so-called continuous quantity of the philosophers; that is to say, the extension of the quantity, or rather of the quantified object, in length, breadth, and depth. I can enumerate different parts of it; to these parts I can assign at will size, shape, position, and local motion; and to these motions I can assign any durations I choose. Not only are these general concepts quite familiar and perspicuous; I perceive also innumerable details as regards shape, number, motion, and so on. The truth of these is obvious and so much in accord with my nature that my first discovery of them appears not as the learning of something new, but as the recollection of what I already knew—as the first occasion of my noticing things that had long been present to me, although I had never previously turned my mind's eye towards them.

The most important point, I think, is that I find within myself innumerable ideas of a kind of objects that, even if perhaps they have no existence anywhere outside me, cannot be called nonentities; my thinking of them (*a me cogitentur*) is in a way arbitrary, but they are no figments of mine; they have their own genuine and unchangeable natures. For example, when I imagine a triangle, it may be that no such figure exists anywhere outside my consciousness (*cogitationem*), or never has existed; but there certainly exists its determinate nature (its essence, its form), which is unchangeable and eternal. This is no figment of mine, and does not depend on my mind, as is clear from the following: various properties can be proved of this triangle, e.g. that its three angles are together equal to two right angles, that its greatest side subtends its greatest angle, and so on; willy-nilly, I now clearly see them, even if I have not thought of them (*cogitaverim*) in any way when I have previously imagined a triangle; they cannot, then, be figments of mine.

It would be irrelevant for me to say that perhaps this idea of a triangle came to me from external objects by way of the sense-organs (since I have sometimes seen bodies of triangular shape); for I can mentally form countless other figures, as to which there can be no suspicion that they ever came my way through the senses, and yet I can prove various properties of them, just as I can of the triangle. All these properties are true, since I perceive them clearly; and so they are something, not mere nothingness; for it is obvious that whatever is true is something; and I have already proved abundantly that whatever I clearly perceive is true. Even apart from that proof, my mind is assuredly so constituted that I cannot but assent to them, at least at the time of clearly perceiving them; moreover, I remember that even previously at a time when I was utterly immersed in the objects of sensation, I regarded this kind of truths as the most certain of all—namely, those that I recognised as evident in regard to figures, and numbers, and other matters of arithmetic, or of geometry, or in general of pure abstract mathematics.

Now if it follows, from my mere ability to elicit the idea of some object from my consciousness (*cogitatione*), that all the properties that I clearly and distinctly perceive the object to have do really belong to it; could not this give rise to an argument by which the existence of God might be proved? I assuredly find in myself the idea of God—of a supremely perfect being—no less than the idea of a figure or a number; and I clearly and distinctly understand that everlasting existence belongs to his nature, no less than I can see that what I prove of some figure, or number, belongs to the nature of that figure, or number. So, even if my meditations on previous days were not entirely true, yet I ought to hold the existence of God with at least the same degree of certainty as I have so far held mathematical truths.

At first sight, indeed, this is not quite clear; it bears a certain appearance of being a fallacy. For, since I am accustomed to the distinction of existence and essence in all other objects, I am readily convinced that existence can be disjoined even from the divine essence, and that thus God can be conceived (*cogitari*) as non-existent. But on more careful consideration it becomes obvious that existence can no more be taken away from the divine essence than the magnitude of its three angles together (that is, their being equal to two right angles) can be taken away from the essence of a triangle; or than the idea of a valley can be taken away from the idea of a hill. So it is not less [1] absurd to think of God (that is, a supremely perfect being) lacking existence (that is, lacking a certain perfection), than to think of a hill without a valley.

[1] [The Latin word is *magis;* but the sense seems to require *minus.* So the French version : *moins de répugnance.*—TR.]

'Perhaps I cannot think of (*cogitare*) God except as existing, just as I cannot think of a hill without a valley. But from my thinking of a hill with a valley, it does not follow that there is any hill in the world; similarly, it appears not to follow, from my thinking of God as existent, that God does exist. For my thought (*cogitatio*) imposes no necessity on things; and just as I can imagine a winged horse, although no horse has wings, so, it may be, I can feign the conjunction of God and existence even though no God should exist.'

There is a lurking fallacy here. What follows from my inability to think of a mountain apart from a valley is not that a mountain and a valley exist somewhere, but only that mountain and valley, whether they exist or not, are mutually inseparable. But from my inability to think of God as non-existent, it follows that existence is inseparable from God and thus that he really does exist. It is not that my thought makes this so, or imposes any necessity on anything; on the contrary, the necessity of the fact itself, that is, of God's existence, is what determines me to think this way. I am not free to think of God apart from existence (that is, of a supremely perfect being apart from the supreme perfection) in the way that I can freely imagine a horse either with or without wings.

Moreover, I must not say at this point: 'After supposing God to have all perfections, I must certainly suppose him to be existent, since existence is one among perfections; but the initial supposition was not necessary. In the same way, there is no necessity for me to think all quadrilaterals can be inscribed in a circle; but given that I do think so, I shall necessarily have to admit that a rhombus can be inscribed in a circle; this, however, is obviously false.' For there is indeed no necessity for me ever to happen upon any thought of (*cogitationem de*) God; but whenever I choose to think of (*cogitare de*) the First and Supreme Being, and as it were bring out the idea of him from the treasury of my mind, I must necessarily ascribe to him all perfections, even if I do not at the moment enumerate them all, or attend to each. This necessity clearly ensures that, when later on I observe that existence is a perfection, I am justified in concluding that the First and Supreme Being exists. In the same way, it is not necessary that I should ever imagine any triangle; but whenever I choose to consider a rectilinear figure that has just three angles, I must ascribe to it properties from which it is rightly inferred that its three angles are not greater than two right angles; even if I do not notice this at the time. When, on the other hand, I examine what figures can be inscribed in circles, it is in no way necessary for me to think all quadrilaterals belong to this class; indeed, I cannot even imagine this, so long as I will admit only what I clearly and distinctly understand. Thus there is a great difference between such false suppositions and my genuine innate ideas, among which the first and chief is my idea of God. In many ways, I can see that this idea is no fiction depending on my way of thinking (*cogitatione*), but an image of a real and immutable nature. First, I can frame no other concept of anything to whose essence existence belongs, except God alone; again, I cannot conceive of two or more such Gods; and given that one God exists, I clearly see that necessarily he has existed from all eternity, and will exist to all eternity; and I perceive many other Divine attributes, which I can in no wise diminish or alter.

Whatever method of proof I use, it always comes back to this: I am not utterly convinced of anything but what I clearly and distinctly perceive. Of the things I thus perceive, some are obvious to anybody; others are discovered only by those who undertake closer inspection and more careful investigation, but, when once discovered, are regarded as no less certain than the others. It is not so readily apparent that the square on the base of a right-angled triangle is equal to the squares on the sides, as it is that the base subtends the greatest angle; but once it has been seen to be so, it is just as much believed. Now as regards God, assuredly there would be nothing that I perceived earlier or more readily, if it were not that I am overwhelmed by prejudices, and my consciousness (*cogitationem*) beset in every direction by images of sensible objects.[1] For what is intrinsically more obvious than that the Supreme Being is; that God, to whose essence alone existence belongs, exists? And though it took careful consideration for me to see this, yet now I am as certain of it as I am of anything else that appears most certain; not only that, but I can further see that the certainty of everything else depends on this, so that apart from this no perfect knowledge is ever possible.

I am indeed so constituted that I cannot but believe something to be true at the time of perceiving it clearly and distinctly. But I am likewise so constituted that I cannot fix my mind's eye constantly on the same object so as to perceive it clearly; and the memory of a previous judgment often comes back to me when I am no longer attending to my arguments for having made it. Consequently, other arguments might now be adduced, which would readily upset my view if I had no knowledge of God; and thus I should never have genuine and certain knowledge of anything, but only unsteady and changeable opinions.[2] For example, when I consider the nature of a triangle, it is most evidently apparent to me, familiar as I am with geometrical principles, that its three angles are equal to two right angles; and so long as I attend to the proof, I cannot but believe that this is true. But as soon as I

---

[1] [Cp. *Princ.* I. 1; below, p. 191, § N.—TR.]

[2] [Cp. *Princ.*, I. xiii; below, p. 184, § C.—TR.]

turn my mind's eye away from the proof, I may still remember, as much as you like, that I did see it very clearly; but I may yet easily come to doubt its truth—supposing I have no knowledge of God. For I can satisfy myself that I am so constituted as to go wrong sometimes about what I think I perceive most evidently; especially when I remember that I have frequently regarded things as true and certain, and yet have later been induced, on account of other arguments, to decide that they were false.

But now I have discerned that God exists, and have understood at the same time that everything else depends on him, and that he is not deceitful; and from this I have gathered that whatever I clearly and distinctly perceive is necessarily true. So even if I am not any longer attending to the arguments for having judged this to be true, yet, so long as I remember that I did perceive it clearly and distinctly, no contrary argument can be brought forward to induce me to doubt it; I have genuine and certain knowledge of the matter. My knowledge extends not only to this, but also to everything else that I remember I have proved—in geometry and so on.

What can now be said on the other side? That I am so made as to be frequently deceived? But I now know that as regards what I clearly understand I cannot be deceived. Or, that I have previously regarded as true and certain many things I have since observed to be false? But I never did perceive these things clearly and distinctly; I was ignorant of this criterion of truth; I believed them for other reasons, whose weakness I discovered later on. What then could be said? Could one raise the objection I made against myself just now—that perhaps I am dreaming, and all that I am now experiencing (*cogito*) has as little reality as what happens in sleep? Even this makes no difference; for assuredly, even if I were dreaming, whatever is evident to my understanding must be wholly true.

Thus I see plainly that the certainty and truth of all knowledge depends entirely on my awareness of the true God; before knowing him I could have no perfect knowledge of anything. And now it becomes possible for countless things to be clearly known and certain to me; both about God himself and other intellectual beings, and about the whole field of corporeal nature that is the subject-matter of pure mathematics.

SIXTH MEDITATION

The Existence of Material Things : the Real Distinction of Mind and Body

It remains for me to examine whether material things exist. I already know at least the possibility of their existence, in so far as they are the subject-matter of pure mathematics, since in this regard I clearly and distinctly perceive them. For God is undoubtedly able to effect whatever I am thus able to perceive; and I have never decided that anything could not be done by him, except on the ground that it would involve contradiction for me to perceive such a thing distinctly. Further, when I am occupied with material objects, I am aware of using the faculty of imagination; and this seems to imply that they exist. For when I consider carefully .what imagination is, it seems to be a kind of application of the cognitive faculty to a body intimately present to it—a body, therefore, that exists.

To explain this, I begin by examining the difference between imagination and pure understanding. For instance, when I imagine a triangle, I do not just understand that it is a figure enclosed in three lines; I also at the same time see the three lines present before my mind's eye, and this is what I call imagining them. Now if I want to think of a chiliagon, I understand just as well that it is a figure of a thousand sides as I do that a triangle is a figure of three sides; but I do not in the same way imagine the thousand sides, or see them as presented to me. I am indeed accustomed always to imagine something when I am thinking of a corporeal object; so I may confusedly picture to myself some kind of figure; but obviously this picture is not a chiliagon, since it is in no way different from the one I should form if I were thinking of a myriagon, or any other figure with very many sides; and it in no way helps me to recognise the properties that distinguish a chiliagon from other polygons. If now it is a pentagon that is in question, I can understand its figure, as I can the figure of a chiliagon, without the aid of imagination; but I may also imagine this very figure, applying my mind's eye to its five sides and at the same time to the area contained by them; and here I clearly discern that I have to make some special effort of mind to imagine it that I do not make in just understanding it; this new mental effort plainly shows the difference between imagination and pure understanding.

I further consider that this power of imagination in me, taken as distinct from the power of understanding, is not essential to the nature of myself, that is, of my mind; for even if I lacked it, I should nevertheless undoubtedly still be the selfsame one that I am; it seems, therefore, that this power must depend on some object other than myself. And if there is a body to which the mind is so conjoined that it can at will apply itself, so to say, to contemplating it, then I can readily understand the possibility of my imagining corporeal objects by this means. The difference between this mode of consciousness and pure understanding would then be simply this: in the act of understanding the mind turns as it were towards itself, and contemplates one of the ideas contained in itself; in the act of imagining, it turns to the body, and contemplates something in it resembling an idea understood by the mind itself or perceived by sense. I can readily understand, I say, that imagination could be performed in this way, if a body exists; and since there does not occur to me any other equally convenient way of explaining it, I form from this the probable conjecture that the body exists. But this is only probable; and, in spite of a careful investigation of all points, I can as yet see no way of arguing conclusively from the fact that there is in my imagination a distinct idea of a corporeal nature to the existence of any body.

Besides that aspect of body which is the subject-matter of pure mathematics, there are many other things that I habitually imagine—colours, sounds, flavours, pain, and so on; but none of these are so distinctly imagined. In any case, I perceive them better by way of sensation, and it is from thence that they seem to have reached my imagination, by the help of memory. Thus it will be more convenient to treat of them by treating of sense at the same time; I must see if I can get any certain argument for the existence of material objects from things perceived in the mode of consciousness that I call sensation.

I will first recall to myself what kinds of things I previously thought were real, as being perceived in sensation, and for what reasons I thought so; then I will set out my reasons for having later on called them in question; finally I will consider what to hold now.

In the first place, then: I had sensations of having a head, hands, feet, and the other members that make up the body; and I regarded the body as part of myself, or even as my whole self. I had sensations of the commerce of this body with many other bodies, which were capable of being beneficial or injurious to it in various ways; I estimated the beneficial effects by a sensation of pleasure, and the injurious, by a sensation of pain. Besides pain and pleasure, I had internal sensations of hunger, thirst, and other such appetites; and also of physical inclinations towards gladness, sadness, anger, and other like emotions. I had external sensations not only of the extension, shapes, and movements of bodies, but also of their hardness, heat, and other tangible qualities; also, sensations of light, colours, odours, flavours, and sounds. By the varieties of these qualities I distinguished from one another the sky, the earth, the seas, and all other bodies.

I certainly had some reason, in view of the ideas of these qualities that presented themselves to my consciousness (*cogitationi*), and that were the only proper and immediate object of my sensations, to think that I was aware in sensation of objects quite different from my own consciousness: viz. bodies from which the ideas proceeded. For it was my experience (*experiebar*) that the ideas came to me without any consent of mine; so that I could neither have a sensation of any object, however I wished, if it were not present to the sense-organ, nor help having the sensation when the object was present. Moreover, the ideas perceived in sensation were much more vivid and prominent, and, in their own way, more distinct, than any that I myself deliberately produced in my meditations, or observed to have been impressed on my memory; and thus it seemed impossible for them to proceed from myself; and the only remaining possibility was that they came from some other objects. Now since I had no conception of these objects from any other source than the ideas themselves, it could not but occur to me that they were like the ideas. Further, I remembered that I had had the use of the senses before the use of reason; and I saw that the ideas I formed myself were less prominent than those I perceived in sensation, and mostly consisted of parts taken from sensation; I thus readily convinced myself that I had nothing in my intellect that I had not previously had in sensation.

Again, I had some reason for holding that the body I called ' *my* body ' by a special title really did belong to me more than any other body did. I could never separate myself entirely from it, as I could from other bodies. All the appetites and emotions I had, I felt in the body and on its account. I felt pain, and the titillations of pleasure, in parts of *this* body, not of other, external bodies. Why should a sadness of the mind follow upon a sensation of pain, and a kind of happiness upon the titillation of sense? Why should that twitching of the stomach which I call hunger tell me that I must eat; and a dryness of the throat, that I must drink; and so on? I could give no account of this except that nature taught me so; for there is no likeness at all, so far as I can see, between the twitching in the stomach and the volition to take food; or between the sensation of an object that gives me pain, and the experience (*cogitationem*) of sadness that arises from the sensation. My other judgments, too, as regards the objects of sensation seemed to have been lessons of nature; for I had convinced myself that things were so, before setting out any reasons to prove this.

Since then, however, I have had many experiences that have gradually sapped the faith I had in the senses. It sometimes happened that towers which had looked round at a distance looked square when close at hand; and that huge statues standing on the roof did not seem large to me looking up from the ground. And there were countless other cases like these, in which I found the external senses to be deceived in their judgment; and not only the external senses, but the internal senses as well. What [experience] can be more intimate than pain? Yet I had heard sometimes, from people who had had a leg or arm cut off, that they still seemed now and then to feel pain in the part of the body that they lacked; so it seemed in my own case not to be quite certain that a limb was in pain, even if I felt pain in it. And to these reasons for doubting I more recently added two more, of highly general application. First, there is no kind of sensation that I have ever thought I had in waking life, but I may also think I have some time when I am asleep; and since I do not believe that sensations I seem to have in sleep come from external objects,

I did not see why I should believe this any the more about sensations I seem to have when I am awake. Secondly, I did not as yet know the Author of my being (or at least pretended I did not); so there seemed to be nothing against my being naturally so constituted as to be deceived even about what appeared to myself most true. As for the reasons of my former conviction that sensible objects are real, it was not difficult to answer them. I was, it seemed, naturally impelled to many courses from which reason dissuaded me; so I did not think I ought to put much reliance on what nature had taught me. And although sense-perceptions did not depend on my will, it must not be concluded, I thought, that they proceed from objects distinct from myself; there might perhaps be some faculty in myself, as yet unknown to me, that produced them.

But now that I am beginning to be better acquainted with myself and with the Author of my being, my view is that I must not rashly accept all the apparent data of sensation; nor, on the other hand, call them all in question.

In the first place, I know that whatever I clearly and distinctly understand can be made by God just as I understand it; so my ability to understand one thing clearly and distinctly apart from another is enough to assure me that they are distinct, because God at least can separate them. (It is irrelevant what faculty enables me to think of them as separate.) Now I know that I exist, and at the same time I observe absolutely nothing else as belonging to my nature or essence except the mere fact that I am a conscious being; and just from this I can validly infer that my essence consists simply in the fact that I am a conscious being. It is indeed possible (or rather, as I shall say later on, it is certain) that I have a body closely bound up with myself; but at the same time I have, on the one hand, a clear and distinct idea of myself taken simply as a conscious, not an extended, being; and, on the other hand, a distinct idea of body, taken simply as an extended, not a conscious, being; so it is certain that I am really distinct from my body, and could exist without it.[1]

Further, I find in myself powers for special modes of consciousness, e.g. imagination and sensation; I can clearly and distinctly understand myself as a whole apart from these powers, but not the powers apart from myself— apart from an intellectual substance to inhere in; for the essential (*formali*) conception of them includes some kind of intellectual act; and I thus perceive that they are distinct from me in the way aspects (*modos*) are from the object to which they belong. I also recognise other powers—those of local motion, and change of shape, and so on; these, like the ones I mentioned before, cannot be understood apart from a substance to inhere in; nor, therefore, can they exist apart from it. Clearly these, if they exist, must inhere in a corporeal or extended, not an intellectual substance; for it is some form of extension, not any intellectual act, that is involved in a clear and distinct conception of them. Now I have a passive power of sensation—of getting and recognising the ideas of sensible objects. But I could never have the use of it if there were not also in existence an active power, either in myself or in something else, to produce or make the ideas. This power certainly cannot exist in me; for it presupposes no action of my intellect, and the ideas are produced without my co-operation, and often against my will. The only remaining possibility is that it inheres in some substance other than myself. This must contain all the reality that exists representatively in the ideas produced by this active power; and it must contain it (as I remarked previously) either just as it is represented,[2] or in some higher form.[2]

[1] [Cp. *Princ.*, i. lx; below, pp. 193-4, § P.—Tr.]
[2] [See p. 81, footnote.—Tr.]

So either this substance is a body—is of corporeal nature—
and contains actually whatever is contained representatively in the ideas; or else it is God, or some creature
nobler than bodies, and contains the same reality in a
higher form.[1] But since God is not deceitful, it is quite
obvious that he neither implants the ideas in me by his
own direct action, nor yet by means of some creature that
contains the representative reality of the ideas not precisely
as they represent it,[1] but only in some higher form.[1]
For God has given me no faculty at all to discern their
origin; on the other hand, he has given me a strong
inclination to believe that these ideas proceed from corporeal objects; so I do not see how it would make sense
to say God is not deceitful, if in fact they proceed from
elsewhere, not from corporeal objects. Therefore corporeal
objects must exist. It may be that not all bodies are such
as my senses apprehend them, for this sensory apprehension
is in many ways obscure and confused; but at any rate their
nature must comprise whatever I clearly and distinctly
understand—that is, whatever, generally considered, falls
within the subject-matter of pure mathematics.

There remain some highly doubtful and uncertain points;
either mere details, like the sun's having a certain size or
shape, or things unclearly understood, like light, sound,
pain, and so on. But since God is not deceitful, there
cannot possibly occur any error in my opinions but I can
correct by means of some faculty God has given me to that
end; and this gives me some hope of arriving at the truth
even on such matters. Indeed, all nature's lessons undoubtedly contain some truth; for by nature, as a general
term, I now mean nothing other than either God himself,
or the order of created things established by God; and by
my nature in particular I mean the complex of all that God
has given *me*.

[1] [See p. 81, footnote.—Tr.]

Now there is no more explicit lesson of nature than that I have a body; that it is being injured when I feel pain; that it needs food, or drink, when I suffer from hunger, or thirst, and so on. So I must not doubt that there is some truth in this. Nature also teaches by these sensations of pain, hunger, thirst, etc., that I am not present in my body merely as a pilot is present in a ship; I am most tightly bound to it, and as it were mixed up with it, so that I and it form a unit. Otherwise, when the body is hurt, I, who am simply a conscious being, would not feel pain on that account, but would perceive the injury by a pure act of understanding, as the pilot perceives by sight any breakages there may be in the ship; and when the body needs food or drink, I should explicitly understand the fact, and not have confused sensations of hunger and thirst. For these sensations of thirst, hunger, pain, etc., are simply confused modes of consciousness that arise from the mind's being united to, and as it were mixed up with, the body.[1]

Moreover, nature teaches me that my body has an environment of other bodies, some of which must be sought for and others shunned. And from the wide variety of colours, sounds, odours, flavours, degrees of hardness, and so on, of which I have sensations, I certainly have the right to infer that in the bodies from which these various sense-perceptions arise there is corresponding, though perhaps not similar, variety. Again, from the fact that some of these perceptions are pleasant to me and others unpleasant, it is quite certain that my body—or rather myself as a whole, who am made up of body and mind—can be variously affected for good or ill by bodies in its environment.

Many other beliefs may seem to be lessons of nature, which I really derive not from nature but from a habit of inconsiderate judgment, so that they may easily be false; e.g. that a region is empty if no occurrence in it affects

[1] [Cp. *Princ.*, I. xlviii *ad fin.*; below, pp. 190-1, § M.—TR.]

117

my senses; that if a body is (say) hot, it has some property just like my idea of heat; that in a white or green object there is the same whiteness or greenness as in my sensation, and in a sweet or bitter body the same flavour as I taste, and so on; that stars and towers and other distant bodies have just the size and shape they manifest to my senses; and the like.[1] But to avoid an indistinct view of this matter, I must define here more accurately just what I mean by a lesson of nature. I am using ' nature ' here in a more restricted sense than the complex of everything that God has given me. For this complex includes much that belongs only to the mind—e.g. my seeing that what is once done cannot be undone, and the rest of what I know by the light of nature; I am not speaking here about this. Again, it includes much that has regard only to the body, e.g. a downward tendency; this again I am not now discussing. I am concerned only with what God has given to me considered as a compound of mind and body. It is a lesson of my ' nature ', in this sense, to avoid what gives me a sensation of pain, and pursue what gives me a sensation of pleasure, and so on. But it does not seem to be also a lesson of nature to draw any conclusion from sense-perception as regards external objects without a previous examination by the understanding; for knowledge of the truth about them seems to belong to the mind alone, not to the composite whole.

Thus, a star has no more effect on my eye than the flame of a small candle; but from this fact I have no real, positive inclination to believe it is no bigger; this is just an irrational judgment that I made in my earliest years. Again, I have a sensation of heat as I approach the fire; but when I approach the same fire too closely, I have a sensation of pain; so there is nothing to convince me that something in the fire resembles heat, any more than the

[1] [Cp. *Princ.*, I. lxx; below, pp. 194-6, § Q.—Tr.]

pain; it is just that there must be something in it (whatever this may turn out to be) that produces the sensations of heat or pain. Again, even if in some region there is nothing to affect the senses, it does not follow that there is no body in it. I can see that on these and many other questions I habitually pervert the order of nature. My sense-perceptions were given me by nature properly for the sole purpose of indicating to the mind what is good or bad for the whole of which the mind is a part; and to this extent they are clear and distinct enough. But I use them as if they were sure criteria for a direct judgment as to the essence of external bodies; and here they give only very obscure and confused indications.[1]

I have already examined sufficiently the reason why, in spite of God's goodness, my judgments are liable to be false. But a new problem arises here about the objects that nature shows me I ought to seek or shun; and also as regards the errors I seem to have observed in internal sensations. For instance, a man is deceived by the pleasant taste of some food, and swallows the poison concealed within it. But what his nature impels him to desire is what gives the food its pleasant taste; not the poison, of which his nature knows nothing. All that can be inferred from this is that his nature is not omniscient; and this is not surprising, for a man is a finite thing and his nature has only a finite degree of perfection.

But we quite often go wrong about the things that nature does impel us towards. For instance, sick men long for drink or food that would soon be harmful to them. It might be said that they go wrong because their nature is corrupted; but this does not remove the problem. A sick man is no less God's creature than a healthy man; and it seems just as absurd that God should give him a nature that deceives him.

[1] [Cp. *Princ.*, I. lxxi; below, pp. 196-7, § R.—TR.]

Now a clock built out of wheels and weights, obeys all the laws of ' nature ' no less exactly when it is ill-made and does not show the right time, than when it satisfies its maker's wishes in every respect. And thus I may consider the human body as a machine fitted together and made up of bones, sinews, muscles, veins, blood, and skin in such a way that, even if there were no mind in it, it would still carry out all the operations that, as things are, do not depend on the command of the will, nor, therefore, on the mind. Now, if, for instance, the body is suffering from dropsy, it has the dryness of the throat that normally gives the mind the sensation of thirst; and this disposes its nerves and other parts to taking drink, so as to aggravate the disease. But I can easily recognise that this is just as ' natural ' as it is for a body not so affected to be impelled by a similar dryness of the throat to take drink that will be beneficial to it.

Of course, if I consider my preconceived idea of the use of a clock, I may say that when it does not show the right time it is departing from its ' nature '. Similarly, if I consider the machine of the human body in relation to its normal operations, I may think it goes astray from its ' nature ' if its throat is dry at a time when drink does not help to sustain it. But I see well enough that this sense of ' nature ' is very different from the other. In this sense, ' nature ' is a term depending on my own way of thinking (*a cogitatione mea*), on my comparison of a sick man, or an ill-made clock, to a conception of a healthy man and a well-made clock; it is something extrinsic to the object it is ascribed to. In the other sense, ' nature ' is something actually found in objects; so this conception has some degree of truth.

' It may be a merely extrinsic application of a term when, considering a body that suffers from dropsy, we call its nature corrupted because it has a dry throat and yet has no need of drink. But if we consider the compound, the mind united to the body, it is not just a matter of terms; there is a real fault in its nature, for it is thirsty at a time when drink would be hurtful to it. So the question remains: how is it that the divine goodness does not prevent " nature " (in this sense) from deceiving us ? '

I must begin by observing the great difference between mind and body. Body is of its nature always divisible; mind is wholly indivisible. When I consider the mind— that is, myself, in so far as I am merely a conscious being— I can distinguish no parts within myself; I understand myself to be a single and complete thing. Although the whole mind seems to be united to the whole body, yet when a foot or an arm or any other part of the body is cut off I am not aware that any subtraction has been made from the mind. Nor can the faculties of will, feeling, understanding and so on be called its parts; for it is one and the same mind that wills, feels, and understands. On the other hand, I cannot think of any corporeal or extended object without being readily able to divide it in thought and therefore conceiving of it as divisible. This would be enough to show me the total difference between mind and body, even if I did not sufficiently know this already.

Next, I observe that my mind is not directly affected by all parts of the body; but only by the brain, and perhaps only by one small part of that—the alleged seat of common sensibility. Whenever this is disposed in a given way, it gives the same indication to the mind, even if the other parts of the body are differently disposed at the time; of this there are innumerable experimental proofs, of which I need not give an account here.

I observe further that, from the nature of body, in whatever way a part of it could be moved by another part at some distance, that same part could also be moved in the same way by intermediate parts, even if the more distant part did nothing. For example, if ABCD is a cord, there is no way of moving A by pulling the end D that could not be carried out equally well if B or C in the middle were pulled and the end D were not moved at all. Now, similarly, when I feel pain in my foot, I have learnt from the science of physic that this sensation is brought about by means of nerves scattered throughout the foot; these are stretched like cords from there to the brain, and when they are pulled in the foot they transmit the pull to the inmost part of the brain, to which they are attached, and produce there a kind of disturbance which nature has decreed should give the mind a sensation of pain, as it were in the foot. But in order to reach the brain, these nerves have to pass through the leg, the thigh, the back, and the neck; so it may happen that, although it is not the part in the foot that is touched, but only some intermediate part, there is just the same disturbance produced in the brain as when the foot is injured; and so necessarily the mind will have the same sensation of pain. And the same must be believed as regards any other sensation.

Finally, I observe that, since any given disturbance in the part of the brain that directly affects the mind can produce only one kind of sensation, nothing better could be devised than that it should produce that one among all the sensations it could produce which is most conducive, and most often conducive, to the welfare of a healthy man. Now experience shows that all the sensations nature has given us are of this kind; so nothing can be found in them but evidence of God's power and goodness. For example: when the nerves of the foot are strongly and unusually disturbed, this disturbance, by way of the spinal cord, arrives at the interior of the brain; there it gives the mind the signal for it to have a certain sensation, viz. pain, as it were in the foot; and this arouses the mind to do its best to remove the cause of the pain, as being injurious to the foot. Now God might have so made human nature that this very disturbance in the brain was a sign to the mind of something else; it might have been a sign of its own occurrence in the brain; or of the disturbance in the foot, or in some intermediate place; or, in fact, of anything else whatever. But there would be no alternative equally conducive to the welfare of the body. Similarly, when we need drink, there arises a dryness of the throat, which disturbs the nerves of the throat, and by means of them the interior of the brain; and this disturbance gives the mind the sensation of thirst, because the most useful thing for us to know in this whole process is that we then need drink to keep healthy. And so in other cases.

From all this it is clear that in spite of God's immeasurable goodness, man as a compound of body and mind cannot but be sometimes deceived by his own nature. For some cause that occurs, not in the foot, but in any other of the parts traversed by the nerves from the foot to the brain, or even in the brain itself, may arouse the same disturbance as is usually aroused by a hurt foot; and then pain will be felt as it were in the foot, and there will be a ' natural ' illusion of sense. For the brain-disturbance in question cannot but produce always the same sensation in the mind; and it usually arises much more often from a cause that is hurting the foot than from another cause occurring somewhere else; so it is in accordance with reason that it should always give the mind the appearance of pain in the foot rather than some other part. Again, sometimes dryness of the throat arises not, as usual, from the fact that drink would be conducive to bodily health, but from some contrary cause, as in dropsy; but it is far better that it should deceive us in that case, than if it always deceived us when the body was in good condition. And so generally.

This consideration is of the greatest help to me, not only for noticing all the errors to which my nature is liable, but also for readily correcting or avoiding them. I know that all my sensations are much more often true than delusive signs in matters regarding the well-being of the body; I can almost always use several senses to examine the same object; above all, I have my memory, which connects the present to the past, and my understanding, which has now reviewed all the causes of error. So I ought not to be afraid any longer that all that the senses show me daily may be an illusion; the exaggerated doubts of the last few days are to be dismissed as ridiculous. In particular, this is true of the chief reason for doubt—that sleep and waking life were indistinguishable to me; for I can now see a vast difference between them. Dreams are never connected by memory with all the other events of my life, like the things that happen when I am awake. If in waking life somebody suddenly appeared and directly afterwards disappeared, as happens in dreams, and I could not see where he had come from or where he went, I should justifiably decide he was a ghost, or a phantasm formed in my own brain, rather than a real man. But when I distinctly observe where an object comes from, where it is, and when this happens; and when I can connect the perception of it uninterruptedly with the whole of the rest of my life; then I am quite certain that while this is happening to me I am not asleep but awake. And I need not doubt the reality of things at all, if after summoning all my senses, my memory, and my understanding to examine them, these sources yield no conflicting information. In such things I am nowise deceived, because God is no deceiver. But since practical needs do not always leave time for such a careful examination, we must admit that in human life errors as regards particular things are always liable to happen; and we must recognise the infirmity of our nature.

124

The Third Set of
OBJECTIONS & REPLIES

containing the Controversy
between
Hobbes and Descartes

First published
with the ' Meditations'
in 1641

Throughout, the Objections are by Hobbes, the Replies by Descartes. Descartes does not mention Hobbes by name.

On Meditation I

FIRST OBJECTION

It is well enough established by what is said in this Meditation that there is no criterion for telling our dreams from waking life and real sensation; and therefore the phantasms we get when we are awake and have sensation are not accidents that inhere in external objects, and are no proof that such external objects exist at all. So, if we are to follow our senses without further reasoning, we shall do well to doubt whether anything exists. I admit the validity of this Meditation. But this very matter of the uncertainty of sensible things has been discussed by Plato and other ancient philosophers; and it is a common observation how hard it is to tell waking life from dreams. So I am sorry that so excellent an author of new speculations should publish this old stuff.

REPLY

The grounds for doubt which the Philosopher here admits as valid were put forward by me only as plausible; and I did not use them in order to hawk them about as novelties. My aim was partly to accustom the reader's mind to consider intelligible objects and distinguish them from corporeal things—and to this end such doubts seem to me quite indispensable; partly, to reply to them in the subsequent Meditations; and partly, also, to show how solid are the truths I set forth later on, since they cannot be sapped by such metaphysical doubts. I sought after no praise for rehearsing them; but I think I could no more leave them out than a medical writer could leave out the description of a disease for which he wanted to explain the method of treatment.

SECOND OBJECTION

§ ' *I am a conscious being* (sum res cogitans) ', he says; quite correctly. From the fact that I experience (*cogito*), or have a phantasm, whether I am awake or dreaming, it is to be inferred that I am something that experiences (*sum cogitans*) ; for *I experience* (*cogito*) and *I am something that experiences* (*sum cogitans*) have the same meaning. But when he adds: *that is, a mind, a soul* (animus), *an intellect, a reason*, there arises a doubt. It seems not to be a valid argument to say ' I am conscious (*cogito*), therefore I am a consciousness (*cogitatio*) ', or ' I am intelligent, therefore I am an intellect '. For I might as well say ' I am walking, therefore I am a walk '. M. Descartes is thus assuming an identity between an intelligent being and intellection, which is the act of an intelligent being; or at any rate between an intelligent being and intellect, which is the power of an intelligent being. But all philosophers distinguish a subject from its faculties and acts, that is from its properties and essential characters; *ens* and *essentia* are different.[1] It may be that the thing that is conscious is the *subject* of a mind, reason, or intellect, and so it may be something corporeal; the contrary is assumed, not proved. Yet this inference is the foundation of the result M. Descartes seems to be trying to establish.

§ ' *I am aware of my own existence ; I want to know what is this " I " of which I am aware. Assuredly, the conception of this*

---

[1] [I leave the Latin because Hobbes is citing a scholastic tag.—Tʀ.]

" I ", precisely as such, does not depend on things of whose existence I am not yet aware.'

It is absolutely certain that the knowledge of the proposition that *I exist* depends on the proposition that *I am experiencing (ego cogito)* ; as the author has rightly shown us. But where do we get the knowledge that it is I who am experiencing *(ego cogito)* ? Surely it can only be from our inability to conceive any act without its subject— a leap without a leaper, knowledge without a knower, experience without one who experiences *(cogitare sine cogitante)*. From this it seems to follow that a conscious being *(rem cogitantem)* is something corporeal; for the subjects of all acts [1] seem to be conceived only in terms of body or matter. This comes out in his example of the wax; its colour, its hardness, its shape, and all its other acts change, but we conceive that there is always the same thing, that is, the same matter, as subject of these changes.

It is not through some further consciousness *(cogitationem)* that it is inferred I am conscious *(me cogitare)* ; a man may be conscious of having been conscious, and this consciousness is simply memory, but it is quite impossible to be conscious that one is conscious, or know that one knows. For otherwise there would be an unending question : how do you know that you know that you know that you know—?

So knowledge of the proposition *I exist* depends on knowledge that it is I that am conscious *(ego cogito)* ; and this knowledge depends on our inability to separate consciousness from matter that is conscious. So it seems one should infer rather that a conscious being is material than that it is immaterial.

---

[1] [In the subsequent discussion *acts* is used in the scholastic sense, comprising not only actions and mental acts, but also positive characters of an object like shape and colour.—Tr.]

REPLY

When I said 'that is a mind, a soul, an intellect, a reason', I took these terms to mean not mere faculties, but beings endowed with a faculty of consciousness (*cogitandi*) ; the first pair of terms are normally so taken by everybody, and the latter pair very often are; I explained this so expressly, and in so many places, that I think there was no room left for doubt.

There is no comparison here between consciousness and a walk; the term *a walk* is usually understood only of the act of walking; whereas *consciousness* is taken sometimes for an act, sometimes for a faculty, sometimes for the subject possessing the faculty.

I do not say that an intelligent being and his intellection are the same; I do not even say that an intelligent being is the same as his intellect, if intellect is taken for a faculty, but only if it is taken for the being who understands. I freely admit that in order to signify such a being or substance I used the most abstract words I could in the effort to strip it of everything irrelevant; whereas this Philosopher uses the most concrete words he can—*subject, matter, body*— to signify it, so that he may not allow it to be severed from the body. I am not afraid of anybody's thinking that his method of joining a number of things together is more fitted to the discovery of truth than my method of distinguishing things as far as possible.

But let us leave terms aside and come to the point. ' It may be,' he says, ' that the thing that is conscious is something corporeal ; the contrary is assumed, not proved.' But I did not ' assume ' the contrary, nor in any way use it as a ' foundation '; I left it quite undecided until the sixth Meditation, where it is proved.

He is right in saying that we cannot conceive any act apart from its subject, e.g. experience (*cogitationem*) apart from a being that experiences (*rem cogitantem*), because that which experiences (*cogitat*) is not nothing. But it is without any reason, and contrary to all usage and all logic, when he adds 'From this it seems to follow that a conscious being (*rem cogitantem*) is something corporeal'. 'The subjects of all acts are conceived' in terms of substance, or even, if he will have it so, 'in terms of matter', i.e. metaphysical matter;[1] but are not therefore conceived as bodies. Logicians, and indeed men in general, usually say that some substances are spiritual, others corporeal. All that I proved by the example of the wax was that colour, hardness, and shape do not belong to the concept of wax as such; I was not dealing with the concept of mind as such, or of body as such.

When the Philosopher says here that one conscious act (*cogitationem*) cannot be the object of another, it is irrelevant. Who ever imagined such a possibility except himself?

To give a brief explanation of the real point: it is certain that experience (*cogitationem*) cannot exist apart from an experiencing being, nor in general can any act or accident exist apart from a substance to inhere in. Now we know substance, not immediately and in its own right, but only as the subject of certain acts; so it is very reasonable, and prescribed by usage, to use different names for substances that we recognise as the subjects of quite different acts or accidents; we may then examine later on whether these different names stand for different things, or for one and the same thing. Now there are certain acts that we call *corporeal*, viz. size, shape, motion and all others that are inconceivable apart from extension in place; we call the substance in which they inhere a *body*. It is unimaginable

---

[1] [Descartes alludes here to a famous dispute in the schools. Many scholastics held that since angels and human minds were persistent subjects of change, there must be in them an aspect corresponding to the persistent matter of bodies, for all that they were unextended and incorporeal; God alone was strictly immaterial. Others, such as St Thomas, rejected this view.—Tr.]

that there is one substance to be the subject of shape, another to be the subject of local motion, and so on; all these acts fall under the common concept of extension. There are also other acts which we call *conscious* (*cogitativos*), e.g. understanding, willing, imagining, feeling; these all fall under the common concept of consciousness or perception or awareness; and we call the substance in which they inhere a *conscious being* or *mind*. The term used does not matter so long as we do not confuse this with corporeal substance; conscious acts have no affinity with corporeal acts, and the common concept of such acts, viz. *consciousness*, is quite different in kind from *extension*, the common concept of the other acts. After forming distinct notions of these two sorts of substance it is easy, according to what is said in the sixth Meditation, to find out whether they are one and the same thing or different things.

THIRD OBJECTION

§ ' *Is any of these something distinct from my consciousness ? Can any of them be called a separate thing from myself?*'

Perhaps someone will reply thus to this question: I myself, who am conscious (*cogito*), am distinct from my consciousness; and my consciousness is distinct, though not separated, from me, just as (*v. supra*) a leap is from one who leaps. If M. Descartes means that the one who understands is identical with his understanding, we shall fall back into the scholastic way of talking; *the understanding understands, the sight sees, the will wills ;* and by a perfectly fair analogy *a walk* (or at any rate *the power of walking*) *walks*. All these expressions are obscure and improper, and most unworthy of M. Descartes's usual clarity.

REPLY

I do not deny that I who am conscious am distinct from my consciousness, as a thing is from its state. But **my**

question : *Is any of these something distinct from my consciousness?*
is meant to refer to the various modes of consciousness
mentioned in that place, not to the substance of myself;
and the further question: *Can any of them be called a
distinct thing from myself?* just means that all these modes
of consciousness inhere in me. I cannot see what imaginable doubt or obscurity there is about this.

FOURTH OBJECTION

§ ' *It remains then for me to admit that I know the nature even of
this piece of wax not by imagination but by purely mental conception.*' [1]

There *is* a great difference between imagining, or
possessing an idea, and mental conception, that is, inferring
by reasoning that a thing is or exists. But M. Descartes
has not explained the difference. Even the old Peripatetics
taught clearly enough that substance is not apprehended
by the senses, but is inferred by reasoning processes.

Now what if perhaps reasoning be nothing but a joining
together and linking of names or appellations by means of
the verb *is*? In that case, we learn by reasoning nothing as
to the nature of things, but only as to their appellations;
we learn, namely, whether or not we are combining the
names of things according to the conventions we have
made at our pleasure about what they are to signify. If so,
reasoning will depend on names, names on imagination,
and imagination perhaps (and this is my opinion) on the
motions of bodily organs; and thus the mind will be
nothing but motions in certain parts of an organic body.

REPLY

I did explain the difference between imagination and
mere mental conception; both in this example, where I

[1] [Hobbes writes *conceptio*: but it is *perceptio* in the sentence he is
quoting.—TR.]

enumerate those characters of the wax that we imagine and those of which we have a mere mental conception; and in another place, where I explained how one and the same thing, say a pentagon, is in different ways an object of intellection and of imagination.

The combination involved in reasoning is not one of names but of things signified by names; I am surprised that the opposite view should have occurred to anybody. Who doubts that a Frenchman and a German can reason about the very same things, although they form quite different words? And surely the Philosopher refutes himself by speaking of conventions we have made at our pleasure about what words are to signify? If he admits that words signify something, why will he not have our reasonings to be about this something that they signify, rather than about mere words?

As for his conclusion that the mind is a motion, he might as well conclude that the earth is the sky, or anything he likes.

FIFTH OBJECTION

§ ' *Some* [human experiences (*cogitationes*)] *are, as it were, pictures of objects, and these alone are properly called ideas ; e.g. when I think of* (cogito) *a man, a chimera, the sky, an angel, or God.*'

When I think of a man, I am aware of an idea, or shaped and coloured image, about which I can ask whether or not it is the likeness of a man. Similarly, when I think of the sky. When I think of a Chimera, I am aware of an idea or image about which I can ask whether or not it is the likeness of a non-existent animal, which yet might exist, or did formerly exist, or perhaps never did.

When, however, I think of an angel, what comes into my mind is the image sometimes of a flame, sometimes of a fair winged child; and I feel certain that this has no likeness to an angel, and is thus not an idea of an angel. I believe there are creatures who minister to God, invisible and immaterial; and I give this thing that I believe or assume to exist the name *angel ;* but the idea by means of which I imagine an angel is made up out of ideas of visible things.

Similarly, the sacred name of God gives us no image or idea of God. And therefore we are forbidden to adore God in an image, lest we should think we conceive of the Inconceivable.

It seems then, that we have no idea of God. We are in the case of a man born blind. When he has several times approached a fire, and felt warm, he recognises that there is something that warms him; he hears this called *fire*, and concludes that fire exists. But he has no knowledge of the shape and colour of fire, no idea of fire, no image occurring in his mind. Similarly, man knows that his images or ideas must have a cause, and this cause another, earlier, cause, and so on; and he is led at last to suppose some eternal cause which never began to be, and so can have no cause earlier than itself; he thus concludes that there must needs be something eternal. But he has no idea that he could say is the idea of the Eternal; he merely believes or admits that it exists, and gives it the name or appellation *God.*

Now M. Descartes proceeds from the assumption that we have an idea of God in our soul to the proof of the theorem that God (that is, One supremely powerful and wise, the Creator of the world) exists. He ought to have given a better explanation of this idea of God; and he ought to have deduced not only the existence of God, but also his creation of the world.

REPLY

Here he will have the term *idea* to mean only the images of material things, formed by means of corporeal phantasy; and granting this he readily proves that there can be no proper idea of an angel or of God. But I have shown again and again throughout the work, and in this passage particularly, that I take the term *idea* to stand for whatever the mind is directly aware of (*a mente percipitur*). For instance, when I wish or am afraid, I am at the same time aware of (*percipio*) wishing or being afraid; thus I count *volition* and *fear* among ideas. I used this term because it was the familiar philosophical term for the forms of which the divine Mind is aware (*formas perceptionum mentis divinae*), although we recognise that in God there is no phantasy; I could find none more suitable.

I think I did explain the idea of God well enough for those

136

who want to attend to my meaning; I could never give an explanation that would satisfy people who choose to take my words otherwise than I intended. What he says further about the creation of the world is quite off the point.

SIXTH OBJECTION

§ ' *Other* [experiences (*cogitationes*)] *have additional properties ; when I will, am afraid, assert, or deny, there is always something that I take as the object of my experience* (cogitationis), *but my experience comprises* (cogitatione complector) *more than the likeness of the thing in question; of these experiences, some are termed volitions or emotions, others are termed judgments.*'

When anybody wills or is afraid, he has an image of the thing he fears or the action he wills; what more is comprised in the consciousness (*cogitatione complectitur*) of one who wills or is afraid, is not explained. Fear is consciousness (*cogitatio*), but so far as I can see it can only be consciousness of the thing a man fears. What is fear of an onrushing lion but the idea of an onrushing lion together with the effect that this idea produces in the heart, which leads the one who fears to make the animal motion called *running away?* Now the motion of running away is not an experience (*cogitatio*); hence we are left to conclude that fear involves only the experience that consists in a likeness of the object. Similarly for will.

As for assertion and denial, they occur only together with language and names; brute beasts cannot assert or deny even in thought (*cogitatione*), and therefore cannot judge. But the experience (*cogitatio*) may be alike in man and beast; when we assert that a man runs, our experience (*cogitationem*) is no different from a dog's on seeing his master run; thus affirmation or negation adds nothing over and above simple experiences (*cogitationibus*) except perhaps the thought (*cogitatio*) that the names of which the assertion consists are used by the one who makes it as names of the same thing; and even then he is not apprehending in his experience (*complecti cogitatione*) something more than the likeness of the thing—he is just apprehending its likeness twice over.

REPLY

It is obvious that seeing a lion and at the same time fearing it is different from just seeing; that seeing a man run is different from asserting to oneself that he runs (and this happens apart from language). I see nothing here worth answering.

SEVENTH OBJECTION

§ ' *It only remains for me to examine how I got this idea from God. I did not derive it from the senses ; it did not at any time come to me unexpectedly,*[1] *as normally happens with the ideas of sensible objects when those objects affect (or seem to affect) the external sense-organs ; and it is not my own invention, for I can neither add anything to it not subtract anything from it. So it can only be innate in me, just as the idea of myself is.*'

It is not proved that there is an idea of God, and there seems to be none; if there be none, the whole discussion falls to the ground. As for the idea of myself; if my body is in question, it arises from sight; if my soul is in question, I have no idea at all of the soul. We infer by reasoning that there is something within the human body that gives it animal motion—something by means of which the body feels and moves; we call this, whatever it is, the *soul*, without having an idea of it.

[1] [Latin *expectanti*; I have supplied *non* from the text of the *Meditations*. —TR.]

REPLY

It is clear that there is an idea of God; if so, the whole objection collapses. As for the further statement that there is no idea of the soul, that the soul is inferred by reasoning, this comes to the same as saying that there is no image of the soul formed in our phantasy, but that there is what *I* call an idea.

EIGHTH OBJECTION

§ ' *The other* [idea of the sun] *I get from astronomical reasoning ; that is, it is derived from my innate notions.*'

I think there is only one idea of the sun at one time, whether one is looking at it with one's eyes or has a reasoned concept of it as being many times bigger than it appears. The ' other idea ' is not an idea of the sun, but a rational inference—that, if one looked at the sun at a much smaller distance, there would be a much larger ' idea '. At different times there may be different ideas of the sun : e.g. if one looks at it at one time with the naked eye and at another time with the telescope. But astronomical arguments do not make the idea of the sun bigger or smaller. What they do is rather to show that an idea got by sensation may be deceptive.

REPLY

Here again is something that is said not to be an idea of the sun, but is nevertheless described. Now this is just what *I* call an idea of the sun.

NINTH OBJECTION

§ ' *For indubitably the ideas that manifest substance to me are something* more—*have, so to say, a greater amount of representative reality*—*than those which merely represent states or accidents ; and again, my conception of a supreme God, eternal, infinite, omniscient, almighty, and Creator of all that exists besides himself, certainly has a greater amount of representative reality than the ideas by which finite substances are manifested.'*

I have already frequently remarked that there is no idea either of God or of the soul; nor is there, I would add, of substance. Substance, being matter that is the subject of accidents and changes, is revealed only by reasoning; it is not conceived, nor does it make manifest any idea to us. If so, how can it be said that the ideas which manifest substances to us are something greater, or have more ' representative reality ', than those which manifest accidents ?

Again, M. Descartes ought to consider over again what ' a greater amount of reality ' means. Does reality admit of *more* and *less ?* If he does think that one thing is more of a thing than another, he ought to consider how this can be made plain, so that we may grasp it with the clarity that is needed in any demonstration, and which he himself has employed elsewhere.

REPLY

I have frequently remarked that what is shown by reasoning, like anything else we are aware of in any way at all, is an idea in my sense. I have sufficiently explained how reality admits of *more* and *less :* a substance is more of a thing than a state; real qualities or again incomplete substances, if there are such things, are things to a greater degree than mere states, but to a less degree than complete substances; and finally, if there is an infinite and independent substance, it is more of a thing than a finite and dependent substance. All this is self-evident.

TENTH OBJECTION

§ ' *It only remains to be considered whether there is some element in the idea of God that could not have originated from myself. By the word " God " I mean a substance that is infinite, independent,*

140

supremely intelligent, supremely powerful, and the Creator of myself and anything else that may exist. The more I consider all these attributes, the less it seems possible for them to have originated from myself. So, by what I said above, it may be inferred that God exists.'

When I consider the attributes of God in order to get an idea of God and see if it involves anything that could not have originated within myself, I find (if I am not mistaken) that what comes into one's mind at the name of God does not indeed originate within oneself, but need not have originated otherwise than in external objects. By the name of God I understand a *substance ;* that is, I understand that God exists; but I do this not through an idea but as a result of reasoning. God is conceived as *infinite ;* that is, I cannot conceive or imagine limits to him, or uttermost parts beyond which I can imagine none further; but from this it follows that the term *infinite* gives rise to an idea not of God's infinity but of my own bounds or limits. God is conveived as *independent ;* that is, I conceive of no cause from which God should arise; clearly, I get no idea from the term *independent* except the memory of my ideas, which begin at different times and are thus dependent.

Thus, to say God is *independent* is just to say that God belongs to the class of things whose origin is not imaginable to me. Similarly, to say God is *infinite* is just to say that he belongs to the class of things whose bounds are not conceivable. This rules out any idea of God; what sort of idea can be without origin and without bounds ?

God is conceived as *supremely intelligent.* What I want to know here is: What is the idea by which M. Descartes understands God's understanding ?

God is conceived as *supremely powerful.* Once more, by what idea do we understand *power ?* Power refers to what is future, i.e. non-existent. I admittedly do understand *power*—by means of an image, or memory, of past actions.

141

I get to the idea thus : ' Something *did* so-and-so ; therefore it *could* do so-and-so ; therefore if it remains the same it can do so-and-so again—that is, it has the *power* to do so-and-so '. Now all these are ideas that may have originated in external objects.

God is conceived as *the Creator of all that exists*. I can form a kind of image of creation from what I have seen ; e.g. from the birth of a man—his growth from a mere point to his present size and shape. No other idea is aroused in anyone by the word *Creator*. It is however not a sufficient proof of creation that we can imagine the world to have been created. So even if one had demonstrated the existence of a Being who was *infinite, independent, supremely powerful,* and so on, it does not follow that a Creator exists. Unless somebody thinks the existence of a Being who *according to our creed* created everything else is a valid proof that he did once create the world.

Again, when he says the ideas of God and the soul are innate, I should like to know if the souls of men in a deep dreamless sleep are conscious. If not, they have at the time no ideas. So no idea is innate ; for what is innate is always present.

REPLY

Nothing that we ascribe to God can have originated from an archetype that is among external objects ; for no divine attribute is like those of external, i.e. corporeal, things ; now if we think of anything unlike external things, clearly they cannot originate this thought in us ; only a cause of this diversity can do that.

And I want to know how the Philosopher deduces God's understanding from external things. I can easily explain how *I* have an idea of it—meaning by *idea* the content of any awareness. For who is not aware of some-times understanding ? Everybody, then, has this content, the idea of understanding; and by indefinitely extending it he forms the idea of God's understanding. And so for God's other attributes.

To prove the existence of God we used the idea of him that is inherent in us. Now this idea comprises power so immeasurable that we see it is a contradiction, if God exists, that anything else should exist without being created by him. It thus plainly follows, when once his existence has been proved, that we have also proved that the whole world, or whatever things there are apart from God, were created by God.

Finally, when I say an idea is innate I do not mean it always occurs in us (in that sense, no idea would be innate) but only that we have in us the power of calling it into being.

ELEVENTH OBJECTION

§ ' *The whole force of the argument lies in this : I realise that I could not possibly exist with the nature I actually have, that is, one endowed with the idea of God, unless there really is a God— the very God, I mean, of whom I have an idea.*'

Therefore, since it has not been proved that we have an idea of God; and since the Christian religion obliges us to believe God is inconceivable (and that means, in my opinion, that we have no idea of him); it follows that God's existence has not been demonstrated; and much less, creation.

REPLY

When God is called inconceivable this refers to a concept that should adequately comprehend him. In what way we have an idea of God, I have repeated *ad nauseam ;* and there is nothing brought forward here to overthrow my demonstrations.

143

On Meditation IV

TWELFTH OBJECTION

§ ' *Thus I know at any rate that error as such is not a positive reality but merely a deficiency ; and in order to go wrong I need no faculty expressly given me by God.*'

It is certain that ignorance is merely a defect—that no positive power is needed in order to be ignorant; but as regards error the matter is not so obvious. Stones and inanimate things seem to be unable to err simply because they have no power of reasoning or imagination. So it is natural to infer that in order to err one needs the power of reasoning, or at least of imagination; both these powers are positive, and they are given always, and only, to those who err.

§ Again, M. Descartes says: ' [My errors], *I observe, depend on two concurrent causes : on my faculty of cognition and my faculty of choice or free will.*'

This seems inconsistent with what goes before. It should be noticed that free will is here assumed without proof, in spite of the Calvinist opinion.

REPLY

Error presupposes the faculty of reasoning (or rather of judgment—of assertion and denial), being a defect of it; but it does not follow that this defect is a reality; in the same way, it does not follow that blindness is a reality, although the mere inability of stones to see does not make us call them blind.

144

I am surprised that so far I have come across not one valid argument in these objections.

No doubt many people, when they consider God's fore-ordaining, are unable to grasp how our liberty is consistent with it. But there is nobody but is aware, when he just considers himself, that *voluntary* and *free* mean one and the same thing. And this is no place to examine what opinion others may have of the matter.

THIRTEENTH OBJECTION

§ ' *For instance, during these last few days I have been considering whether anything in the world exists, and have observed that from the very fact that I examine the question it necessarily follows that I do exist. I could not but judge to be true what I understood so clearly ; not because I was compelled to do so by any external cause, but because the great illumination of my understanding was followed by a great inclination of the will ; and my belief was the more free and spontaneous for my not being indifferent in the matter.*'

This phrase, *a great illumination of the understanding,* is metaphorical, and thus no ground for argument. Anybody who feels no doubt claims such an ' illumination ' and has an inclination of the will to assert what he has no doubt about, no less than one who really knows. So this ' illumination ' may be the reason why a man obstinately defends or holds an opinion; but cannot be ground for knowledge of its truth.

Again, not only knowledge that something is true, but even belief or assent, is independent of the will. What is validly proved or credibly reported we believe, whether we will or no. Admittedly, assertion and denial, defence or refutation of propositions, are voluntary acts; but it does not follow that inward assent depends on the will.

So there is no sufficient proof of the subsequent conclusion: *There is inherent in this wrong use of free will the privation in which the nature of error consists.*

REPLY

It is not to the point to enquire whether the phrase ' a great illumination ' is a ground for argument or no, so long as it is (as it is in fact) self-explanatory. Everybody knows that illumination of the understanding means clarity of knowledge; perhaps not everybody has it who thinks he has, but this does not prevent its being far different from an obstinate opinion formed without self-evident awareness.

As for saying that we assent to what we are clearly aware of, ' whether we will or no ', this is like saying that we desire what we clearly see to be good, *whether we will or no.* The words *or no* are out of place in such contexts; they imply that we can both will and not will the same thing.

On Meditation V

FOURTEENTH OBJECTION

§ ' *For example, when I imagine a triangle, it may be that no such figure exists anywhere outside my consciousness, or ever has existed ; but there certainly exists its determinate nature (its essence, its form) which is unchangeable and eternal. This is no figment of mine, and does not depend on my mind, as is clear from the following : various properties can be proved of this triangle. . . .*'

If a triangle exists nowhere, I do not understand how it can have a ' nature '; for what is nowhere, *is not*, and therefore has not a being or a nature. A triangle in the mind arises from our seeing a triangle, or forming one from what we have seen. Now when once we have given the name *triangle* to the thing from which we think the idea of a triangle comes, then even though the triangle ceases to be, the name remains. Similarly, if we have once conceived in our mind that the angles of a triangle are together equal to two right angles, and given a triangle the further name *having its three angles equal to two right angles*, then even if no angle existed in the world, the name would remain; and thus the truth of the proposition *a triangle is something having its three angles equal to two right angles* is everlasting. But the nature of a triangle is not everlasting; all triangles might cease to be. Similarly, the proposition *man is an animal* is true for ever, because names are everlasting; but when the human race ceases to be, human nature will be no more.

From this it is clear enough that essence as opposed to existence is merely a combination of names by means of the verb *is ;* essence apart from existence is a fiction of ours.

It should seem that essence is to existence as the mental image of a man is to a man; or again, the essence of Socrates is to his existence as the proposition *Socrates is a man* is to the proposition *Socrates is* or *exists*. Now *Socrates is a man*, when Socrates does not exist, stands only for a connexion of names; and *is*, or the verb *to be*, represents the oneness of a thing that has two names.

REPLY

Everybody is familiar with the distinction of essence and existence; and this talk about names as being everlasting (instead of our having notions or ideas of eternal truths) has already been sufficiently refuted.

FIFTEENTH OBJECTION

§ ' *God has given me no faculty to discern their origin* [sc. whether ideas are derived from bodies or not]; *on the other hand, he has given me a strong inclination to believe that these ideas proceed from corporeal objects ; so I do not see how it would make sense to say God is not deceitful if in fact they proceed from elsewhere, not from corporeal objects. Therefore corporeal objects must exist.*'

It is the common opinion that doctors do not sin when they deceive sick men for their health's sake; nor fathers, when they deceive their children for their own good; that the guilt of deceit consists not in the falsity of what is said, but in the injury done by those who deceive. M. Descartes ought to consider whether the universal proposition *God can in no case deceive us* is true; if it is not universally true, his conclusion *therefore corporeal objects exist* does not follow.

REPLY

My conclusion does not presuppose that we can in no case be deceived; I have readily admitted that we often are deceived; but only, that we are in fact not deceived when error would argue a will in God to deceive us, such as it is self-contradictory that he should have. Bad reasoning again.

SIXTEENTH OBJECTION

§ ' *I can now see a vast difference between them* [sc. waking life and dreams]. *Dreams are never connected by memory with all the other events of my life.*'

149

I want to know whether it is certain that a man who dreams of wondering whether he is dreaming or not may not dream that his dream fits together with a long series of past events. If this is possible, then what the dreamer thinks are events in his past life may be counted as real, just as though he were awake. Moreover, by the author's assertions, the certainty and truth of all knowledge depends on knowledge of the true God; but then either an atheist must be incapable of inferring that he is awake, from memory of his past life, or somebody can know he is awake apart from knowledge of the true God.

REPLY

A dreamer cannot really connect his dream with ideas of the past; it is just that he may dream he does. But who denies that a man may be mistaken in his sleep? And on waking afterwards he will readily recognise his mistake.

An atheist can infer that he is awake from memory of his past life; but he cannot know that this sign is enough to give him certainty that he is not mistaken, unless he knows he was created by a God who is not a deceiver.

RULES
FOR THE DIRECTION
OF THE MIND

Written before 1630
First published in the ' Opera Posthuma'
in 1701

RULE I

*The aim of our studies must be the direction of our mind so that it may form solid and true judgments on whatever matters arise.**

RULE II

*We must occupy ourselves only with those objects that our intellectual powers appear competent to know certainly and indubitably.**

RULE III

As regards any subject we propose to investigate, we must inquire not what other people have thought, or what we ourselves conjecture, but what we can clearly and manifestly perceive by intuition or deduce with certainty. For there is no other way of acquiring knowledge.

We must read the works of the ancients; for it is an extraordinary advantage to have available the labours of so many men, both in order to recognise what true discoveries have already long since been made and also to become aware of what scope is still left for invention in the various disciplines. There is, however, at the same time a great danger that perhaps some contagion of error, contracted from a too attentive reading of them, may stick to us against our will, in spite of all precautions. For authors are ordinarily so disposed that whenever their heedless credulity has led them to a decision on some controverted opinion, they always try to bring us over to the same side, with the subtlest arguments; if on the other hand they have been fortunate enough to discover something

* [The asterisk indicates that a comment follows which has been omitted in this selection.—Tr.]

153

certain and evident, they never set it forth without wrapping
it up in all sorts of complications. (I suppose they are
afraid that a simple account may lessen the importance
they gain by the discovery; or perhaps they begrudge
us the plain truth.)

But in fact, even if all writers were honest and plain; even
if they never passed off matters of doubt upon us as if they
were truths, but set forth everything in good faith; nevertheless, since there is hardly anything that one of them says
but someone else asserts the contrary, we should be continually uncertain which side to believe. It would be no
good to count heads, and then follow the opinion that has
most authorities for it; for if the question that arises is a
difficult one, it is more credible that the truth of the matter
may have been discovered by few men than by many. But
even if all agreed together, it would not be enough to have
their teachings. For we shall never be mathematicians,
say, even if we retain in memory all the proofs others have
given, unless we ourselves have the mental aptitude of
solving any given problem; we shall never be philosophers,
if we have read all the arguments of Plato and Aristotle but
cannot form a solid judgment on matters set before us;
this sort of learning would appear historical rather than
scientific.

Further, this Rule counsels us against ever mixing up any
conjectures with our judgments as to the truth of things.
It is of no small importance to observe this; for the chief
reason why in the common philosophy there is nothing to
be found whose certitude is so apparent as to be beyond
controversy is that those who practise it have not begun
by contenting themselves with the recognition of what is
clear and certain, but have ventured on the further assertion
of what was obscure and unknown and was arrived at
only through probable conjectures. These assertions
they have later on themselves gradually come to hold with

complete confidence, and have mixed them up indiscriminately with evident truths; and the final result was their
inability to draw any conclusion that did not seem to
depend on some such proposition, and consequently to
draw any that was not uncertain.

In order to avoid our subsequently falling into the same
error, the Rule enumerates all the intellectual activities
by means of which we can attain to knowledge of things
without any fear of deception; it allows of only two such—
intuition and induction (*sic*).[1]

By *intuition* I mean, not the wavering assurance of the
senses, or the deceitful judgment of a misconstructing
imagination, but a conception, formed by unclouded mental
attention, so easy and distinct as to leave no room for
doubt in regard to the thing we are understanding. It
comes to the same thing if we say: It is an indubitable
conception formed by an unclouded and attentive mind;
one that originates solely from the light of reason, and is
more certain even than deduction, because it is simpler
(though, as we have previously noted,[2] deduction, too,
cannot go wrong if it is a human being that performs it).
Thus, anybody can see by mental intuition that he himself
exists, that he thinks, that a triangle is bounded by just
three lines, and a globe by a single surface, and so on;
there are far more of such truths than most people observe,
because they disdain to turn their mind to such easy topics.

Some people may perhaps be troubled by this new use of
the word *intuition*, and of other words that I shall later on
be obliged to shift away from their common meaning.
So I give at this point the general warning that I am not

[1] [The term is ' deduction ' in the Rule itself, and in the later exposition. It is probable that *inductio* is a misprint.—TR.]

[2] [This refers to Descartes's comment on Rule II, where he stated that
while our opinions based on experience are often mistaken, deduction
cannot be wrong if performed by ' human beings, not brutes '.—TR.]

in the least thinking of the usage of particular words that has prevailed in the Schools in modern times, since it would be most difficult to use the same terms while holding quite different views; I take into account only what a given word means in Latin, in order that, whenever there are no proper words for what I mean, I may transfer to that meaning the words that seem to me most suitable.

The evidentness and certainty of intuition is, moreover, necessary not only in forming propositions but also for any inferences. For example, take the inference that 2 and 2 come to the same as 3 and 1; intuition must show us not only that 2 and 2 make 4, and that 3 and 1 also make 4, but furthermore that the above third proposition is a necessary conclusion from these two.

This may raise a doubt as to our reason for having added another mode of knowledge, besides intuition, in this Rule —namely, knowledge by *deduction*. (By this term I mean any necessary conclusion from other things known with certainty.) We had to do this because many things are known although not self-evident, so long as they are deduced from principles known to be true by a continuous and un-interrupted movement of thought, with clear intuition of each point. It is in the same way that we know the last link of a long chain is connected with the first, even though we do not view in a single glance (*intuitu*) all the intermediate links on which the connexion depends; we need only to have gone through the links in succession and to remember that from the first to the last each is joined to the next. Thus we distinguish at this point between intuition and certain deduction; because the latter, unlike the former, is conceived as involving a movement or succession; and is again unlike intuition in not requiring something evident at the moment, but rather, so to say, borrowing its certainty from memory. From this we may gather that when propositions are direct conclusions from first principles, they may be said to be known by intuition or by deduction, according to different ways of looking at them; but first principles themselves may be said to be known only by intuition; and remote conclusions, on the other hand, only by deduction.

These are the two most certain ways to knowledge; and on the side of the mind no more must be admitted; all others must be rejected as suspect and liable to mislead. This, however, does not prevent our believing that divine revelation is more certain than any knowledge; for our faith in it, so far as it concerns obscure matters, is an act not of the mind but of the will; and any intellectual foundations that it may have can and must be sought chiefly by one or other of the two ways I have mentioned. Perhaps I shall later on show this to be so at greater length.

RULE IV

*There is need of a method for investigating the truth about things.**

RULE V

*The method consists entirely in an orderly arrangement of the objects upon which we must turn our mental vision in order to discover some truth. And we shall be observing this method exactly if we reduce complex and obscure propositions step by step to simpler ones, and then, by retracing our steps, try to rise from intuition of all of the simplest ones to knowledge of all the rest.**

RULE VI

*In order to distinguish what is most simple from what is complex, and to deal with things in an orderly way, what we must do, whenever we have a series in which we have directly deduced a number of truths one from another, is to observe which one is most simple, and how far all the others are removed from this—whether more, or less, or equally.**

157

RULE VII

In order to complete our knowledge we must scrutinise all the several points pertinent to our aim, in a continuous and uninterrupted movement of thought, and comprise them all in an adequate and orderly enumeration.

The observance of these precepts is necessary in order that we may admit to the class of certitudes those truths which, I previously said, are not immediate deductions from the first self-evident principles. For sometimes the succession of inferences is so long that when we arrive at our results we do not readily remember the whole road that has led us so far; and therefore I say that we must aid the weakness of our memory by a continuous movement of thought. For instance, suppose that by successive mental acts I have learnt first the relation between the magnitudes A and B, then that between B and C, then that between C and D, and finally that between D and E; I do not on this account see the relation between A and E; and I cannot form a precise conception of it from the relations I know already, unless I remember them all. So I will run through these several times over in a continuous movement of the imagination, in which intuition of each relation is simultaneous with transition to the next, until I have learnt to pass from the first to the last so quickly that I leave hardly any parts to the care of memory and seem to have a simultaneous intuition of the whole. In this way memory is aided, and a remedy found for the slowness of the understanding, whose scope is in a way enlarged.

I add that the movement must be ' uninterrupted ', because it often happens that people who try to make some deduction in too great haste and from remote principles do not run over the whole chain of intermediate conclusions with sufficient care to avoid making many unconsidered jumps. But assuredly the least oversight immediately breaks the chain and destroys all the certainty of the conclusion. Further, I say that 'enumeration' is required 'in order to complete our knowledge'. For other precepts are helpful in resolving very many questions, but it is only enumeration that enables us to form a true and certain judgment about anything whatever that we apply our mind to, and, by preventing anything from simply escaping our notice, seems to give us *some* knowledge of everything.

This enumeration, or induction, ranging over everything relevant to some question we have set before us, consists in an inquiry so careful and accurate that it is a certain and evident conclusion that no mistaken omission has been made. When, therefore, we perform this, if the thing we are looking for still eludes us, we are at any rate so much the wiser, that we can see with certainty the impossibility of our finding it by any way known to us; and if we have managed to run over all the ways of attaining it that are humanly practicable (as will often be the case) then we may boldly affirm that knowledge of it has been put quite out of reach of the human mind.

It must further be observed that by 'adequate' enumeration or induction I mean exclusively the sort that makes the truth of conclusions more certain than any other type of proof, apart from simple intuition, makes it. Whenever a piece of knowledge cannot be reduced to simple intuition (if we throw off the fetters of syllogism), this method is the only one left to us that we must entirely rely on. For whenever we have deduced one thing from others, if the inference was an evident one, the case is already reduced to genuine intuition. If on the other hand, we make a single inference from many separate data, our understanding is often not capacious enough to grasp them all in one act of intuition, and in that case we must content ourselves with the certitude of this further operation. In the same way, we cannot visually distinguish all the links of a longish chain in one glance (*intuitu*); but nevertheless, if we have seen the connexion of each with the next, this will justify us in saying that we have actually seen how the first is connected to the last.

I said this operation must be ' adequate ', because it may often be defective, and consequently liable to error. For sometimes our enumeration includes a number of very obvious points; nevertheless, the least omission breaks the chain and destroys all the certainty of the conclusion. Again, sometimes our enumeration covers everything but the items are not all distinguished, so that we have only a confused knowledge of the whole.

Sometimes, then, this enumeration must be complete, and sometimes it must be distinct; but sometimes neither condition is necessary. This is why I say merely that the enumeration must be ' adequate '. For example, if I want to establish by enumeration how many kinds of things are corporeal, or are in some way the objects of sensation, I shall not assert that there are just so many without first assuring myself that my enumeration comprises all the kinds and distinguishes each from the others. But if I want to show in the same way that the rational soul is not corporeal, a complete enumeration will not be needed; it will be enough to comprise all bodies in a certain number of classes and show that the rational soul cannot be referred to any of these. Again, if I want to show by enumeration that the area of a circle is greater than the areas of all other figures of equal periphery, I need not give a list of all figures; it is enough to prove this in some particular cases, and then we may inductively extend the conclusion to all other figures.

I added further that the enumeration must be ' orderly '; for the defects already enumerated cannot be remedied more directly than they are by an orderly scrutiny of all

items. Again, it is often the case that nobody could live
long enough to go through each several item that concerns
the matter in hand; either because there are too many
such items, or because we should keep going back to the
same items. But if we arrange these items in the ideal
order, then as a rule they will be reduced to certain classes;
and it may be enough to have an exact view of one class,
or of some member of each class, or of some classes rather
than others; at any rate, we shall not ever go futilely over
and over the same point. This is a great help; a proper
arrangement often enables us to deal rapidly and easily
with an apparently unmanageable multitude of details.

This order of enumeration is variable, and depends on
the free choice of the individual; skill in devising it requires
that we bear in mind the terms of Rule V. There are,
indeed, a good many ingenious trivialities where the device
wholly consists in effecting this sort of arrangement.
For example, suppose you want to make the best anagram
you can by transposing the letters of a certain name.
Here there is no need to advance from· easy to difficult
cases, or to distinguish between what is underived and what
is dependent; for these problems do not arise here. It will
be enough to determine an order for examining trans-
positions of letters, so that you never go over the same
arrangement twice over, and to divide the possible arrangements into certain classes in a way that makes the most
likely source of a solution immediately apparent. The
task will then often be no long one—child's play, in fact.

Really, though, these last three Rules are inseparable;
in most cases they have all to be taken into account at once,
and they all go together towards the completeness of the
method. The order of setting them forth did not much
matter; I have explained them here briefly because almost
all the rest of this treatise will be a detailed exposition of
what is here summed up in a general way.

RULE VIII

*If in the series of subjects to be examined we come to a subject of which our intellect cannot gain a good enough intuition, we must stop there; and we must not examine the other matters that follow, but must refrain from futile toil.**

RULE IX

*We ought to turn our entire attention upon the smallest and easiest points, and dwell on them a long time, until we get accustomed to behold the truth by distinct and clear intuition.**

RULE X

*To gain sagacity, our mind must be trained on the very problems that other men have already solved, and it must methodically examine even the most trivial of human devices, but especially those which manifest or imply an orderly arrangement.**

RULE XI

If, after gaining intuitive knowledge of several simple propositions, we are to draw some further inference from them, it is useful for us to run through them in a continuous and uninterrupted movement of thought, to reflect on their interrelations and to form, so far as we can, distinct conceptions of several at once. For this adds much to the certainty of our knowledge, and it greatly increases the scope of our mind.

It is in place here to give a clearer exposition of what I said before about intuition (Rules III and VII). In the one place I contrasted intuition with deduction; in the other, merely with enumeration. (I defined enumeration as an inference made from many separate data put together; the simple deduction of one thing from another is made, I said, by intuition.) This procedure was necessary because intuition must satisfy two conditions: first, our understanding of a proposition must be clear and distinct;

secondly, it must be one simultaneous whole without succession. Now if we are thinking of the act of deduction, as in Rule III, it has not the appearance of being a simultaneous whole; rather, it involves a movement of the mind in which we infer one thing from another. Here, then, we were justified in distinguishing it from intuition. If on the other hand we attend to deduction as something already accomplished, as in the notes on Rule VII, then the term does not stand any longer for such a movement, but for the result of the movement. In that sense, then, I assume that a deduction is something intuitively seen, when it is simple and clear, but not when it is complex and involved; for that, I used the term ' enumeration ' or ' induction '. For the latter sort of deduction cannot be grasped all at once; its certainty depends in a way on memory, which must retain judgments about the various points enumerated in order that we may put them all together and get some single conclusion.

All these distinctions had to be made in order to bring out the meaning of the present Rule. Rule IX dealt only with intuition, and Rule X only with enumeration; then comes this Rule, explaining how these two activities co-operate and supplement one another—seem, in fact, to merge into a single activity, in which there is a movement of thought such that attentive intuition of each point is simultaneous with transition to the next.

I mention two advantages of this: the greater certainty in our knowledge of the conclusion we have in view, and the greater aptitude of our mind for making further discoveries. As I said, when conclusions are too complex to be held in a single act of intuition, their certainty depends on memory; and since memory is perishable and weak, it must be revived and strengthened by this continuous and repeated movement of thought. For example, suppose I have learnt, in a number of successive mental acts, the relations

between magnitudes 1 and 2, magnitudes 2 and 3, magnitudes 3 and 4, and, finally, magnitudes 4 and 5; this
does not make me see the relation between magnitudes 1 and
5, nor can I deduce it from the ones I already know, unless
I remember them all; accordingly, I must run over them
in thought again and again, until I pass from the first to the
last so quickly that I have hardly any parts to the care of
memory, but seem to have a simultaneous intuition of the
whole.

In this way, as no-one can fail to see, the slowness of the
mind is remedied, and its capacity enlarged. But it must
further be noticed, as the chief advantage of this Rule,
that by reflection upon the interdependence of simple
propositions we acquire the practice of rapidly discerning
their degrees of derivativeness and the steps of their reduc-
tion to what is underived. For example, if I run through
a series of magnitudes in continued proportion, I shall
reflect on all the following points: it is by concepts of the
same level that I discern the ratio of term 1 to term 2, of
term 2 to term 3, of term 3 to term 4, and so on, and there
are no degrees of difficulty in conceiving these ratios;
but it is more difficult for me to conceive the way that
term 2 depends on terms 1 and 3 together, and still more
difficult to conceive how the same term 2 depends on terms
1 and 4, and so on. This shows me the reason why, given
merely terms 1 and 2, I can easily find terms 3, 4, etc.;
for this is done by means of particular and distinct concepts.
But given merely terms 1 and 3, I cannot so easily find their
(geometric) mean; this can be done only by means of a
concept involving two together of the concepts just mentioned. Given only terms 1 and 4, it is still more difficult
to get an intuition of the two mean (proportionals), since
this involves three simultaneous concepts. Consequently
it might seem to be even more difficult to find three mean
(proportionals) given terms 1 and 5; but, for a further

reason, this is not the case. Although we have here four concepts joined together, they can be separated, because 4 is divisible by another number; so I can begin by trying to find term 3 from terms 1 and 5, and then go on to find term 2 from terms 1 and 3 ⟨and then term 4 from terms 3 and 5⟩. He who is accustomed to reflect on such matters recognises at once, when he examines each new problem, the source of the difficulty and the simplest method ⟨of solution[1]⟩; and this helps very much towards knowledge of the truth.

RULE XII

Finally, we must make use of all the aids of understanding, imagination, sense, and memory; and our aims in doing this must be, first, to gain distinct intuitive knowledge of simple propositions; secondly, to relate what we are looking for to what we already know, so that we may discern the former; thirdly, to discover those truths which should be correlated with each other, so that nothing is left out that lies within the scope of human endeavour.

This Rule sums up all that has been said already, and gives a general account of the various particulars that had to be explained: as follows.

Only two things are relevant to knowledge: ourselves, the subjects of knowledge; and the objects to be known. In ourselves there are just four faculties that can be used for knowledge: understanding, imagination, sense, and memory. Only the understanding is capable of perceiving truth, but it must be aided by imagination, sense, and memory, so that we may not leave anything undone that lies within our endeavour. On the side of the object of knowledge, it is enough to consider three points: first, what is obvious on its own account; secondly, the means of knowing one thing by another; lastly, the inferences that can be made from any given thing. This enumeration

---

[1] [Hiatus in the text.—TR.]

seems to me to be complete, and not to leave out anything that can be attained by human endeavour.

Turning therefore to the first point ⟨the subjective aspect of knowledge⟩, I should like to expound here the nature of the human mind and body, the way that the soul is the form of[1] the body, the various cognitive faculties that exist in the whole composed ⟨of mind and body⟩ and their several activities; but I think I have not enough space to contain all that would have to be premised before the truth on these matters could be made clear to everybody. For it is my aim always to write in such a way that, before making any assertion on the ordinary controversial points, I give the reasons that have led me to my view and might, in my opinion, convince other people as well.

Since such an exposition is now impossible, I shall content myself with explaining as briefly as possible the way of conceiving our means of knowledge that is most useful for our purpose. You need not, if you like, believe that things are really so; but what is to stop us from following out these suppositions, if it appears that they do not do away with any facts, but only make everything much clearer? In the same way, geometry makes certain suppositions about quantity; and although in physics we may often hold a different view as to the nature of quantity, the force of geometrical demonstrations is not in any way weaker on that account.

My first supposition, then, is that the external senses *qua* bodily organs may indeed be actively applied to their objects, by locomotion, but their having sensation is properly something merely passive, just like the shape (*figuram*) that wax gets from a seal. You must not think this expression is just an analogy; the external shape of the sentient organ must be regarded as really changed by the object, in exactly the same way as the shape of the surface

_____
[1] [Latin *informet*, a scholastic term. See the note on p. 229.—TR.]

of the wax is changed by the seal. This supposition must be made, not only as regards tactual sensations of shape, hardness, roughness, etc., but also as regards those of heat, cold, and so on. So also for the other senses. The first opaque part of the eye receives an image (*figuram*) in this way from many-coloured illumination; and the first membrane of the ears, nostrils, or tongue that is impervious to the object perceived similarly derives a new shape from the sound, odour, or savour.[1]

It is of great help to regard all these facts in this way; for no object of sense is more easily got than shape, which is both felt and seen. And no error can follow from our making this supposition rather than any other, as may be proved thus: The concept of shape is so common and simple that it is involved in every sensible object. For example, on any view of colour it is undeniably extended and therefore has shape. Let us then beware of uselessly assuming, and rashly imagining, a new entity; let us not deny anyone else's view of colour, but let us abstract from all aspects except shape, and conceive the difference between white, red, blue, etc., as being like the difference between such shapes as these:

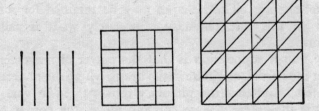

What trouble can this lead us into? And so generally; for assuredly the infinite multiplicity of shapes is adequate to explain all varieties of sensible objects.

[1] [Conceived as physical stimuli, not as sensations.—Tr.]

My second supposition is that when the external sense
⟨organ⟩ is disturbed by the object, the image (*figuram*) it
receives is transmitted to another part of the body, called
the ⟨organ of⟩ common sensibility; this happens instantaneously, and no real entity travels from one organ to the
other. In just the same way (I conceive) while I am now
writing, at the very moment when the various letters are
formed on the paper, it is not only the tip of the pen that
moves; there could not be the least movement of this that
was not at once communicated to the whole pen; and all
these various movements are also described in the air by
the top end of the pen; and yet I have not an idea that
something real travels from one end of the pen to the other.
For who could suppose that the parts of the human body
have less interconnexion than those of the pen? and what
simpler way of explaining the matter could be devised?

My third supposition is that the ⟨organ of⟩ common
sensibility also plays the part of a seal, whereas the phantasy
or imagination is the wax on which it impresses these
images or ideas, which come from the external sense
⟨organs⟩ unadulterated and without ⟨the transmission of⟩
any body; and this phantasy is a genuine part of the body,
large enough for its various parts to assume a number of
distinct shapes. These shapes may be retained for some
time; in this case phantasy is precisely what is called
memory.

My fourth supposition is that the power of movement,
in fact the nerves, originate in the brain, where the phantasy
is seated; and that the phantasy moves them in various
ways, as the external sense ⟨organ⟩ moves the ⟨organ of⟩
common sensibility, or as the whole pen is moved by its tip.
This illustration also shows how it is that the phantasy can
cause various movements in the nerves, although it has not
images of these formed in itself, but certain other images,
of which these movements are possible effects. For the pen

as a whole does not move in the same way as its tip; indeed, the greater part of the pen seems to go along with an altogether different, contrary motion. This enables us to understand how the movements of all other animals are accomplished, although we suppose them to have no consciousness (*rerum cognitio*) but only a bodily ⟨organ of⟩ phantasy; and furthermore, how it is that in ourselves those operations are performed which occur without any aid of reason.

My fifth and last supposition is that the power of cognition properly so called is purely spiritual, and is just as distinct from the body as a whole as blood is from bone or a hand from an eye; and that it is a single power. Sometimes it receives images from the common sensibility at the same time as the phantasy does; sometimes it applies itself to the images preserved in memory; sometimes it forms new images, and these so occupy the imagination that often it is not able at the same time to receive ideas from the common sensibility, or to pass them on to the locomotive power in the way that the body left to itself would. In all these processes the cognitive power is sometimes passive, sometimes active; it plays the part now of the seal, now of the wax; here, however, these expressions must be taken as merely analogical, for there is nothing quite like this among corporeal objects. The cognitive power is always one and the same; if it applies itself, along with the imagination, to the common sensibility, it is said to see, feel, etc.; if it applies itself to the imagination alone, in so far as that is already provided with various images, it is said to remember; if it does this in order to form new images, it is said to imagine or conceive; if, finally, it acts by itself, it is said to understand. (The manner of this last operation will be explained at more length in the proper place). In accordance with these diverse functions the same power is called now pure intellect, now imagination, now memory, now sense; and it is properly called mind (*ingenium*) when it is either forming new ideas in the phantasy or attending to those already formed. We regard it as capable of these various operations; and the distinction between these terms will have to be observed in what follows. In terms of these conceptions, the attentive reader will easily gather how we must seek to aid each faculty, and how far human endeavour can supply what is lacking to the mind.

For the understanding may be set in movement by the imagination, or on the other hand may set it in movement. Again the ⟨organ of⟩ imagination may act on the senses by means of the locomotive power, by applying them to their objects; or on the other hand they may act upon it, since it is upon it that they trace images (*imagines*) of bodies. Further, memory (considered, that is, as a corporeal faculty like the recollections of brutes) is nothing distinct from imagination. From this it is a certain inference that if the understanding is occupied with objects that have no corporeal or quasi-corporeal aspect, it cannot be aided by these faculties; on the contrary, we must prevent it from being hindered by them; sense must be banished, and imagination stripped (so far as possible) of every distinct impression. If, on the other hand, the understanding intends to examine something that can be referred to ⟨the concept of⟩ body, then we must form in the imagination as distinct an idea of this thing as we can; and in order to provide this in a more advantageous way, the actual object represented by this idea must be presented to the external senses. There are no further means of aiding the distinct intuition of individual facts. The inference of one fact from several, which often has to be carried out, requires that we should discard any element in our ideas that does not need our attention at the moment, in order to make it easier to keep the remainder in our memory; and then we must similarly present to the external senses, not the actual objects of our ideas, but rather compendious diagrams of them; so long as these are adequate to guard against a lapse of memory, the less space they take up the better. And anybody who observes all these precepts will, I think, have left nothing undone as regards the first point ⟨the subjective conditions of knowledge⟩.

We must now take the second point ⟨the conditions relating to the object of knowledge⟩. Here we must make a careful distinction between simple and compound notions, and try to discern, as regards each class, the possible sources of error, in order to avoid it, and the possible objects of assured knowledge, in order to occupy ourselves with these alone. Here, as previously, I shall have to make some assumptions that are perhaps not generally received; but it does not matter much, even if they are no more believed in than the imaginary circles by which astronomers describe their phenomena, so long as they enable you to distinguish the sort of apprehension of any given thing that is liable to be true or false.

In the first place, we must think differently when we regard things from the point of view of our knowledge and when we are talking about them as they are in reality. For example, take a body that has shape and extension. We shall admit that objectively there is one simple fact; we cannot call it, in this sense, ' a compound of the natures *body, extension,* and *figure* ', for these ' parts ' have never existed separate from one another. But in respect of our understanding we do call it a compound of these three natures; for we had to understand each one separately before judging that the three are found in one and the same subject. Now we are here concerned with things only in so far as they are perceived by the understanding; and so we use the term ' simple ' only for realities so clearly and distinctly known that we cannot divide any of them into

171

several realities more distinctly known, for example, shape, extension, motion, etc.; and we conceive of everything else as somehow compounded out of these. This principle must be taken quite generally, without even excepting the concepts that we sometimes form by abstraction even from simple ones. For example, we may say that figure is the terminus of an extended thing, meaning by ' terminus ' something more general than ' figure ', since we may also say ' terminus of a duration ', ' terminus of a motion ', etc. But although in this case the meaning of ' terminus ' is abstracted from figure, it is not therefore to be regarded as simpler than figure; on the contrary, since it is predicated also of other things, e.g. the end of a duration or motion, which are wholly different in kind from figure, it must have been abstracted from these too, and is thus something compounded out of quite diverse natures— in fact, its various applications to these are merely equivocal.

Secondly, the things that are termed simple (in relation to our understanding) are either purely intellectual, or purely material, or common ⟨to both realms⟩. The purely intellectual objects are those that the understanding knows by means of an innate light, without the help of any corporeal image. For there certainly are some such objects; no corporeal idea can be framed to show us the nature of knowledge, doubt, ignorance, or the action of the will (which we may call volition), or the like; but we really do know all these things, and quite easily at that; we need only have attained to a share of reason in order to do so. Those objects of knowledge are purely corporeal which are known to occur only in ⟨the realm of⟩ bodies: e.g. shape, extension, motion, etc. Finally, we must term common ⟨to both realms⟩ what is predicated indiscriminately now of corporeal things and now of spirits; e.g. existence, unity, duration, etc. We must also refer to this class axioms that form connecting links between other simple natures, and on whose self-evident character all conclusions of reasoning depend. For example: things that are the same as a single third thing are the same as one another; things that cannot be related in the same way to a third thing are in some respect diverse, etc. The understanding may know these common properties either by its own bare act, or by an intuition of images of material things.

Further, among these simple natures I wish to count also privations or negations of them, in so far as we conceive of such; for my intuition of nothingness, an instant, or rest is not less genuine knowledge than my concept of existence, duration, or motion. This way of regarding them will be helpful, for it enables us to say by way of summary that everything else we get to know will be a compound of these simple natures; for example, if I judge that some figure is not moving, I shall say that my thought is in a way a compound of ' figure ' and ' rest '; and so in other cases.

Thirdly, the knowledge of each of these simple natures is underived, and never contains any error. This is easily shown if we distinguish the intellectual faculty of intuitive knowledge from that of affirmative or negative judgment. For it is possible for us to think we do not know what in fact we do know; namely, we may be of opinion that besides the actual object of intuition, or what is grasped in our experience (*cogitando*), some further element hidden from us is involved, and this opinion (*cogitatio*) of ours may be false. Hence it is evident that we go wrong if we ever judge that one of these simple natures is not known to us in its entirety. For if our mind grasps the least thing to do with such a nature—as is necessary *ex hypothesi* if we are forming some judgment about it—this of itself entails that we know it in its entirety; otherwise it could not be termed simple, but would be compounded of the element perceived by us and the supposed unknown element.

Fourthly, the conjunction of these simple natures with one another is either necessary or contingent. It is necessary when one is implicitly contained in the concept of the other, so that we cannot distinctly conceive of either if we judge that they are separated; it is in this way that figure is conjoined with extension, motion with duration or time, etc., since an extensionless figure or a durationless motion is inconceivable. Again, if I say 'four and three are seven' this is a necessary conjunction; for we have no distinct concept of the number seven that does not implicitly include the numbers three and four. Similarly, any demonstrated property of figures or numbers is necessarily connected with that of which it is asserted. It is not only in the sensible world that we find this sort of necessity, but we have also cases like this: from Socrates's assertion that he doubts everything there is a necessary consequence 'therefore he understands at least what he doubts', or again 'therefore he knows that there is something that can be true or false', or the like; for these are necessarily bound up with the nature of the doubt. A combination of natures is contingent when they are not conjoined by any inseparable relation; as when we say that a body is animated, that a man is clothed, etc. Many necessary conjunctions, moreover, are generally counted as contingent, because their real relation is generally unobserved, e.g. the proposition 'I am, therefore God is', or again, 'I understand, therefore I have a mind distinct from the body', and the like. Finally, it is to be observed that very many necessary propositions have contingent converses; e.g. although God's existence is a certain conclusion from mine, my existence cannot be asserted on account of God's existence.

Fifthly, we can never have any understanding of anything apart from these single natures and their blending or composition. It is often easier to attend to a conjunction of

several than to separate out one from the others; for I may,
e.g. know a triangle without ever having thought that this
involves knowledge of angle, line, the number three,
figure, extension, etc. But this in no way goes against our
saying that the nature of a triangle is composed of all these
natures, and that they are prior to ' triangle ' in the order of
knowledge, since they are the very natures that are understood to occur in a triangle. Moreover, there may well be
many other natures implicit in ' triangle ' that escape our
notice; e.g. the size of the angles (their being equal to
two right angles), and an infinity of relations between the
sides and the angles, the sides and the area, etc.

Sixthly, the natures called ' compound ' are known
to us either because we have experience (*experimur*) of them
or because we ourselves compound them. By our experience I mean sense-perception, hearsay, and in general
everything that is either brought to our understanding
from outside or arises from its own self-contemplation.
It must here be remarked that no experience can deceive
the understanding if it confines itself to intuition of what is
presented to it—of what it itself contains, or what is given
by means of a brain-image—and does not go on to judge
that imagination faithfully reproduces the objects of the
senses, or that the senses give us true pictures (*figuras*) of
things, in short, that external things are always what they
seem. On all such matters we are liable to go wrong;
e.g. if somebody tells us a tale and we believe the thing
happened; if a man suffering from jaundice thinks
everything is yellow because his eye is suffused with yellow;
if again, there is a lesion in the organ of imagination, as in
melancholia, and we judge that the disordered images it
produces represent real things. But the understanding
of a sage (*sapientis*)[1] will not be misled by such things;
for as regards any datum of the imagination, he will

[1] [Perhaps a reference to the Stoic conception of the sage.—TR.]

indeed judge that there really is such a picture in that faculty, but he will never assert that this picture has been transmitted in its entirety and unchanged from the external object to the senses and from the senses to the phantasy, unless he has antecedently had some other means of knowing this fact. I say that an object of understanding is ' compounded by ourselves ' whenever we believe that something is involved in it that has not been directly perceived by the mind in experience. For example, the jaundiced man's conviction that what he sees is yellow is a mental state (*cogitatio*) compounded of the representation in his phantasy and an assumption that he makes on his own account, viz. that the yellow colour appears not through a defect in the eye but because what he sees really is yellow. From this we conclude that we can be deceived only so long as the object of our belief is, in a way, of our own compounding.

Seventhly, this ' compounding ' may take place in three ways; on impulse, or from conjecture, or by deduction. People compound their judgments about things ' on impulse ' when their own mind[1] leads them to believe something without their being convinced by any reasoning; they are determined to do so either by a higher power, or by their own spontaneity, or by the disposition of the phantasy; the first never misleads, the second rarely, the third almost always. But the first does not concern us here, since it is not something attainable by our technique. The following is an example of conjecture: Water, which is further from the centre than earth, is also rarer; air, which comes above water, is still more rare; we conjecture that above air there is only a very pure aether, far thinner even than air. Views ' compounded ' in this way are not misleading, so long as we regard them only as probable and never assert them as truth; they actually add to our stock of information.

[1] [*Ingenium*. For the shade of meaning cp. p. 170.—Tr.]

There remains deduction—the only way of 'compounding' things so that we may be certain that the result is true. But even here all sorts of faults are possible. For example, from the fact that this region (which is full of air) contains nothing that we perceive by sight or touch or any other sense, we may conclude that it is empty, and thus wrongly conjoin the natures 'this region' and 'vacuum'. This error occurs whenever we judge that a general and necessary conclusion can be got from a particular or contingent fact. But it lies within our powers to avoid it; we can do so by never conjoining things unless we see intuitively that their conjunction is absolutely necessary, as we do when we infer that nothing can have shape without extension because shape has a necessary connexion with extension.

From all this the first conclusion to be drawn is that we have now set forth in a distinct way, and with what seems to me to be an adequate enumeration, the truth that we were previously able to establish only confusedly and roughly; viz. that there are no ways of attaining truth open to man except self-evident intuition and necessary inference; and it is moreover clear what 'simple natures' are. . . . It is obvious, furthermore, that the scope of intuition covers all these, and knowledge of their necessary connexions; and, in sum, covers everything that is comprised precisely in the experience (*experitur*) of the understanding, as a content either of its own or of the phantasy. About deduction we shall say more in the sequel. . . . °

For the rest, in case anybody should miss the interconnexion of my rules, I divide all that can be known into simple propositions and problems (*quaestiones*). As regards simple propositions, the only rules I give are those that prepare the mind for more distinct intuition and more sagacious examination of any given objects; for such propositions must come to one spontaneously—they cannot be sought for. This was the content of my first twelve Rules, and I think that in these I have set forth all that can facilitate the use of reason. As regards problems, they consist, first, of those that are perfectly understood, even if the solution is unknown; we shall deal exclusively with these in the next twelve Rules;[1] and, secondly, of those that are not perfectly understood; these we reserve for the last twelve. We have made this division on purpose, both in order to avoid having to speak of anything that presupposes an acquaintance with what follows, and also to teach those matters first which, in our view, should be studied first in developing our mental powers. Among ' problems perfectly understood ', be it observed, I count only those as regards which we see three things distinctly: first, the criteria for recognising what we are looking for, when we come upon it; secondly, the precise premise from which to infer it; thirdly, the way to establish their interdependence—the impossibility of modifying one without the other. We must, then, be in possession of all the premises; nothing must remain to be shown except the way of finding the conclusion. This will not be a question of a single inference from a single simple premise (which, as I have said, can be performed without rules), but of a technique for deriving a single conclusion from many premises taken together without needing a greater mental capacity than for the simplest inference. These problems are for the most part abstract ones, and are almost confined to arithmetic and geometry; so novices may regard them as comparatively useless. But I urge the need of long use and practice in acquiring this technique for those who wish to attain a perfect mastery of the latter part of the Method, in which we shall treat of all these other matters.

[1] [Descartes intended the work to consist of thirty-six Rules falling into three parts. It was never completed.—Tr.]

RULE XIII

*If we are to understand a problem perfectly, we must free it from any superfluous conceptions, reduce it to the simplest terms, and by a process of enumeration, split it up into the smallest possible parts.**

RULE XIV

*The same rule must be applied to the real extension of bodies, and it must be set before the imagination by means of plain diagrams. For in this way it will be far more distinctly perceived by the understanding.**

RULE XV

*It is also often helpful to draw these diagrams and to display them to the external senses, so that in this way our attention may be held more easily.**

RULE XVI

*Matters, on the other hand, that do not demand our attention at the moment, though they are needed for drawing conclusions, are best represented by very brief symbols rather than by complete diagrams. For in this way our memory cannot be misled, and at the same time our thought will not be distracted by having to keep these things in mind while we are engaged in other deductions.**

RULE XVII

*When we are dealing with a problem we must run over it in a direct course; in so doing, we must abstract from the fact that some of its terms are known, others unknown; and by valid processes, step by step, we must apprehend the interdependence of the terms.**

RULE XVIII

*To this end only four operations are needed : addition, subtraction, multiplication, and division. The last two of these must, at this stage, not be performed too often, in order to avoid gratuituous complications, and also because they can be carried out more easily later on.**

RULE XIX

In this method of reasoning we must try to get expressed in two different ways each as many magnitudes as there are unknown terms; we treat the latter as though they were known when we are running over the problem in a direct course. For we shall thus have the same number of equations [1] *as there are unknowns.*

RULE XX

Having found the equations, [2] *we must perform the operations which we have left out, never making use of multiplication when there is scope for division.*

RULE XXI

If there are several such equations, all of them must be reduced to a single one : namely to the one whose terms occupy fewest places in a series of magnitudes in continued proportion ; and its terms must be set out in the order followed by the series. [3]

THE END [4]

[1] [Literally, ' comparisons between two equals '.—Tr.]

[2] [The word is here *aequatio*.—Tr.]

[3] [The modern term would be ' the equation of lowest degree,' i.e. the one involving the lowest power of the 'unknown' x. x, x^2, x^3, . . . are of course ' a series of magnitudes in continued proportion '; the equation of lowest degree is thus the one that involves fewest terms in the series. The last part of the Rule means that the equation must be set forth in *descending* powers of x, e.g. $x^2 - 3x + 2 = 0$.—Tr.]

[4] [This is found both in Leibniz's MS and in the Amsterdam edition. However, in both these texts it is noted, immediately before Rule XIX: ' the rest is missing '.—Ed.]

Extracts from

PRINCIPLES OF PHILOSOPHY

illustrating Descartes's Use of certain Terms
and his Principles in Physics

*From the Latin text
first published in 1644*

FIRST PHILOSOPHY

Extracts from ' Principles of Philosophy ' Part I

A

IX.[1] By the term *conscious experience* (*cogitationis*) I understand everything that takes place within ourselves so that we are aware of it (*nobis consciis*), in so far as it *is* an object of our awareness (*conscientia*). And so not only acts of understanding, will, and imagination, but even sensations, are here to be taken as experience (*cogitare*). Suppose I say *I see* (or *I am walking*) *therefore I exist*. If I take this to refer to vision (or walking) as a corporeal action, the conclusion is not absolutely certain; for, as often happens during sleep, I may think I am seeing though I do not open my eyes (or think I am walking although I do not change my place); and it may even be that I have no body. But if I take it to refer to the actual sensation or awareness (*conscientia*) of seeing (or walking), then it is quite certain; for in that case it has regard to the mind, and it is the mind alone that has a sense or experience (*cogitat*) of itself seeing (or walking).

B

X. . . . I have often observed that philosophers make the mistake of trying to explain by logical definitions those things which are most simple and self-evident; they thus only make them more obscure. When I said that the proposition *I experience* (*cogito*) *therefore I am* is the first

---

[1] [These are the numbers originally given to the sections in Descartes's *Principles of Philosophy* Pt. 1—Tr.]

and the most certain of those we come across when we philosophise in an orderly way, I was not denying that we must first know what is meant by *experience, existence, certainty;* again, we must know such things as that *it is impossible for that which is experiencing to be non-existent;* but I thought it needless to enumerate these notions, for they are of the greatest simplicity, and by themselves they can give us no knowledge that anything *exists.*

C

XIII. . . . [The mind] finds within itself ideas of many things; and so long as it merely contemplates these, and neither asserts nor denies the existence of something like them outside itself, it cannot be in error. Further, it finds certain axioms, and from these it makes up various demonstrations; and so long as it attends to them, it is wholly convinced of their truth. For instance, the mind has within itself ideas of numbers and figures, and has also such axioms as *if you add equals to equals the results will be equal;* from these it is easily proved that the three angles of a triangle are equal to two right angles, and so on; and the mind is convinced of such truths, so long as it is attending to the premises from which it deduced them. But it cannot always be attending to them; and when it goes on to recollect that so far it does not know but that it was so created as to be liable to go wrong even about what appears most evident, it sees that it does well to doubt such conclusions—that certainty in knowledge is impossible until it has come to know the Author of its being.

D

XVII. When we consider further the ideas we possess, we see that in so far as they are states (*modi*) of consciousness they do not differ much from one another; but in so far as they represent different things, they are very various; and the greater amount of representative perfection they comprise, the more perfect must their cause be. For example, when somebody possesses the idea of a highly complicated machine, we are justified in asking from what cause he derived it; did he somewhere see such a machine made by somebody else ? or is it that he has made such a careful study of mechanics, or is so clever, that he could invent it on his own account, although he has never seen it anywhere ? Any device that is found in the idea representatively, in a picture so to say, must occur in the cause (whatever this turns out to be) not just representatively or by way of reproduction, but actually; either the device as such must occur, or it must exist in some higher form; at least, this holds good as regards the first and principal cause.

E

XXIII. There are many properties in which we do indeed discern an element of perfection, but also an element of imperfection or limitation; these, therefore, cannot belong to God. Thus, the nature of body includes divisibility as well as extension in place; and it is an imperfection to be divisible; so it is certain that God is not a body. Again, in us sense is a perfection; but every sensation involves being acted on, and to be acted on is to be dependent on something; so we must not think there is any sensation in God, but only intellection and will. And we must not regard these as taking place in God by distinct operations as they do in us; we must hold that there is a single, constant, and supremely simple activity by which God simultaneously understands, wills and effects everything. (By 'everything' I mean every *thing*; God does not will the wickedness of sin, for that is not a thing.)

185

XXIV. . . . We must always be careful to bear it specially in mind that God the Author of things is infinite, and we ourselves in every way finite. XXV. . . . We shall then not wonder at all that there are many things, both in the immeasurable nature of God and among his creatures, which exceed our grasp.

XXVI. And so we shall never be troubled by arguments about infinity. Since we ourselves are finite, it would be absurd for us to try to determine something about infinity, and thus, so to say, to make it finite and comprehend it. We shall therefore not take the trouble to give a reply to people who ask: *Given an infinite line, is half of it infinite too? Is an infinite number odd or even?* and so on. Nobody, I think, is obliged to think of such matters, unless he thinks his own mind is infinite.

Whatever is such that in some aspect we can find no bounds to it we shall not assert to be infinite, but shall regard as indefinitely great (*indefinita*). For instance, we cannot imagine any extension so great that we do not conceive the possibility of one still greater; so we shall say that the magnitude of possible things is indefinitely great (*indefinitam*). Again, a body cannot be divided into so many parts that we do not conceive of each of these parts as being again divisible; so we shall consider quantity as indefinitely divisible. Again, we cannot imagine the number of the stars to be so great that we do not think God could have created any more; so we shall suppose the number to be indefinitely great (*indefinitum*). And so on.

XXVII. We shall use the term *indefinitely great* (*indefinita*) rather than *infinite* in order to confine the term *infinite* to God; only as regards God is it a matter of our not merely failing to apprehend any limits in any respect, but positively knowing there are none. We have no such positive knowledge that other things are in some respect unlimited; we merely make the negative admission that, if they have limits, at any rate they are not discoverable by us.

F

XXXII. All forms of consciousness (*modi cogitandi*) that we experience (*experimur*) can be brought under two general heads: viz. cognition (*perceptio*), or the operation of the intellect, and volition, or the operation of the will. Sensation, imagination, and pure intellection are just various forms (*modi*) of cognition (*percipiendi*); desire, aversion, assertion, denial, doubt, are various forms (*modi*) of volition.

G

XXXIV. Judgment presupposes intellect, since we can make no judgment about an object that we do not in any way cognise (*percipimus*); it also presupposes the power of will, so that we may assent to what we somehow cognise. But judgment (at least, the occurrence of some sort of judgment) does not presuppose complete cognition (*perceptio*) of a thing under every aspect. We may well assent to many things when we have only a highly obscure and confused cognition (*cognoscimus*) of them.

H

XXXV. Intellectual cognition (*perceptio*) has for its scope only the few objects presented to it, and is always extremely limited. But the will may in a sense be termed infinite; for we never observe any possible object of another will (even of the immeasurable Will of God) that does not also fall within the range of our own will. So it is easy for us to extend our will beyond what we clearly cognise (*percipimus*); and when we do this, it is not surprising if we happen to go wrong. XXXVII. This vast range of our will belongs to its very nature. It is a supreme perfection in man to act voluntarily or freely, and thus to be in a special sense the author of his own actions, and to deserve praise for them. We do not praise automata for precisely carrying out all the movements for which they were designed, since they carry them out by necessity; we rather praise the maker for fashioning such precise machines, because he fashioned them not by necessity but freely. Similarly, it is more to our credit that we embrace the truth when we do, because we do this freely, than it would be if we could not but embrace it.

I

XXXVIII. . . . God could have endowed our intellect with such a power of discernment that we never were wrong; but we cannot claim this from him by any right. Among us men, if somebody has the power to prevent an evil, and nevertheless does not prevent it, we say he causes it; but we must not similarly consider that, because God could have made us never to be wrong, he is the cause of our errors. For the power of one man over others was established to the end that he should use it to ward them away from evil; but God's power over all men is utterly unrestricted and free.

J

XXXIX. The existence of freedom in our will, and our power in many cases to assent or dissent at our pleasure, is so clear that it must be counted among the first and most axiomatic (*communes*) of our innate notions. This came out just now when we were trying to doubt everything: we reached the point of imagining some most powerful author of our being who was trying in all ways to deceive us;

but even so we were conscious (*experiebamur*) of freedom to abstain from believing what was not quite certain and thoroughly examined. And nothing can be more self-evident or more manifest that what appeared beyond doubt even in those conditions.

XL. Now that we recognise a God, we see that his power is so immeasurable that we hold it impious to believe we can ever do anything but what God has fore-ordained. And so we may easily entangle ourselves in great difficulties if we try to reconcile God's preordination with our free will, and to comprehend both at once. XLI. We shall get out of these if we remember the finitude of our own mind, and the infinity of God's power, whereby he not only foreknew all actual or possible beings from eternity, but also willed and fore-ordained them. Our minds are adequate to arrive at this power—we clearly and distinctly perceive that it exists in God; but not to comprehend it—we cannot see how it leaves human free actions undetermined. On the other hand, we are so conscious (*conscios*) of the freedom and indetermination that occurs in us, that there is nothing we comprehend more evidently or more perfectly. Now it would be absurd if our not comprehending one thing, which we know must from its very nature be incomprehensible to us, led us to doubt something else, which we intimately comprehend and of which we have personal experience.

K

XLII. We now see that all our errors depend on our will; so it may seem surprising that we ever go wrong, since nobody chooses to go wrong. But there is a great difference between choosing to go wrong, and choosing to assent to something that in fact involves error. And although certainly nobody expressly chooses to go wrong, there is hardly anyone but frequently chooses to assent to

what, unbeknownst to him, contains error. Indeed, the
very eagerness to attain truth often leads people who do
not know the right way of attaining it to form judgments
about what they do not discern (*percipiunt*), and thus to
fall into error.

L

XLV. . . . For a perception to be a possible foundation
for a certain and indubitable judgment, it must be not only
clear but also distinct. I call a perception *clear* when, if
the mind attends to it, it is present and manifest; just
as we say we see clearly what is present to the gaze of our
eye and has a sufficiently strong and manifest effect upon
it. I call a perception *distinct* if it is not only clear but
also precisely distinguished from all others, so that it
contains no element that is not clear. XLVI. For instance,
when a man feels great pain, he has a very clear perception
of pain, but not always a distinct one; for men commonly
confuse this perception with an obscure judgment as to the
nature of pain; they think there is something in the painful
spot resembling the sensation of pain, but the sensation is
all that they perceive clearly. So a perception may be
clear without being distinct, though not distinct without
being clear.

M

XLVIII. . . . I recognise only two *summa genera* of
realities: intellectual or mental (*cogitativarum*) realities, i.e.
such as belong to a mind or conscious (*cogitantem*) substance;
and material realities, i.e. such as belong to an extended
substance, a body. Cognition (*perceptio*), volition, and all
cognitive (*percipiendi*) and volitional states (*modi*) are
referred to a conscious substance; to an extended substance
are referred size (i.e. actual extension in length, breadth,

and depth), shape, motion, position, divisibility of its parts, and so on. But we also have experience (*experimur*) of other things, which should not be referred to the mind alone nor yet to the body alone; they arise, as we shall see, from a close and intimate union of body and mind. To this class belong (1) appetites—hunger, thirst, etc.; (2) impulses or passions of the mind, which do not consist in mere consciousness (*cogitatione*)—impulses towards anger, joy, sorrow, love, etc.; (3) all sensations—the sensations of pain, enjoyment, light and colours, sounds, odours, flavours, heat, hardness, and other tactile qualities.

N

XLIX. . . . When we recognise the impossibility of some-thing coming out of nothing, then we are considering the proposition *Nothing comes out of nothing* not as an existent thing, or an aspect (*modus*) of a thing, but as an eternal truth that dwells in our mind; we call such truths common notions, or axioms. To this class belong: *It is impossible that a given thing should at once be and not be ; What has happened cannot not have happened ; One who is experiencing* (cogitat) *cannot but exist while he is experiencing ;* and countless others. It would not be easy to enumerate them all; but one is not, either, likely to be ignorant of them when occasion arises to think of them and when we are not blinded by prejudice. L. There is no doubt but these common notions can be clearly and distinctly perceived; . . . but some of them are not equally perceived by all men. It is not, in my opinion, that one man's power of knowledge has a greater scope than another's, but rather that these axioms happen to be opposed to some men's preconceived opinions and thus cannot be readily grasped by them, although other men, who are free from such prejudices, perceive them most evidently.

O

LI. . . . We can mean by *substance* nothing other than a thing existing in such a manner that it has need of no other thing in order to exist. There can indeed be only one substance conceived as needing absolutely no other thing in order to exist; namely, God. We can see that all other substances are able to exist only by means of God's co-operation. So the term *substance* does not (to use scholastic language) apply univocally to God and other things; that is, there is no distinctly conceivable meaning of the term that is a common property of God and creatures. LII. But corporeal substance and mind (i.e. created conscious substance) can be brought under this common concept: things that need only the co-operation of God in order to exist.

Our first knowledge of a substance cannot come from the mere fact that it is an existent thing; for this in itself has no effect on us. But from any attribute we readily apprehend substance, because of the axiom (*communem notionem*) that a nonentity can have no attributes, properties, or qualities. From perceiving the presence of an attribute we conclude to the necessary presence also of some existing thing or substance to which it may be attributed. LIII. Any attribute gives us knowledge of substance; but every substance has a principal property that constitutes its essential nature, and all others are reduced to this. Extension in length, breadth, and depth is what constitutes the very nature of corporeal substance; consciousness is what constitutes the very nature of a conscious substance. For any other possible attribute of body presupposes extension and is, so to say, an aspect (*modus*) of an extended thing; and likewise whatever is found in the mind is merely one aspect or another of consciousness (*diversi modi cogitandi*). For example, shape is not conceivable except in an extended thing, nor motion except in an extended space; whereas imagination, sensation and will are inconceivable except in a conscious being. But on the other hand extension is conceivable apart from shape or motion, and so is consciousness apart from imagination and sense, and so on; this is clear to anyone on reflection. LIV. We can thus readily get two clear and distinct notions or ideas: one of created conscious substance, the other of corporeal substance; provided that we carefully distinguish all attributes of consciousness from attributes of extension.

We can likewise get a clear and distinct idea of uncreated and independent conscious substance, that is, God; provided that we do not suppose that this idea is an adequate manifestation of all that exists in God, and do not falsely imagine that something is comprised in it, but merely observe what it really does involve—what we evidently see belongs to the nature of a supremely perfect being. And assuredly nobody can deny that there is within us such an idea of God, unless he should think that there is no knowledge of God in the human mind at all.

P

LX. . . . Real distinction between two or more substances . . . is discovered from the mere fact that we can clearly and distinctly conceive one without the other. For when we come to know God, we are certain that he can do whatever we distinctly understand. For example, our having the idea of extended or corporeal substance, though not enough to assure us that any such substance in fact exists, is enough to assure us that it can exist; and further, that if it does, any portion of it delimited by us in thought (*cogitatione*) is really distinct from other parts of the same substance. Again, each of us conceives of himself as a conscious being, and can in thought exclude from himself any other substance, whether conscious or extended; so from this mere fact it is certain that each of us, so regarded, is really distinct from every other conscious substance and from every corporeal substance. And even if we supposed that God had conjoined some corporeal substance to such a conscious substance so closely that they could not be more closely joined, and had thus compounded a unity out of the two, yet even so they remain really distinct. For however closely he had united them, he could not deprive himself of his original power to separate them, or to keep one in being without the other; and things that can be separated, or kept in being separately, by God are really distinct.

Q

LXVIII. . . . Pain, colour, and so on are clearly and distinctly perceived when they are considered merely as sensations or experiences (*cogitationes*). When they are judged to be realities existing outside our mind, their nature is quite unintelligible; if someone says he sees colour in a body, or feels pain in a limb, it is just as though he said he saw or felt in that place something of a completely unknown nature—i.e. as if he said he did not know what he saw or felt. It is true that if he is careless he may easily persuade himself that he has some notion of what it is, because he may suppose it to be something like the sensation of colour or pain of which he is aware within himself. But if he examines the question what is represented by the sensation of colour or pain, which looks as though it existed in the coloured body or the painful part, he will see he is wholly ignorant of this. LXIX. This point is specially clear from a consideration of the vast difference, as regards our knowledge of their real nature, between, on the one hand, the size, shape, motion,[1] position, duration, number, etc., of a visible body—the properties that I have said we clearly perceive in bodies—and, on the other hand, colour, painfulness, odour, flavour, and any other such characteristics of the body in question, which I have said are to be referred to sensation. It is true that, upon seeing a body, we are no less certain of its existence *qua* that which appears coloured than *qua* that which appears with a shape; but we know far more evidently what shape is, than what colour is, as inherent in the body.

LXX. Clearly, then, when we say we perceive colours in objects, it is really just the same as though we said that we perceive in objects something as to whose nature we are ignorant, but which produces in us a very manifest and obvious sensation, called the sensation of colour. But as regards the manner of making the judgment there is a very great difference. So long as we merely judge that there is in objects (that is, the things, whatever they may turn out to be, from which we get the sensation) something of whose nature we are ignorant, we do not go wrong; on the contrary, we guard against error in advance, for on observing our ignorance we are less inclined to form rash judgments. It is otherwise when we think we perceive colours in objects. True, we are in fact ignorant as to the nature of what we then call colour, and we cannot conceive of any likeness between the colour supposed to be in objects and the colour of which we have sense-experience; but we do not take account of this; and there are many other characteristics (size, shape, number, etc.) about which we clearly perceive that they appear to in sensation or intellection just as they are, or at any rate could be, in the objects. So we easily fall into the mistake of judging

---

[1] I.e. *local* motion. Philosophers have fancied other kinds of motion, distinct from local motion; they have thus only made the nature of motion less intelligible to themselves.

that the feature of objects that we call colour is something just like the colour in our sensation; i.e. of thinking that we clearly perceive something which in fact we do not perceive at all.

R

LXXI. . . . In our infancy our mind was so tightly bound to the body as not to be open to any experiences (*cogitationibus*) except mere feelings of what affected the body. As yet it did not refer these feelings to anything situated outside itself; it merely had sensations of pain in places where something unbeneficial, and of pleasure where something beneficial, happened to the body; and in places where the body was affected without any greatly beneficial or unbeneficial result, it had a variety of sensations, according to the various parts where, and ways in which, the body was so affected—sensations, as we call them, of flavours, odours, sounds, heat, cold, light, colours, etc.; sensations representing nothing outside our consciousness (*cogitationem*). At the same time the mind perceived sizes, shapes, motions, etc., which were made manifest to it not as mere sensations, but as things (or aspects of things) existing (or at least capable of existing) outside consciousness; as yet, however, it was unaware of the distinction.

Later on, since the bodily mechanism is naturally so constituted as to be capable of various movements by its own power, its random wrigglings this way and that, as it followed after something beneficial or shrank from something unbeneficial, led the mind conjoined to it to observe the external existence of what the body thus followed after or shrank from; and to this reality the mind ascribed not only size, shape, motion, etc., which it perceived as things or aspects of things, but also flavours, odours, and other qualities, sensations of which it observed to be caused in it by the external reality.

196

Further, since our mind related everything to the interest of the body in which it was immersed, it judged of the degree of reality of objects that affected it by the magnitude of their effects. Thus, it judged that there was much more substance or body in stones and metals than in water or air, because it had a greater sensation of hardness and heaviness; and in fact it considered air as mere nothingness, so long as it had no awareness of wind or cold or heat in the air. Again, since there was no more light shining on it from the stars than from the small flames of lamps, it had no picture of stars bigger than such flames. Again, it did not observe the Earth's rotation, nor the globular curvature of its surface; so it was the more prone to judge that the Earth was motionless and flat. There are a thousand other prejudices that our mind absorbed in infancy; and later on in childhood, forgetting that these views were accepted as a result of insufficient examination, it regarded them as the evidence of the senses, or as a natural endowment, and held them to have the highest degree of truth and evidentness.

LXXII. In adult life the mind is no longer wholly a slave to the body, and does not relate everything to that; it enquires after the truth of things considered in themselves; and it thus discerns the falsity of very many of its former views. But for all that it cannot so readily blot them out of its memory; and as long as they stay there, they may cause a variety of errors. For example, in our infancy we imagined the stars to be very small; astronomical arguments may show clearly that they are in fact very large, but our preconceived opinion still has the power of making it very hard to imagine them except as we did before.

§

LXXIII. Attention to any subject is impossible for our mind without some difficulty and fatigue; and is specially

difficult as regards what is not present either to sense or
even to imagination. This may be because of the mind's
very nature, as conjoined to a body; or again because of its
having acquired special practice and facility with sensations
and images in its earliest years, when it was wholly occupied
with them. This is the reason why so many people cannot
even now conceive of any substance but is imaginable,
corporeal and even sensible. They do not realise that
imagination cannot go beyond what is extended and
movable, and has shape, whereas many other things are
conceivable. They suppose that nothing can exist
(*subsistere*) except body; and even that no body can,
unless it is sensible. And since in fact we do not perceive
the nature of anything by sensation alone, . . . the result
is that many people have nothing but confused perceptions
throughout their lives.

T

LXXIV. On account of using language, we associate all
our concepts with the words we use to express them, and
commit them to memory only along with those words.
Later on we remember the words more readily than the
realities; and we hardly ever have such a distinct conception
of any reality that we abstract it from any conception of
words; most men's thoughts are concerned with words
rather than realities. And very often people assent to
words they do not understand, because they think they
did once, or think they got them from others who did
understand them properly. . . .

PRINCIPLES OF MATERIAL THINGS

A Selection from ' Principles of Philosophy ' Part II.

IV. . . . The nature of matter, or of body considered in general, does not consist in its being a thing that has hardness or weight, or colour, or any other sensible property, but simply in its being a thing that has extension in length, breadth, and depth. For as regards hardness, our sensation tells us no more than that the parts of a hard body resist the movement of our hands when they encounter it; if, whenever our hands moved in a given direction, all the bodies lying that way were always to retreat with the same speed as our hands approached, we should never have any sensation of hardness. Now it is inconceivable that, if bodies did retreat in this way, they would thereby lose their nature as bodies; so this nature cannot consist in hardness. By the same reasoning it may be shown that weight, colour and all other such sensible qualities of corporeal matter can be removed from body while it itself remains in its entirety; so it follows that its real nature depends upon none of them.

V. There remain, however, two possible reasons for doubting whether the real nature of body consists merely in extension. First, many people hold that various bodies can be rarefied and condensed, so that when rarefied they have more extension than when condensed; some people are indeed so subtle as to distinguish the substance of a body from its quantity, and even the quantity from its extension. Secondly, if we conceive a place to contain nothing but extension in length, breadth, and depth, we do not usually say there is a body there; we just say there is space there—

empty space, which almost everyone is convinced is mere nonentity.

VI. But as regards rarefaction and condensation, anybody who thinks attentively, and will admit only what he clearly perceives, will hold that all that happens here is change of shape. What I mean is this: rarefied bodies are those that have many gaps between their particles, which are occupied by other bodies; and increase of density results merely from these particles approaching one another, so as to diminish these gaps or altogether obliterate them. In the latter case the body becomes so dense that it is contradictory to suppose it could be any denser. A body is, however, not of less extent in this case than when it occupies a greater space through the separation of its particles; for the extension comprised in the pores or gaps that remain between its particles must be assigned not to it but to the other bodies, whatever they may be, that fill the gaps. It is just as when we see a sponge swollen with water or some other fluid; we do not think its several parts have any greater extension than when it is squeezed dry; we just think that its pores are open wider, so that it is spread over a bigger space.

VII. I really cannot see the motive of people who chose to say that rarefaction happens by an increase of quantity, rather than explain it by this example of the sponge. Of course when air or water is rarefied we cannot see any pores growing bigger, nor yet any new body coming to fill them up; but it is irrational to invent something unintelligible as a merely verbal account of rarefaction, rather than infer from rarefaction that there are pores or gaps that grow bigger, that there is some new body that comes and fills them up, although we do not perceive this body by any of our senses. For there is no compelling reason to believe that all bodies that exist must affect our senses. Again, we can very easily see how rarefaction can come about in this way, but not how it could in any other way. Finally, it is a flat contradiction that anything should be increased by new quantity, new extension, without a simultaneous addition of new extended substance, that is new body. No increment of extension or quantity is conceivable without an increment of substance to which this quantity and extension shall belong. This will be made clearer by what follows.

VIII. Quantity differs from the extended substance, not in actuality, but only as regards our way of conceiving them; just as number does from what is numbered. We may consider the entire nature of the corporeal substance that in fact occupies a space of ten feet, without attending to the magnitude *ten feet;* for this nature is conceived as being just the same in any given part of the space as in the whole space. Conversely, the number ten, and similarly the continuous quantity *ten feet,* may be conceived without our attending to this definite substance. The concept of the number ten is just the same whether it is referred to this ten-foot magnitude or to anything else; and although the continuous quantity *ten feet* cannot be conceived apart from some substance whose quantity it shall be, it can be conceived without this definite substance. But in actuality it is not possible to subtract the least bit of the quantity or extension without likewise removing just as much of the substance; or conversely, to remove never so little of the substance without subtracting just as much of the quantity or extension.

IX. People may speak otherwise, but I do not think they have any conception other than this. When they distinguish substance from extension or quantity, either they mean nothing by the term substance; or they simply have a confused notion of an incorporeal substance, which they falsely attach to corporeal substance; the genuine notion of corporeal substance falls for them under extension, which, however, they call an accident. Thus what they express in words is quite different from what they grasp in their minds.

X. A space, or intrinsic place, does not differ in actuality from the body that occupies it; the difference lies simply in our ordinary ways of thinking. In reality the extension in length, breadth, and depth that constitutes the space is absolutely the same as that which constitutes the body. The difference lies in this: when we consider the extension as belonging to the body, we regard it as something individual, so that there is a new extension in the place as often as there is a new body; but when we consider the extension as belonging to the space, we are ascribing to it only a generic identity, so that when a new body comes to occupy the space, the extension of the space is deemed not to be a new extension, but to be just the same as before. (So long, that is, as it still has the same size and shape, and keeps the same position relatively to certain external bodies that we use to determine the space.)

XI. It is easy to see that it is the same extension that essentially constitutes (*naturam . . . constituit*) a body and a space; that there is no more difference here than there is between the essence (*natura*) of a genus or species and the essence (*natura*) of the individual. We have only to attend to our idea of some body, e.g. a stone, and remove from it whatever we know is not entailed by the very nature of body. We first reject hardness; for if the stone is melted, or divided into a very fine powder, it will lose this quality without ceasing to be a body. Again, we reject colour; we have often seen stones so transparent as to be colourless. We reject heaviness; fire is extremely light, but none the less conceived as a body. Finally, we reject coldness and heat and all other such qualities; either they are not what we are considering in thinking of the stone, or at least their changing does not mean that the stone is regarded as having lost the nature of a body. We may now observe that absolutely no element of our idea remains, except extension in length, breadth, and depth. Now this is just what is implied in the idea of space; not merely of a space occupied by bodies, but even of a so-called vacuum.

XII. There is, however, a conceptual difference. When a stone is removed from the space or place where it is, we think of its extension as being likewise removed; for we are then regarding the extension as something individual, and inseparable from the stone. At the same time, we regard the extension of the place where the stone was as something persisting and identical, although the place of the stone is now occupied by wood, water, air, or any other body, or is believed to be empty; for now we are considering the extension as a general property, and it is deemed to be ' the same ' extension in stone, wood, water, or any other body (or even in a vacuum, if such there be) so long as it still has the same shape and size, and keeps the same position relatively to the external bodies that determine this space.

XIII. The terms *place* and *space* do not signify something different from the body that is said to be in a place; they merely mean its size, shape, and position relative to other bodies. To determine the position we have to look to some other bodies, regarded as unmoving; and we may say— relatively to different sets of bodies—that the same thing is simultaneously changing and not changing its place. E.g. when a ship is sailing at sea, a man sitting in the poop remains in one place relatively to the parts of the ship, for he keeps in one position among these; and yet he is con- tinually changing his place relatively to the shore, for he is continually receding from one shore and approaching the other. Again, if we conceive of the Earth as moving, and as travelling from West to East exactly as far as the ship travels from East to West in the same time, we shall again say that the man sitting in the poop ' is not changing his place ' ; we shall now be deriving the determination of place from some unmoving points in the heavens. But we may well end by thinking that no such genuinely unmoving points are to be found in the universe . . . ; and in that case we shall conclude that no object has a permanent place except by the determination of our thought (*cogitatione*).

XIV. The terms *place* and *space* differ in that *place* signifies position more expressly than size or shape, and these features, conversely, are rather what we have in mind when we speak of space. We often say that one body takes the ' place ' of another, even if it has not exactly the same size or shape ; but we then say it does not occupy the same space. On the other hand, when the position is changed, we say the place is changed, even if the body keeps the same shape and size. When we say an object is ' in ' a place we are merely thinking of its occupying a position relatively to other objects ; when we add that it ' fills ' the place or space, we are also thinking of it as having a definite size and shape.

XV. Thus we always take *a space* to mean an extension in length, breadth, and depth. Place is considered sometimes as intrinsic to the object that is in a place, and sometimes as extrinsic to it. Intrinsic place is just the same as space ; extrinsic place may be taken to mean the surface immediately surrounding the body that is in the place. It should be noticed that *surface* here does not mean a part of the surrounding body, but only the common boundary of the surrounding and surrounded bodies, which is a mere aspect of them ; at least, what is meant is the surface as a common property, which is not part of one body rather than the other, and is deemed to be always ' the same ' so long as it keeps the same size and shape. For even if the body, and the surface of the body, surrounding a given object, should completely change, yet the object so surrounded is not considered as changing its place, provided that it meanwhile retains the same position relatively to the bodies that are taken as unmoving. E.g. if we suppose that a ship is equally impelled in one direction by the flow of the river and in the opposite direction by the wind, so that its position relative to the banks is unchanged, it will readily be held to be staying in the same place, although the surface surrounding it is entirely changed.

XVI. The impossibility of a vacuum in the philosophical sense—a place in which there is absolutely no substance—is obvious from the fact that the extension of a space or intrinsic place is in no way different from the extension of a body. For the extension of a body in length, breadth and depth justifies us in concluding that it is a substance, since it is wholly contradictory that there should be extension that is the extension of nothing ; and we must draw the same conclusion about the supposedly empty space—viz. that since there is extension there, there must necessarily be substance there as well.

XVII. In common speech the term *empty* usually means, not a place or space where there is no object at all, but simply a place where there is no object such as we think there ought to be. Since e.g. a jug is made to hold water, it is called ' empty ' when it is only full of air. A fish-pond ' has nothing in it ', although there is plenty of water in it, if there are no fish. A ship fitted out to carry merchandise is ' empty ' if it is loaded only with sand to break the force of the wind. Finally, a space containing nothing sensible is ' empty ', even if it is full of created and self-subsistent matter ; for we ordinarily consider only such things as our senses attain to. If, then, we neglect the proper meaning of the terms *empty* and *nothing*, and suppose that when we call a space ' empty ' it contains, not just nothing that is sensible, but no object at all, we shall be falling into the same error as though we inferred, from our way of calling a jug that contains only air an 'empty' jug, that the air contained in it is not a substantial reality.

XVIII. Almost all of us have fallen into this error at an early age. We could discern no necessary connexion between a vessel and the body it contains ; so we thought there was nothing to prevent a body's being removed from the vessel it fills without any other taking its place ; that at any rate God could bring this about. To correct this error, we must reflect that, whereas there is no connexion between a vessel and this or that particular body contained in it, there is a very close, and absolutely necessary, connexion between the concave shape of the vessel and the general concept of the extension that must be contained in that concavity. It is no less contradictory than to think of a mountain without a valley, if we conceive that there can be this concavity without extension contained in it, or that there can be this extension without a substance whose extension it shall be ; for, as I have often said, there can be no extension that is extension of nothing. It may be asked what would happen if God removed all the body contained in a vessel, and allowed no other body to come and take the place of what was removed. The answer must be that in that case the sides of the vessel would *ipso facto* be in contact ; for when there is nothing between two bodies, they must necessarily touch each other. It is manifestly contradictory for them to be apart, or to have a distance between them, while at the same time the distance is nothing ; for any distance is an aspect (*modus*) of extension, and thus cannot exist without an extended substance.

XIX. We have thus seen that the nature of corporeal substance consists in its being something extended (*res extensa*), and that its extension is none other than is commonly ascribed to a space however 'empty'. From this we readily see that it is impossible for any part of matter

206

to occupy more space at one time than at another; thus rarefaction is not possible except in the way already explained. And, again, there can be no more matter (corporeal subs;ance) in a vessel filled with lead, gold, or some other such body, as heavy and solid (*duro*) as you will, than there is when it just contains air and is considered ' empty '. The quantity of a piece of matter depends not on its heaviness or solidity (*duritie*), but simply on its extension; and in a given vessel this is constant.

XX. We see also the impossibility of atoms—pieces of matter that are by their nature indivisible. If they exist, they must necessarily be extended, however small they are imagined to be; so we can still divide any one of them in thought (*cogitatione*) into two or more smaller ones, and thus we can recognise their divisibility. There is nothing we can divide in thought but we can see to *be* divisible; if we were to judge that it was indivisible, our judgment would go against what we knew. Even if we imagined a Divine decree that some particle of matter could not be divided into smaller ones, it would not be properly speaking indivisible. Even if God made it not to be divisible by any creatures, he could not take away his own power of dividing it; for it is quite impossible for God to diminish his own power. . . . So, speaking absolutely, it will still be divisible, being such by its very nature.

XXI. We see, furthermore, that this world—the totality of corporeal substance—has no limits to its extension. Wherever we imagine the boundaries to be, there is always the possibility, not merely of imagining further space indefinitely extended,[1] but also of seeing that this imagination is true to fact—that such space actually exists. And hence there must also be indefinitely extended [1] corporeal substance contained in this space. For, as has already been abundantly shown, the idea of the extension that we

---

[1] [Cp. *Princ.*, I. xxvi-vii; above, pp. 185-7, § E.—Tr.]

conceive any given space to have is identical with the idea of corporeal substance.

XXII. We can also readily derive the result that celestial and terrestrial matter do not differ; if these were an infinity of worlds, they could not but consist of one and the same kind of matter; and thus there cannot be a plurality of worlds, but only one. For we clearly understand that matter, whose nature consists merely in being extended substance, already occupies every imaginable space where ' other ' worlds would have to exist; and there is not to be found in us any idea of any other sort of matter.

XXIII. Thus it is one and the same matter that exists throughout the universe; its one distinctive characteristic everywhere is extension. All the properties that we clearly perceive in it are reducible to divisibility and a capacity for varying motions in the various parts; from this there follows the potentiality of all the states (*affectionum*) that we see may arise from the motion of its parts. Merely mental partition changes nothing; all variegation of matter, all differences of forms of matter, depend on motion. This seems to have been generally recognised by philosophers; for they have called nature ' the principle of motion and rest ', and by ' nature ' here they meant the source of the observed properties of all corporeal objects.

XXIV. Motion [1] in the vulgar sense is simply *the activity by which a body travels from one place to another*. Thus, just as I remarked above that the same thing may be said to be simultaneously changing and not changing its place, so also the same thing may be said to be moving and not moving. E.g. a man sitting in a ship as she leaves the harbour considers himself as moving relatively to the shore, if he takes that as unmoving; but not relatively to the ship, for

---

[1] Local motion, that is; there is no other sort I can think of (*sub cogitationem meam cadit*) and I see no reason to imagine any other to exist in nature.

he is keeping the same position relatively to the parts of the ship. Indeed, since the vulgar idea is that all motion involves activity, and rest the cessation of activity, the man is in this case more properly said to be at rest than to be moving, since he is conscious of no activity in himself.

XXV. If, however, we consider what *motion* ought to mean, not according to the vulgar usage, but according to the facts of the case, and we want to assign to it a definite nature, we may say that it is *the translation of a piece of matter (a body) from the neighbourhood of the bodies immediately touching it, these being regarded as at rest, to the neighbourhood of others.* Here, when I speak of *a* body or *a* piece of matter, I mean something that is all transferred at once; this may, however, again consist of many parts with various motions relatively to one another. I say that motion is *translation,* not the force or action of transference, to show that motion inheres always in a moving body, not in the body that moves it (an accurate distinction between these two things is not ordinarily made); and to show that it is a mere aspect (*modum*), not a substantial reality (*rem subsistentem*), just as shape is an aspect of the object that has shape, and rest of the thing that rests.

XXVI. It should be observed that here we are encumbered by a serious prejudice: we think more activity is needed for motion than for rest. We got this conviction in our earliest years; our bodies usually move by our will, of which we are intimately aware, and they remain at rest simply through adhering to the earth and by the force of gravity, of which we have no sensation. Further, gravity and various other unobserved causes offer resistance to our initiating voluntary motions of our limbs, and make us tired; so we think more activity or force is needed to start motion than to arrest it; by activity we mean here the effort by which we move our limbs and, by means of them, other bodies. An easy way to get rid of this prejudice is to consider that effort is needed not only to move external bodies but also, quite often, to arrest their movement, if it is not arrested by gravity or some other cause. We employ, e.g. no more activity in pushing a boat that is at rest in still water, than in suddenly stopping it when once it is moving. At least, not much more; for in the latter case we have to subtract the combined effect of the weight of water displaced and the viscosity (*lentor*) of the water, which could bring the boat gradually to rest.

XXVII. What is in question at present is not the activity conceived to exist in the object that produces or arrests motion, but simply translation, and absence of translation or rest. Plainly this translation can have no being outside the moving body; and the body is in a different condition when it is being transferred and when it is not being transferred or is at rest. Thus motion and rest are simply two different states (*modi*) of a body.

XXVIII. I added furthermore that the translation takes place *from the neighbourhood of contiguous bodies to that of others*, not *from one place to another*. The meaning of *place*, as I said just now, is variable, and depends on our way of thinking (*cogitatione*); but if we mean by *motion* translation that takes place from the neighbourhood of contiguous bodies, then we cannot ascribe to the moving body several motions simultaneously, but only a single motion; for only one set of bodies can be contiguous to a given moving body at a given moment of time.

XXIX. Finally, I added that the translation takes place from the neighbourhood, not of any contiguous bodies, but precisely of such as are *regarded as at rest*. In itself, translation is reciprocal; we cannot conceive the body AB as transferred out of the neighbourhood of the body CD without simultaneously conceiving the body CD as transferred out of the neighbourhood of the body AB; and just the same force and activity is needed on both sides. So if we wanted to assign to motion its proper, non-relative nature, we should say that when two bodies are contiguous and then undergo translation in opposite directions, there is as much motion in one as in the other. But this would do too much violence to our ordinary way of speaking; for normally we consider the Earth we stand on as resting; and although we observe that some parts of the Earth, to which other smaller bodies are contiguous, are transferred from the neighbourhood of these bodies, we do not on that account regard the Earth as in motion.

XXX. The chief reason for this is as follows: motion is conceived as qualifying the moving body as a whole; and this makes it impossible to ascribe it to the Earth as a whole on account of the translation of some of its parts from the neighbourhood of smaller contiguous bodies; for often one may observe several such translations happening on the Earth in opposite directions. Let the body EFGH be the Earth, and let there be simultaneously on its surface a trans-

lation of the body AB from E towards F and of the body CD from H towards G. *Ipso facto*, the parts of the Earth contiguous to AB undergo a translation from B towards A, and there need not be in them any less activity, or any other sort of activity, in order to effect this translation, than there is in the body AB. But we do not on that account conceive the Earth as moving from B towards A, or from West to East; for by parity of reasoning, since the parts of the Earth that are contiguous to the body CD undergo translation from C to D, we should have to conceive the Earth as also moving the other way, from East to West; and these two conceptions are inconsistent. So, to avoid too great a departure from the ordinary use of language, we shall say here that it is not the Earth that moves, but only the bodies AB and CD; and so in other cases. At the same time we must remember that the real positive characteristic of moving bodies— that which makes us call them moving bodies—is also fully to be found in the other bodies contiguous to them, although these are regarded only as being at rest.

XXXI. A given body has only one proper motion; for it can be conceived as departing from only one set of contiguous, resting bodies. It may however share in any number of other motions, if it is a part of other bodies that have these other motions. Suppose somebody walks on board ship with a watch in his pocket; the watch-wheels have only one proper motion; but they will share in another motion, since they are connected to the man who is walking, and form along with him a single piece of matter; and in another motion again, by being connected to the ship tossing in the sea; and in yet another, by being connected to the sea; and finally, in yet another motion, by being connected to the Earth, if the Earth as a whole moves. All these motions will really exist in the wheels; but since it is not easy to conceive of so many all at once— indeed, we cannot know of all of them—it will be enough to consider in each body only one motion—its proper motion.

XXXII. This single proper motion of any given body may be considered as though it were a plurality of motions. We may e.g. distinguish two different motions of carriage-wheels: a circular motion around the axle, and a rectilinear motion along the road by which they are travelling. But this distinction between motions is not a real one, as is obvious from the fact that any given point of the moving body just describes one given line. It is irrelevant that this line may often look as though it were generated by a plurality of different motions, because it is very twisty; for we can similarly imagine any line (even the simplest of

all, a straight line) as arising from an infinity of different
motions. Suppose the line AB travels towards CD and
at the same time the point A travels towards B; the straight
line AD described by this point depends
on two rectilinear motions, from A to B
and from AB to CD, in just the same
way as the curve described by any
point on the wheel depends on a
rectilinear and a circular motion. It
is indeed often useful to distinguish
various parts of a single motion in
this way; but absolutely speaking,
we must reckon only one motion in any given body.

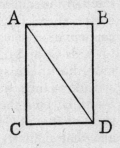

XXXIII. I observed above that all places are full of
body, and an identical piece of matter always occupies an
equal place. It follows that the only possible movement
of bodies is a circulation; a body pushes another out of the
place it enters, and this pushes another, and that another,
till at last we come to a body that is entering the place left
by the first body at the very moment when the first body
is leaving it. In the case of a perfect circle this is readily

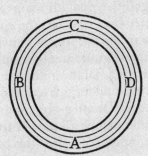 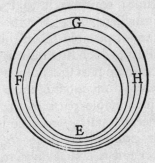

understood; we can see that no vacuum, and no rarefaction or condensation either, is needed in order that there
may be a simultaneous motion of the part A of the circle
towards B, B towards C, C towards D, and D towards A.

But the same thing is conceivable in the case of an imperfect circle, however irregular; we only have to notice
the way that all the inequalities of place may be compen-
sated by inequalities of velocity. The matter contained
in the space EFGH may move in a circle without any
condensation or vacuum; the part that is at E may travel
towards G, and the part that is at G towards E; provided
only that if the space at G is supposed to be four times
as wide as the space at E and twice as wide as the space at
F and H, then the velocity of motion at E is four times as
great as it is at G, and twice as great as it is at F and H;
and that similarly at all places a narrower space is com-
pensated by a greater velocity. For with this proviso the
amounts of matter passing through different parts of the
circle in any given time will always be equal.

XXXIV. I must admit that in this movement we come
upon something that our mind recognises to be true, but
whose way of coming to pass is inconceivable. There is an
infinite or indefinite division of matter into small parts; and
the number of these is so great that, however small a
particle of matter we mentally (*cogitatione*) determine,
we must conceive it as undergoing actual division into
still smaller parts. For the matter that now fills the space
G cannot possibly fill in succession all the spaces between
G and E, which diminish by infinitely gradual stages, unless
it has some part that adjusts its shape to all the innumerable
different dimensions of these spaces; and for this to happen,
all imaginable parts of this piece of matter—in fact, innumerable parts—must be to some degree displaced from
their positions relative to one another; and this dis-
placement is actual division.

XXXV. . . . Our thought is unable to comprehend the
manner of this indefinite division. But we should not
therefore doubt that it occurs; we can see clearly that it is
a necessary consequence of what we know self-evidently

to be the nature of matter, and we also see that it is the sort of thing our finite minds cannot grasp.[1]

XXXVI. After considering the nature of motion, we must treat of its cause; in fact, of two sorts of cause. First, the universal and primary cause—the general cause of all the motions in the universe; secondly the particular cause that makes any given piece of matter assume a motion that it had not before.

As regards the general cause, it seems clear to me that it can be none other than God himself. He created matter along with motion and rest in the beginning; and now, merely by his ordinary co-operation, he preserves just the quantity of motion and rest in the material world that he put there in the beginning. Motion, indeed, is only a state (*modus*) of the moving body; but it has a certain definite quantity, and it is readily conceived that this quantity may be constant in the universe as a whole, while varying in any given part. (We must reckon the quantity of motion in two pieces of matter as equal if one moves twice as fast as the other, and this in turn is twice as big as the first; again, if the motion of one piece of matter is retarded, we must assume an equal acceleration of some other body of the same size.) Further, we conceive it as belonging to God's perfection, not only that he should in himself be unchangeable, but also that his operation should occur in a supremely constant and unchangeable manner. Therefore, apart from the changes of which we are assured by manifest experience or by divine revelation, and about which we can see, or believe [by faith], that they take place without any change in the Creator, we must not assume any others in the works of God, lest they should afford an argument for his being inconstant. Consequently it is most reasonable to hold that, from the mere fact that God gave pieces of matter various movements at their first

[1] [Cp. *Princ.*, I. xxvi–vii; above, pp. 185–7, § ᴇ.—Tʀ.]

creation, and that he now preserves all this matter in being in the same way as he first created it, he must likewise always preserve in it the same quantity of motion.

XXXVII. From God's immutability we can also know certain rules or natural laws which are the secondary, particular causes of the various motions we see in different bodies. The *first law is*: *Every reality, in so far as it is simple and undivided, always remains in the same condition so far as it can, and never changes except through external causes.* Thus if a piece of matter is square, one readily convinces oneself that it will remain square for ever, unless something comes along from elsewhere to change its shape. If it is at rest, one thinks it will never begin to move, unless impelled by some cause. Now there is equally no reason to believe that if a body is moving its motion will ever stop, spontaneously that is, and apart from any obstacle. So our conclusion must be: *A moving body, so far as it can, goes on moving.*

We, however, live on the Earth, and the constitution of the Earth is such that all motions in her neighbourhood are soon arrested—often by insensible causes. Thus from our earliest years we have held the view that these motions (which in fact are brought to rest by causes unknown to us) come to an end spontaneously. And we tend to hold in all cases what we think we have observed in many cases—that motion ceases, or tends towards rest, by its very nature. Now this is in fact flatly opposed to the laws of nature; for rest is the opposite of motion, and nothing can by its own nature tend towards its opposite, towards its own destruction.

XXXVIII. Our everyday observation of projectiles completely confirms this rule. The reason why projectiles persist in motion for some time after leaving the hand that throws them is simply that when they once move they go on moving, until their motion is retarded by bodies that get in the way. Obviously the air, or other fluid in which they are moving, gradually retards their motion, so that it cannot last long. The resistance of air to the movement of other bodies may be verified by the sense of touch if we beat it with a fan; and the flight of birds confirms this. And the resistance of any fluid other than air to the motion of projectiles is even more obvious.

XXXIX. The *second* natural law is: *Any given piece of matter considered by itself tends to go on moving, not in any oblique path, but only in straight lines.* (Of course many pieces of matter are constantly being compelled to swerve by meeting with others; and, as I said, any motion involves a kind of circulation of matter all moving simultaneously.) The reason for this rule, like that for the last one, is the immutability and simplicity of the operation by which God preserves motion in matter. For he preserves the motion in the precise form in which it occurs at the moment when he preserves it, without regard to what it was a little while before. *In* the instant, of course, no motion can take place; but obviously the motion of any moving body is determined *at* any assigned instant of its duration as capable of being continued in a given direction; continued, that is, in a straight line, not some sort of curve. For example, a stone A is moving in a sling EA in a circle ABF. At the moment when it is at the point A, it has motion in a definite direction, viz. in a straight line towards C, where the straight line AC is a

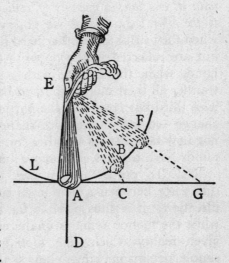

tangent to the circle. It cannot be imagined that the stone has any definite curvilinear motion; it is true that it arrived at A from L along a curved path, but none of this curvature can be conceived as inherent in its motion when it is at the point A. Observation confirms this; for if the stone leaves the sling just then, it goes on towards C, not towards B. . . .[1]

XL. The *third* natural law is this. *When a moving body collides with another, then if its own power of going on in a straight line is less than the resistance of the other body, it is reflected in another direction and retains the same amount of motion, with only a change in its direction ; but if its power of going on is greater than the resistance, it carries the other body along with it, and loses a quantity of motion equal to what it imparts to the other body.* Thus we observe that hard projectiles, when they strike some other hard body, do not stop moving but are reflected in the opposite direction; on the other hand, when they collide with a soft body, they readily transfer all their motion to it, and are thus at once stopped. This third law covers all the particular causes of corporeal change—so far as they are themselves corporeal; I am not now considering whether, or how, human or angelic minds have the power to move bodies. . . .

XLI. To prove the first part of this law: there is a difference between a motion as such and its determinate direction; it is thus possible for the direction to change while the motion remains unaltered. Now, as I said, any given reality which, like motion, is not complex but simple, persists in being so long as it is not destroyed by any external cause. In a collision with a hard body, there is an obvious reason why the motion of the other body that collides with it should not continue in the same direction; but there is no obvious reason why this motion should be

[1] [Descartes resumes this subject elsewhere, at *Principles* III. lv-lvii, lix.—Tr.]

stopped or lessened, for one motion is not the opposite of another motion; so the motion ought not to be diminished.

XLII. The second part is proved from the immutability of the divine operation; God preserving the world by the same activity by which he once created it. For all places are filled with body, and at the same time the motion of every body is rectilinear in tendency; so clearly, when God first created the world, he must not only have assigned various motions to its various parts, but also have caused their mutual impulses and the transference of motion from one to another; and since he now preserves motion by the same activity and according to the same laws, as when he created it, he does not preserve it as a constant inherent property of given pieces of matter, but as something passing from one piece to another as they collide. Thus the very fact that creatures are thus continually changing argues the immutability of God.

XLIII. It must be carefully observed what it is that constitutes the power of a body to act on another body or resist its action; it is simply the tendency of everything to persist in its present state so far as it can (according to the first law). Thus what is joined to another thing has some power of resisting separation from it; what is separate has some power of remaining separate; what is at rest has some power of remaining at rest, and consequently resisting everything that might change its state of rest; what is moving has some power of persisting in its motion—in a motion constant as regards velocity and direction. This last power must be estimated according to the size of the body, and of its surface, which separates it from others, and the velocity of the motion, and the kind and degrees of opposition of state (*modi*) involved in the collision of bodies.

XLIV. Here we must observe that one motion is in no way opposite to another of equal velocity. Properly speaking, there are two sorts of opposition. First, motion is opposite to rest, and likewise a swift motion to a slow one, since slowness has something of the nature of rest. Secondly, the determinate direction of a motion is opposed to the body's meeting with another that lies in that direction and is at rest or is moving differently. The degree of this opposition depends on the direction in which a body is moving when it collides with another.

XLV. To determine from this how collision increases or diminishes the amounts of motion in bodies, or how it alters the direction of their motion, we need only calculate the power of each body to move or to resist motion, and use the principle that the greater power always produces its effect. The calculation would be easy if there were just two bodies colliding, and these were perfectly solid (*dura*)[1] and entirely separated from all others, so that no surrounding bodies impeded or assisted their motion. . . .

LIII. In fact, no bodies in the universe can be thus separated from all others; and in our environment we do not ordinarily get perfectly solid (*dura*) bodies; so it is much harder to calculate how the motions of bodies are changed by collision with others. For we have to take into account all the bodies that touch a body on every side; and the effect of these is very different according as they are solid (*dura*) or fluid.

We must now consider what constitutes this distinction.

LIV. According to the evidence of the senses, the only distinction we can discern is that the parts of fluids readily leave their place, and so offer no resistance when our hands move towards them; whereas the parts of solids (*durorum*) cohere together so that they can be separated only by a force sufficient to overcome their cohesion. If we inquire further why some bodies readily abandon their place

---

[1] [*Sensible* hardness is not in question here, as it is in Part II, Section IV.—Tr.]

for others, while other bodies do not, we can easily see that what is already in motion does not hinder the occupation by another body of the place that it is in any case leaving, whereas what is at rest cannot be driven from its place except by some force. Hence we may infer that bodies divided into many small particles that are agitated by a variety of motions are *fluids;* while those whose particles are at rest relatively to their neighbours are *solids (dura).*

LVI. As regards fluids, we cannot observe any sensible motion of their particles, because they are too small; but such motion is readily inferred from its effects, especially in the case of air and water. For these fluids corrupt many other bodies; and no corporeal activity such as corruption is possible apart from local motion. . . .

LXIV. I will not here say anything further about [geometrical] figures, or as to how there follow from their infinite variety countless varieties of kinds of motion; these points will be sufficiently clear in themselves when we have to treat of them. I presuppose in my readers either a familiarity with elementary geometry, or at least a mental aptitude for following mathematical proofs. I must here make it clear that I recognise no kind of ' matter ' in corporeal objects except that ' matter ' susceptible of every sort of division, shape, and motion, which geometers call quantity, and which they presuppose as the subject-matter of their proofs. Further, the only properties I am considering in it are these divisions, shapes and motions; and about them I assume only what can be derived in a self-evident way from indubitably true axioms so that it can be counted as a mathematical proof. All natural phenomena, as I shall show, can be explained in this way; I therefore do not think any other principles need be admitted in physics or are to be desired.

THE VISIBLE WORLD

A Selection from 'Principles of Philosophy' Part III

I. We have thus discovered certain principles as regards material objects, derived not from the prejudices of our senses but from the light of reason, so that their truth is indubitable; we must now consider whether they suffice to explain all natural phenomena. We must begin with the most general facts on which the rest depend—the construction of the visible universe as a whole. For correct theorising about this, two cautions are needed. First, we must consider the infinite power and goodness of God, and not be afraid that we are imagining his works to be too vast, too beautiful, too perfect; what we must beware of is, on the contrary, the supposition of any bounds to God's works that we do not certainly know, lest we may seem not to have a sufficiently grand conception of the power of the Creator.

II. Secondly, we must beware of thinking too proudly of ourselves. We should be doing this, not merely if we imagined any limits to the universe, when none are known to us either by reason or by divine revelation (as if our powers of thought could extend beyond what God has actually made); but also, and that in a special degree, if we imagined everything had been created by God for our sake; or even if we thought our minds had the power to comprehend the ends God set before himself in creating the world.

III. In ethics indeed it is an act of piety to say that God made everything for our sake, that we may be the more impelled to thank him, and the more on fire with love of him; and in a sense this is true; for we can make *some* use of all things—at least we can employ our mind in contemplating them, and in admiring God for his wonderful works. But it is by no means probable that all things were made for our sake in the sense that they have no other use. In physical theory this supposition would be wholly ridiculous and absurd; for undoubtedly many things exist (or did exist formerly and now do so no longer) that have never been seen or thought of by any man, and have never been any use to anybody.

IV. The principles we have discovered so far are so vast and so fertile, that their consequences are far more numerous than the observable contents of the visible universe; far too numerous, indeed, to be ever exhaustively considered. For an investigation of causes, I here present a brief account of the principal phenomena of nature. Not that we should use these as grounds for proving anything; for our aim is to deduce an account of the effects from the causes, not to deduce an account of the causes from the effects. It is just a matter of turning our mind to consider some effects rather than others out of an innumerable multitude; all producible, on our view, by a single set of causes.

XLII. . . . To discern the real nature of this visible universe, it is not enough to find causes in terms of which we may explain what we see far away in the heavens; we must also deduce from the same causes everything that we see close at hand on earth. We need not indeed consider all of these phenomena in order to determine the causes of more general effects; but *ex postfacto* we shall know that we have determined these causes correctly only when we see that we can explain in terms of them, not merely the effects we had originally in mind, but also all other phenomena of which we did not previously think.

XLIII. But assuredly, if the only principles we use are such as we see to be self-evident; if we infer nothing from them except by mathematical deduction; and if these inferences agree accurately with all natural phenomena: then we should, I think, be wronging God if we were to suspect this discovery of the causes of things to be delusive. God would, so to say, have made us so imperfectly that by using reason rightly we nevertheless went wrong.

XLIV. However, to avoid the apparent arrogance of asserting that the actual truth has been discovered in such an important subject of speculation, I prefer to waive this point; I will put forward everything that I am going to write just as a hypothesis. Even if this be thought to be false, I shall think my achievement is sufficiently worth while if all inferences from it agree with observation (*experimentis*) ; for in that case we shall get as much practical benefit from it as we should from the knowledge of the actual truth.

XLV. Moreover, in order to explain natural objects the better, I shall pursue my inquiry into their causes further back than I believe the causes ever in fact existed. There is no doubt that the world was first created in its full perfection; there were in it a Sun, an Earth, a Moon, and the stars; and on the Earth there were not only the seeds of plants, but also the plants themselves; and Adam and Eve were not born as babies, but made as full-grown human beings. This is the teaching of the Christian faith; and natural reason convinces us that it was so; for considering the infinite power of God, we cannot think he ever made anything that was not peerless. Nevertheless, in order to understand the stature of plants or man, it is far better to consider how they may now gradually develop from seed, rather than the way they were created by God at the beginning of the world; and in just the same way we may conceive certain elements, very simple and very easily understood, and from these seeds, so to say, we may prove that there could have arisen stars, and an Earth, and in fact everything we observe in this visible universe; and although we know perfectly well they never did arise in this way, yet by this method we shall give a far better account of their nature than if we merely describe what they now are. . . .

XLVI. From what has already been said it is established that all bodies in the universe consist of one and the same matter; that this is divisible arbitrarily into parts, and is actually divided into many pieces with various motions; that their motion is in a way circular, and that the same quantity of motion is constantly preserved in the universe. We cannot determine by reason how big these pieces of matter are, how quickly they move, or what circles they describe. God might have arranged these things in countless different ways; which way he in fact chose rather than the rest is a thing we must learn from observation. Therefore, we are free to make any assumption we like about them, so long as all the consequences agree with experience. So, by your leave, I shall suppose that all the matter constituting the visible world was originally divided by God into unsurpassably equal particles of medium size—that is, of the average size of those that now form the heavens and the stars ; that they had collectively just the quantity of motion now found in the world ; that . . . each turned round its own centre, so that they formed a fluid body, such as we take the heavens to be; and that many revolved together around various other points . . . and thus constituted as many different vortices as there now are stars in the world. XLVII. These few assumptions are, I think, enough to supply causes from which all effects observed in our universe would arise by the laws of nature previously stated; and I think one cannot imagine any first principles that are more simple, or easier to understand, or indeed more likely. The actual arrangement of things might perhaps be inferable from an original Chaos, according to the laws of nature; and I once undertook to give such an explanation. But confusion seems less in accord with the supreme perfection of God the Creator of all things than proportion or order, and we can form a less distinct notion of it. . . . In any case, it matters very little what supposition we make; for change must subsequently take place according to the laws of nature; and it is hardly possible to make a supposition that does not allow of our inferring the same effects (perhaps with more labour) according to the same laws of nature. For according to these, matter must successively assume all the forms of which it admits; and if we consider these forms in order, we can at last come to that which is found in this universe. So no error is to be apprehended from a false supposition at this point.

LV. It is a law of nature that *all bodies moving in a circle move away from the centre of their motion so far as they can.* I shall at this point explain as accurately as I can this force by which [bodies] try to move away from these centres. . . . LVI. When I say [they] 'try' to move away from the centres around which they revolve, I must not, therefore, be thought to be fancying that they have some consciousness (*cogitationem*) from which this 'effort' proceeds; I just mean that their positions, and the forces that impel them to motion, are such that they would in fact go in that direction, if no other cause hindered them.

LVII. It very often happens that a number of different causes are acting simultaneously upon the same body, and hinder one another's effects; and so, according as we consider this cause or that, we may say that the body is 'tending' or 'trying' to go different ways. For example the stone A in the sling EA tends to go from A to B if we consider all the causes that go to determine its motion. But if we take into account only the stone's intrinsic power of moving, we shall say that when it is at the point A its tendency is towards C, according to the law of motion stated above. . . . For if the stone left the sling at the moment when it arrives from L at the point A, it would in fact go on towards C, not towards B; and although the sling prevents this from happening, it does not prevent the tendency. Finally, if we take into account, not the stone's whole intrinsic power of movement, but only the part of it that is hindered by the sling (as opposed to the other part, which produces actual motion), we shall say that when the

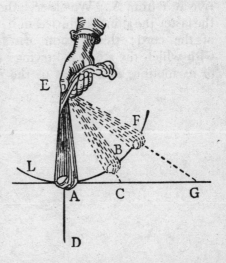

stone is at the point A its tendency is just towards D—that it is 'trying' to move away from the centre E along the straight line EAD.

LIX. . . . Let us take another case. Let EY be a tube containing a little ball A. If this tube is rotated around the centre E, the ball A will at first move only very slowly towards Y; but next moment it will go a little faster, retaining its original power of movement and acquiring a greater power

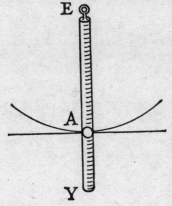

227

from its renewed effort to depart from the centre E; for as long as the circular motion lasts, so does this effort, and it is as it were renewed at every moment. Observation confirms this; for if the tube EY is very rapidly whirled around the centre E, the ball that is in it will very soon arrive at Y from A. We observe the same thing in the sling; the faster the stone is whirled in it, the greater is the tension of the cord; this tension arises merely from the force with which the stone is ' trying ' to depart from the centre of its motion, and shows us the degree of this force.

THE EARTH

A Selection from 'Principles of Philosophy' Part IV

CLXXXVIII. . . . I have described the Earth and the whole visible universe in the manner of a machine, having regard only to the shape and movement of its parts. Now our senses manifest many other things to us: colours, odours, sounds, etc. If I were to pass over these in silence, I might be thought to have left out an important part of the explanation of natural phenomena.

CLXXXIX. We must realise that, although the human soul gives form to (*informet*)[1] the whole body, its chief seat is in the brain; it is there alone that it performs, not only intellection and imagination, but even sensation. It does this by means of the nerves, which extend like threads from the brain to all the other members. They are so attached that hardly any part of the human body can be touched without at once disturbing several of the nerve-endings distributed throughout its extent; and this disturbance is transmitted to the other ends of the nerves, which are all collected together in the brain around the seat of the soul. . . .

The various disturbances that the nerves thus produce in the brain have various effects on the mind or soul, which is intimately united to the brain. The various states (*affectiones*) of mind, or experiences (*cogitationes*), that immediately follow upon the disturbances are called sense-perceptions, or in ordinary language, sensations.

[1] [This term is scholastic. Descartes is making a polite concession to the scholastic view that the soul is the ' substantial form ' of the body, i.e. is what makes it *this* sort of body, rather than a stone or a tree or a cat.—TR.]

CXC. The variety of sensations arises first from the differences between nerves, secondly from diverse distur-bances that may occur in a given nerve. But there is not a special, distinct sensation for every nerve; there are only seven main classes of sensation—the two internal and the five external senses. One kind of internal sensation, the so-called *appetitus naturalis*, is produced by the nerves that go to the stomach, oesophagus, throat, and the other internal organs that subserve the fulfilment of natural needs. The nerves that go to the heart and breast, small as they are, produce another kind of internal sensation; this is what constitutes all the emotions or passions (*pathemata*) of the soul—joy, sorrow, love, hate, etc.

For example, when blood of the right composition is expanding in the heart readily and to an unusual degree, it causes a relaxation, a disturbance, of the nerves around the valves, from which there follow further disturbances in the brain, giving the mind a sensation of joy; and other causes produce the same nervous disturbance and the same sensation of joy. So the imagination of enjoying some good does not intrinsically involve a feeling of joy; animal spirits [1] pass from the brain to the muscles in which these nerves are inserted, and dilate the valves of the heart; and this causes in the nerves of the heart such a disturbance as must be followed by the feeling of joy. When we hear good news, the mind first forms a judgment and rejoices with the intellectual joy that may occur without any bodily dis-turbance—the sort of joy that the Stoics said on this account might occur in a sage. Following upon this imagination, the animal spirits flow from the brain to the muscles of the thorax; they there cause a nervous disturbance, and so excite another disturbance in the brain, which gives the mind a feeling of animal joy. . . . Other disturbances of

[1] [The physiology of Descartes's time held that animal spirits were a fluid passing along the nerves to and from the brain.—Tr.]

these nerves produce other emotions—[sorrow], love, hate, fear, anger, etc. I am here considering these simply as emotions, or passions of the mind—as confused experiences (*cogitationes*), which the mind does not get from its own nature but from being acted on by the body to which it is intimately united. Distinct consciousness (*cogitationes*) of what must be embraced, sought after, shunned, etc., is wholly different from these emotions.

The same applies to 'natural appetites'—hunger, thirst, etc. They are produced by the nerves of the stomach, throat, and so on; and they are wholly different from a volition to eat, drink, or the like. They are called appetites because they are most often accompanied by such volition or appetition.

CXCI. There are commonly reckoned five external senses, according to the kinds of objects that affect the sensory nerves and the corresponding kinds of confused consciousness (*cogitationum*) that these motions produce in the soul. . . . When these nerves are unusually strongly disturbed, but not so that any lesion results in the body, there is produced the feeling of enjoyment; this is naturally pleasant to the mind because it bears witness to the health of the body united to the mind. If a lesion results, there is a feeling of pain. It is thus clear why bodily pleasure and pain, although opposite feelings, correspond to such a small objective difference.

CXCVI. Now it is conclusively proved that the soul has sensations of what affects various members of the body, not by its presence in those members, but only by its presence in the brain. Various diseases affect only the brain, but destroy or disturb all sensation. Again, sleep occurs only in the brain; and every day we lose a great part of our sensory powers in sleep and regain them on awaking. Again, if the brain is intact, a mere obstruction of the paths by which the nerves reach it from the external parts is enough to destroy sensation in those parts. Finally, pain is some-times felt in a limb when there is no cause of pain in it, but only in another part traversed by the nerves from that limb to the brain.

The last point may be shown by innumerable obser-vations; it will be enough to mention one here. A girl with a seriously diseased hand used to have her eyes bandaged when the surgeon came, lest she should be afraid on seeing the surgical instruments. After some days her arm was amputated at the elbow because of a creeping gangrene; napkins were put in its place, so that she did not in the least know she had lost it. At this time she com-plained of feeling pains now in one, now in another finger of the amputated hand. The only possible reason is this: the nerves that formerly led down from the brain to the hand, and that now ended in the arm near the elbow, were undergoing the same disturbances as would formerly have had to arise in the hand, so as to produce in the soul, seated in the brain, the sensation of pain in this or that finger.

CXCVII. Again, it is proved that our mind is such that the mere occurrence of certain movements in the body can excite all sorts of consciousness (*quaslibet cogitationes*) bearing no likeness to those movements; this is specially true of the confused consciousness we call sense or sen-sations. We observe that spoken or even written words excite all sorts of thoughts and emotions in us. With the same paper, pen, and ink, if the tip of the pen travels one way over the paper, it will trace out letters that excite in the reader's mind thoughts (*cogitationes*) of battle, tempest, and riot, and emotions of indignation and sorrow, but if the pen performs some other, very similar, movement, it will produce quite different thoughts (*cogitationes*) of tranquillity, peace, and pleasure, and quite opposite emotions of love and joy.

It may be replied to this that writing or speech does not directly produce any emotions, or any imagination of anything other than itself; it has first to be understood in various ways, and only then does the mind form pictures of various objects. But what about the feelings of pain and enjoyment? A sword is applied to our body and cuts it; and from this mere fact pain results. Now pain is certainly no less different from the local motion of the sword, or of the body that is cut, than colour, sound, odour, or flavour is from local motion. Since, therefore, we clearly see that the sensation of pain is produced in us merely by the local motion of certain parts of our body when in contact with another body, we may conclude that our mind is such as to be liable to all other kinds of sensation merely as a result of local motions.

CXCVIII. Moreover, we observe no difference between nerves to justify the view that something different is transmitted along different nerves from the external sense-organs to the brain; or that anything is transmitted to the brain at all, except the local motion of the nerves themselves. And we observe that this local motion can produce not only sensations of pain and enjoyment, but also those of light and sound. If somebody is struck in the eye, so that the vibration of the blow reaches the retina, he will see, just from this, a large number of dazzling sparks; and this light will have no existence outside the eye. Again, if someone stops his ear with his finger, he will hear a trembling murmur, arising merely from the motion of the air contained in the ear.

Finally, we often observe that heat and other sensible qualities, in so far as they are objective, and even the [substantial] forms [1] of purely material objects, e.g. the form [1] of fire, arise from the local motion of certain bodies, and themselves produce other local motions in other bodies.

1 [See footnote on p. 234.—Tr.]

233

Now we understand very well how the varying size, shape, and motion of the particles of one body arouse various local motions in another body; but we can by no means understand how these properties (size, shape, and motion) should produce something else of wholly different nature, like the substantial forms [1] and real qualities that many people suppose to exist in objects; nor yet, how these qualities or forms [1] could subsequently arouse local motions in other bodies. . . .

We therefore must on all counts conclude that the objective external realities that we designate by the words *light, colour, odour, flavour, sound,* or by names of tactile qualities such as *heat* and *cold,* and even the so-called *substantial forms,*[1] are not recognisably anything other than the powers that objects have to set our nerves in motion in various ways, according to their own varied disposition.

CXCIX. Thus it is easily shown, by an enumeration of subjects, that I have not neglected any natural phenomena in this treatise. Only what is apprehended by sense is to be counted among natural phenomena. Now I have explained the several sizes, shapes, and motions of bodies; and the only other objects of external sensation are light, colour, odour, flavour, sound, and tactile qualities. And I have just shown that these are nothing objective (at least so far as we can tell) apart from dispositions [of matter] constituted by size, shape, and motion. . . . CC. . . . I have considered the shapes, motions, and sizes of bodies, and examined the necessary results of interaction between bodies, by means of the laws of mechanics, which are confirmed every day by reliable observations (*experimentis*).

---

[1] [In scholastic language the substantial form, to which Descartes is here referring, is what makes a body to be this *kind* of body; it is contrasted with the matter of which the body consists; e.g. a flame has continually the same ' substantial form ' of fire though its matter is continually changing. On Descartes's rejection of substantial forms see below, p. 274.—TR.]

Now who has ever doubted that bodies move; that they have various sizes and shapes, and correspondingly varied motions; that the mutual collision of bodies results in the division of a bigger body into many smaller ones, and in changes of shape? These facts are observable not just by one sense but by several—by sight, touch, and hearing; moreover, our imagination and conception of them is distinct. The same does not apply to other sensible qualities such as colour and sound; they are not observed by several senses, but each by one sense only; and the images of them in our consciousness (*cogitatione*) are always confused, and we are ignorant of their real nature.

CCI. In considering every body as containing a multitude of particles that are not perceived by any sense, I may not win the approval of those who take their senses as the measure of what can be known. But who can doubt the existence of a multitude of bodies so small as to be undetectable by sensation? One only has to consider the question what it is that is added to a thing that is gradually growing, or is taken away from a thing that is diminishing. A tree grows day by day; its becoming bigger than it was before is unintelligible, unless we conceive that some body is being added to it. Now who has ever detected by his senses which particles are added to a growing tree in a single day? Again, at least those who recognise the infinite divisibility of matter must admit that its parts may be rendered so small as to be quite imperceptible to the senses. And it ought not to be surprising that we cannot have sensations of very minute bodies; our nerves, which have to be set in motion in order to produce sensation, are not the smallest possible bodies; for they are like tiny cords, consisting of many particles that are even smaller; and thus they cannot be set in motion by the very smallest bodies.

Again, I do not see how any reasonable man can deny the great advantage of forming ideas about microscopic events (*in minutis corpusculis*), which elude our senses by their mere minuteness, on the pattern of sensibly observed macroscopic events (*in magnis corporibus*), instead of bringing into our explanation some new conception of things wholly dissimilar to sensible objects. CCIII. But my assigning definite shapes, sizes and motions to insensible particles of bodies, just as if I had seen them, and this in spite of admitting that they are insensible, may make some people ask how I can tell what they are like. My answer is this. Starting from the simplest and most familiar principles which our minds know by their innate constitution, I have considered in general the chief possible differences in size, shape, and position between bodies whose mere minuteness makes them insensible, and the sensible effects of their various interactions. When I have observed similar effects among sensible objects, I have assumed that they arose from similar interactions of insensible bodies; especially as this seemed the only possible way of explaining them. And I have been greatly helped by considering machines. The only difference I can see between machines and natural objects is that the workings of machines are mostly carried out by apparatus large enough to be readily perceptible by the senses (as is required to make their manufacture humanly possible), whereas natural processes almost always depend on parts so small that they utterly elude our senses. But mechanics, which is a part or species of physics, uses no concepts but belong also to physics; and it is just as ' natural ' for a clock composed of such-and-such wheels to tell the time, as it is for a tree grown from such-and-such seed to produce a certain fruit. So, just as men with experience of machinery, when they know what a machine is for, and can see part of it, can readily form a conjecture about the way its unseen parts are fashioned; in the same way, starting from sensible effects and sensible parts of bodies, I have tried to investigate the insensible causes ard particles underlying them.

CCIV. This may give us an idea of the possible constitution of Nature; but we must not conclude that this is the actual constitution. There might be two clocks made by the same craftsman, equally good time-keepers, and with absolutely similar outsides; and yet the train of wheels inside might be completely different. Similarly, the supreme Craftsman might have produced all that we see in a variety of ways. I freely admit the truth of this; I shall think I have done enough if only what I have written is such as to accord accurately with all natural phenomena. This will suffice for practical application; for medicine, mechanics, and all other arts that may be brought to perfection by the aid of physics are concerned only with the sensible—with what can be reckoned as phenomena of nature. . . .

CCV. In fairness to the truth, however, it must be borne in mind that some things are considered as morally certain —certain for all practical purposes—although they are uncertain if we take into account God's absolute power. Suppose somebody is trying to read a letter written in Roman characters, but in cipher, and guesses that he must throughout substitute B for A, C for B, and in general replace any given letter by the one next following it; and suppose he finds that the result makes up Latin words; then he will have no doubt that the true meaning of the letter is contained in these words. He knows this, of course, only by a guess; the writer of the letter may have put different letters, not the next following, in place of the real ones, so that the meaning of the cipher is quite different; but this could scarcely happen, and appears incredible. Now those who notice how many deductions are here made from a few principles . . . even if they thought my

237

assumption of these principles haphazard and groundless, would perhaps recognise that so many things could hardly hang together if they were false.

CCVI. Moreover, even as regards natural objects, there are some things that we regard as absolutely, not just morally, certain; relying on the metaphysical ground that, since God is supremely good and in no wise deceitful, the faculty he has given us for distinguishing truth from falsehood cannot err, so often as we use it properly, and perceive something distinctly by means of it. To this class belong mathematical proofs; the knowledge that material objects exist; and all self-evident reasonings about natural objects. And with these my own assertions may perhaps find a place, when it is considered how they have been inferred in an unbroken chain from the simplest primary principles of human knowledge. And the more so, if it is sufficiently realised that we can have no sensation of external objects unless they excite some local motion in our nerves, and that the fixed stars, being at a vast distance from us, can excite no such motion unless there is also some motion taking place in them and in the whole of the intermediate heavens; for once this is granted, then, at least as regards the general account I have given of the universe and the Earth, an alternative to the rest of my explanation seems hardly conceivable.

CCVII. Mindful, however, of my own weakness, I make no assertion. I submit everything to the authority of the Catholic Church, and to the judgment of wiser heads; and I would have no one believe anything without being persuaded by evident and invincible reasoning.

FINIS

Extracts from
THE DIOPTRICS
illustrative of Descartes's
Theory of Vision

From the French text
published in 1637

Extracts from

THE DIOPTRICS

[DISCOURSE I]. It has doubtless some time happened that you were walking across difficult country by night without a torch and had to use a stick to guide yourself; and you may then have noticed that you felt, by means of the stick, the objects in your neighbourhood, and that you could even distinguish the presence of trees, stones, sand, water, grass, mud, etc. True, without long practice this kind of sensation is rather confused and dim; but if you take men born blind, who have made use of such sensations all their life, you will find they feel things with such perfect exactness that one might almost say that they see with their hands, or that their stick is the organ of a sixth sense, given to them to make up for the lack of sight.

We may use this as an analogy. I would have you conceive of the light in a ' luminous ' body as being simply a certain very rapid and lively movement or activity, transmitted to our eyes through air and other transparent bodies, just as the movement or resistance of the bodies a blind man encounters is transmitted to his hand through his stick. This may prevent your finding it strange . . . that in this way we can see all sorts of colours; you may even be prepared to believe that in so-called coloured bodies the colours are simply the different ways in which the bodies receive light and send it on to our eyes; for you have only to consider that by means of his stick a blind man observes differences between trees, stones, water, and so on, apparently just as great as those between red, yellow, green and other colours, and that there is nothing in these various bodies to make these differences except their different ways of moving the stick or resisting its movements.

You will thus be in a position to decide that it is not necessary to assume the transmission of something material from the object to our eyes in order that we may see colours and light, nor even the occurrence in the object of anything resembling our ideas or sensations of it. For in just the same way, when a blind man is feeling bodies, nothing has to issue from them and be transmitted along his stick to his hand; and the resistance or movement of the bodies, which is the sole cause of his sensations of them, is nothing like the ideas he forms of them. . . .

[DISCOURSE IV]. In order to facilitate the explanation of the special sense of sight, I must at this point say something about the nature of the senses in general. First, we know for certain that it is to the soul that sense belongs, not to the body; for we observe that when the soul is distracted by ecstasy or deep contemplation, the whole body remains devoid of sensation, in spite of being in contact with various objects. Again, we know that sensation occurs, properly speaking, not in view of the soul's presence in the parts that serve as external sense-organs, but only in view of its presence in the brain, where it employs the faculty called *sensus communis*;[1] for we observe injuries and diseases which attack the brain alone, and yet stop all sensation whatsoever; and this does not mean that the rest of the body ceases to be animated [by the soul]. Finally, we know that it is through the nerves that the impressions made by objects upon the external organs are transmitted to the soul in the brain; for we observe various accidents which, without injuring anything but some nerve, destroy sensibility in all

---

[1] [Descartes here writes *sens commun* ; but this is a French version of the scholastic term given above, which means a central co-ordinating sensory faculty, as opposed to the special senses of sight, hearing, etc.—TR.]

parts of the body to which this nerve sends branches, but do not even diminish it elsewhere.

So that you may know in more detail how the soul, seated in the brain, is able to receive through the nerves impressions of external objects, . . . I would have you conceive [nerves as] tiny fibres . . . stretching from the brain to the extremities of all parts capable of sensation. Thus the slightest touch that sets in motion a point of attachment of a nerve in these parts also simultaneously sets in motion the point of origin of the nerve in the brain; just as pulling one end of a taut string instantly sets the other end in motion. . . .

Further, you must beware of assuming, as philosophers ordinarily do, that it is necessary for sensation that the soul should contemplate certain images transmitted by objects to the brain; or at any rate you must conceive the nature of these images quite differently from their way of thinking. For since they have no notion of the images except that they must be like the objects they represent, they cannot possibly explain how they can be produced by these objects, and received by the external sense-organs, and transmitted by the nerves to the brain. Their sole reason for the assumption is that they have noticed that a picture readily induces us to think of the object depicted, and have thus thought we must be led to conceive of the objects that affect our senses by tiny pictures formed within our head. But we have to consider that thought may be induced by many things besides pictures—e.g. by signs and words, which in no way resemble the things signified.

Even if we think it best, in order to depart as little as possible from received opinions, to admit that the objects of sensation actually do transmit images of themselves to the interior of the brain, we must at least observe that no images have to resemble the objects they represent in all respects (otherwise there would be no distinction between the object

243

and its image) ; resemblance in a few features is enough, and very often the perfection of an image depends on its not resembling the object as much as it might. For instance, engravings, which consist merely of a little ink spread over paper, represent to us forests, towns, men and even battles and tempests. And yet, out of an unlimited number of different qualities that they lead us to conceive the objects, there is not one in respect of which they actually resemble them, except shape. Even this is a very imperfect resemblance; on a flat surface, they represent objects variously convex or concave; and again, according to the rules of perspective, they often represent circles by ovals rather than by other circles, and squares by diamonds rather than by other squares. Thus very often, in order to be more perfect *qua* images, and to represent the object better, it is necessary for the engravings not to resemble it.

Now we must hold a quite similar view of the images produced on our brain; we must observe that the problem is to know how they can enable the soul to have sensations of all the various qualities in the objects to which the images refer; not, how they can resemble the objects. When our blind man touches bodies with his stick, they certainly transmit nothing to him; they merely set his stick in motion in different ways, according to their different qualities, and thus likewise set in motion the nerves of his hand, and the points of origin of these nerves in his brain; and this is what occasions the soul's perception of various qualities in the bodies, corresponding to the various sorts of disturbance that they produce in the brain.

[DISCOURSE V]. You see, then, that sensation does not require that the soul should contemplate any images resembling the objects of sensation. For all that, the objects we look at do in fact produce very perfect images in the back of the eyes. This has been explained by a most ingenious comparison. If a room is quite shut up apart from a single hole, and a glass lens is put in front of the hole, and behind that, some distance away, a white cloth, then the light coming from external objects forms images on the cloth. Now it is said that this room represents the eye; the hole, the pupil; the lens, the crystalline humour—or rather, all the refracting parts of the eye; and the cloth, the lining membrane, composed of optic nerve-endings.

But you may make yourself more certain of the fact. Take the eye of a newly dead man (or, failing that, of an ox or some other large animal); carefully cut away the three enveloping membranes at the back, so as to expose a large part of the humour without shedding any; then cover the hole with some white body, thin enough to let daylight through (e.g. a piece of paper or eggshell). Now put this eye in the hole of a specially made shutter,[1] so that its front faces a spot where there are a number of objects lit up by the sun, and the back, where the white body is, faces the inside of the room you are in. (No light must enter the room except through the eye. . . .) If you now look at the white body, you will see (I dare say with surprise and pleasure) a picture representing in natural perspective all the objects outside. You must indeed see that the eye keeps its natural shape, according to the distance of the objects; if you squeeze it never so little more or less than you ought, the picture becomes less distinct. And it should be noticed that the eye must be squeezed a little more—made proportionally a little longer—when the objects are very near than when they are further away. . . .[2]

Now when you have seen this picture in a dead animal's eye, and considered its causes, you cannot doubt that a

---

[1] [French *fenestre*; but ' window '. would hardly do, since this *fenestre* (*v. infra*) lets in no light except through the hole where the eye is. And in the Latin version we read *asseris*, ' lath ' or ' board '.—Tr.]

[2] [I have omitted letters in the text referring to a diagram not here reproduced.—Tr.]

quite similar picture is produced in a living man's eye, on the lining membrane, for which we substituted the white body; indeed, a much better one, seeing that the humours, being full of [vital] spirits, are more transparent and more exactly of the right shape to effect this. (And perhaps in the ox's eye the shape of the pupil, which is not round, prevents the picture from being so perfect). . . .

Further, the images of objects are not only produced in the back of the eye but also sent on to the brain. . . .

[DISCOURSE VI]. And when it is thus transmitted to the inside of our head, the picture still retains some degree of its resemblance to the objects from which it originates. But we must not think that it is by means of this resemblance that the picture makes us aware of the objects—as though we had another pair of eyes to see it, inside our brain; I have several times made this point; rather, we must hold that the movements by which the image is formed act directly on our soul *qua* united to the body, and are ordained by Nature to give it such sensations.

I will explain this in more detail. The perceived qualities of seen objects can all be brought under six main heads: light, colour, position, distance, size and shape. First, then, as regards light and colour (the only qualities belonging specially to the sense of sight): it must he held that our soul is of such a nature that a sensation of light is determined by the strength of the disturbance that occurs at the points of origin of the optic nerve-fibres in the brain; and one of colour, by the kind of disturbance. In the same way, the disturbance of the nerves that supply the ears determines the hearing of sounds; the disturbance of the nerves in the tongue determines the tasting of flavours; and in general, disturbance of nerve anywhere in the body determines, if it is moderate, a feeling of enjoyment, and if it is too violent, a pain. But there need be no resemblance here between the ideas conceived by the soul and the disturbances that cause them. You will readily believe this if you observe that people hit in the eye think they see a great number of fiery flashes in front of them, in spite of shutting their eyes or being in a dark place; this sensation can be ascribed only to the force of the blow, which sets the optic nerve-fibres in motion as a strong light would do. The same force might cause one to hear a sound, if applied to the ears, or to feel pain, if applied to other parts of the body.

Another confirmation of this view is that if some time you force your eyes to look at the sun, or at some other very strong light, the impression remains in the eye for some time afterwards; even if you keep the eyes shut, you seem to be seeing various colours, one changing into and giving place to another as they fade. This can only be caused by the optic nerve-fibres not being able to come to rest as soon as they usually can, because they have undergone an extraordinarily strong disturbance. The agitation remaining where the eyes are closed is not great enough to represent the strong light that caused it, and thus it represents less lively colours. And the changes of these colours as they fade away show that (as I supposed above) their nature consists simply in various sorts of motion. Another proof of this is the frequent appearance of colours in transparent bodies; for it is certain that here there is no possible cause except the different ways that light-rays are received. An example is the appearance of the rainbow in the clouds; a still clearer one is the likeness of a rainbow that you see in glass cut with several facets. . . .

The parts of a body you are looking at can be discriminated only in so far as they somehow differ in colour; and distinct vision of these colours depends, not only on the approximate concentration of all the rays from the various points of the object at corresponding points in the back of the eye, and the absence of rays reaching the same points from other sources, . . . but also on the number of optic nerve-fibres in the space occupied by the image in the back of the eye. Let an object VXY be composed of ten thousand parts, capable of emitting rays to RST at the back of the eye in ten thousand different ways, and so making ten thousand colours simultaneously visible; their effect on the soul, nevertheless, can only be the discrimination of at most a thousand colours, if we suppose that in the space RST there are only a thousand optic nerve-fibres. Each fibre will be acted upon by ten parts of the object simultaneously; but they will be able to produce only a single disturbance, the resultant of their several disturbances, so that the space occupied by each fibre has to be considered as though it were a mere point. This is why a field decked with an infinity of colours appears from a distance wholly white or wholly blue; and why, in general, bodies are less distinctly seen at a distance than close at hand. Later on, we must specially attend to this. . . .

As regards position, that is, the direction in which the various parts of an object lie relatively to our body, we perceive it by means of our eyes just as we do by means of our hands; our knowledge of it does not depend on any image, nor on any action proceeding from the body, but merely on how the minute points of origin of the nerves are situated in the brain. For this position changes, however slightly, every time that there is a change in the position of the members into which the nerves are inserted; and Nature has appointed this as a means for the soul, not only to know the position of each part of the body it animates in relation to the other parts, but besides that to be able to shift attention to any places lying on the straight lines that may be imagined to be drawn from the extremities of each part and produced to infinity. When our blind man, of whom we have already spoken so much, turns his hand A towards E, or again his hand C towards E, the nerves

inserted in the hand cause a change in his brain, and this
enables his soul to know not only the places A or C, but
also any other places lying on the straight line AE or CE;

he may, e.g. turn his attention to
the objects B and D, and determine
their places, without in any way
having to know or think of the
position of his two hands. Similarly, when our eye or head is
turned in a given direction, our
soul is made aware of it by the
change in the brain that is pro-
duced by the nerves inserted in the muscles that execute
the movement. . . .

You must not, therefore, be surprised that objects can be
seen in their real position, although the picture they impress
upon the eye is inverted; this is just like our blind man's
being able to have simultaneous perception of B, which is to
the right, by means of his left hand, and of D, which is to the
left, by means of his right hand. And just as the blind man
does not judge an object to be double even if he is touching
it with two hands, so likewise when both our eyes are disposed in the right way to carry our attention to one and the
same place, they need only make us see one object, in
spite of the formation of a picture in each of them.

The seeing of distance, as of position, does not depend on
any images emitted from objects but, in the first place, on
the shape of the eye. As I said, this shape must be slightly
different for near and distant vision, and when we adjust
it according to the distance of the objects, we also produce a
change in a certain part of our brain, which is the means
appointed by nature to make our soul perceive the distance.
Ordinarily this happens without our attending to it; just
as, when we squeeze a body in our hand, we adjust it to
the size and shape of the body, and thus feel the body,

without having to be conscious (*que nous pensions*) of these movements of the hand.

Secondly, we know distance by the mutual relation of the two eyes. Our blind man holding the two sticks AE, CE (whose lengths I am assuming him not to know) can tell, as it were by natural geometry, where the point E is, given merely the distance AC between his hands and the size of the angles ACE, CAE. Similarly if our two

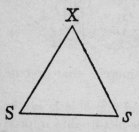

eyes, S*s*, are turned upon the point X; from the length of the line S*s* and the size of the angles XS*s*, X*s*S, we are able to tell where the point X is. We can do the same thing by means of a single eye if we make it change its place; if we keep the eye turned towards X and place it first at the point S and directly afterwards at the point *s*, this will be enough to ensure the co-existence in our imagination of the length of the line S*s* and the size of the angles XS*s* and X*s*S, and thus to make us perceive the distance of the point X.[1] The act of consciousness (*action de la pensée*) involved is a simple act of imagination; but it contains implicitly a reckoning like that made by surveyors, who measure inaccessible places by means of two different observation-posts.

There is a further means of perceiving distance—by the clearness or confusion of the shape seen, and by the strength or weakness of the light. If we are fixing our gaze upon X, the rays from the objects 10 and 12 are not focused so exactly in the back of our eye as they would be if these objects were at the points V and Y; so we see that these objects are either nearer or farther away than X is. Now the light coming from the object 10 to our eye is stronger

[1] [Descartes's own diagram is not reproduced here, being too complex. —Tr.]

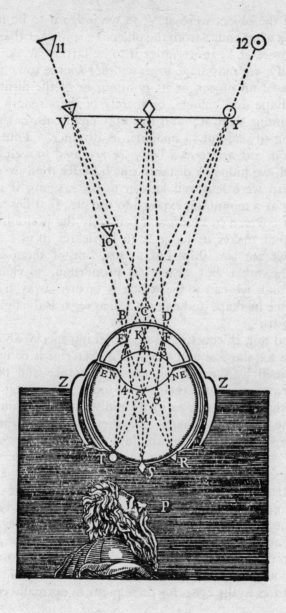

than if the object were at V, so we judge it to be nearer; whereas what comes from the object 12 is weaker than if the object were at Y, so we judge it to be farther away.

Finally, we may have from another source some idea of the size of an object, or its position, or of the distinctness of its shape and colours, or merely of the strength of the light coming from it; and this may enable us, not strictly speaking to see, but to imagine, its distance. Thus, if we look from a distance at a body we are used to seeing close at hand, we judge its distance much better than we should if its size were less well known to us. Again, if we are looking at a mountain, exposed to the sun, that lies beyond a forest covered in shadow, it is merely the position of the forest that makes us judge it to be nearer to us. Again, when we see two ships out at sea, one of them smaller than the other but nearer in proportion, so that they look equal, we can judge which is farther away by their difference in shape and colours and as regards the light they send to us.

I need not, in conclusion, say anything special about the way we see the size and shape of objects; it is completely determined by the way we see the distance and position of their parts. Thus, their size is judged according to our knowledge or opinion as to their distance, in conjunction with the size of the images that they impress on the back of the eye. It is not the absolute size of the images that counts. Clearly they are a hundred times bigger when the objects are very close to us than when they are ten times farther away; but they do not make us see the objects a hundred times bigger; on the contrary, they seem almost the same size, at any rate so long as we are not deceived by [too great] a distance. Again, our judgments of shape clearly come from our knowledge, or opinion, as to the position of the various parts of the objects, and not in accordance with the pictures in the eye; for these pictures normally contain ovals and diamonds when they cause us to see circles and squares.

To remove any doubt you may have whether vision occurs in the way I have explained, I will here consider the reasons why sight sometimes deceives us. First, it is the soul that sees, not the eye; and only by means of the brain does the immediate act of seeing take place. This is why maniacs and men asleep often see, or think they see, objects that are not before their eyes; certain vapours disturb the brain, and produce the same disposition of the region normally employed for sight as though the objects were present.

. . . Again we normally judge that the impressions that affect our sight come from the places towards which we have to look in order to be aware of them; when they come from elsewhere, we may easily make mistakes. For example, people whose eyes are infected with jaundice, or who are looking through yellow glass, or who are shut up in a room where no light enters except through such glass, ascribe this colour to all the bodies they look at. Again, a man in the dark room I described just now ascribes the colours of the outside objects to the white body [stuck on the back of the ox's eye], because he turns his sight only upon that. Again, if our eyes . . . see objects . . . through lenses . . . or in mirrors . . . they judge them to be at [certain] points because these lenses and mirrors deflect the rays that come from the objects, and so our eyes cannot see the objects distinctly except by adjusting themselves to look towards the points [in question].[1] . . . It was a great mistake of the ancients in their catoptrics to try to determine the place of images formed by concave and convex mirrors.[2]

[1] [Departures from the original are made here to avoid reproducing complicated diagrams.—TR.]

[2] [Sc. because there is no such thing as an image, in external space; there is only the place on which an *eye* must focus to see an *object*.—TR.]

It should further be remarked that all our means of knowing distance are highly unreliable. The shape of the eye undergoes hardly any sensible change when the object is more than four or five feet away; even when it is closer, the change is so slight that no very precise knowledge can be got from it. As for the angles between the line joining the two eyes (or two positions of the same eye [1]) and the lines from eye to object, these also vary very little, if one is looking at all far away. Consequently, our sensibility seems actually incapable of receiving the idea of a distance greater than about a couple of hundred feet. This may be verified in the case of the Sun and Moon. They are among the most distant bodies that we can see, and their diameters are to their distances roughly as one to one hundred; but they normally appear to us as only a foot, or at most a couple of feet, across, although our reason assures us that they are exceedingly large and exceedingly remote. This does not happen because we cannot imagine them to be any bigger; we imagine many towers and mountains that are far bigger. But since we cannot imagine them to be more than one or two hundred feet away, they cannot seem to be more than one or two feet across.

Here their position helps to deceive us; normally these heavenly bodies seem smaller when they are high in the heaven at noon than when they are rising and setting; for then there are various objects intermediate between them and our eyes, and their distance is more noticeable. Astronomical measurements with instruments show clearly that their apparently greater size does not result from their being seen to subtend a greater angle, but from their being judged to be farther away. Hence the axiom of the ancient

---

[1] [French *d'un mesme obiet*; but the Latin *ejusdem oculi* gives the sense clearly required; *obiet* may well be an error for *oeil*. See also pp. 250-251.—Tr.]

optics—*The apparent size of objects is proportional to the angle of vision*—is not always true.

We are also deceived because white or luminous bodies, or in general bodies with a great power of affecting the sense of sight, always seem rather closer and bigger than they would if they had less of such power. The reason for their appearing closer is that the movement by which the pupil contracts to avoid their strong light is so bound up with the adjustment of the whole eye for distinct vision of near objects—an adjustment by means of which we judge their distance—that we can hardly carry out one without the other's occurring to some extent; just as we cannot completely close the first two fingers of the hand without the third finger's bending a little as if in order to close too. The reason why these white or luminous bodies appear bigger is not just that our estimate of their size depends on that of their distance, but also that they impress bigger images on the back of the eye. For the optic nerve-endings that line the eye, although very small, have some size; each ending may be affected by different objects in its different parts. But the ending can react only in one way at a time; so if the least part of it is affected by a very brilliant object, and other parts by less brilliant ones, it obeys the impulse of the brilliant object entirely, and forms a representative image of it, not of the other objects.

Suppose 1, 2, 3, are nerve-endings; and suppose the rays that come e.g. from a star to form an image in the back of the eye are spread over 1, and also, if never so little, over the six nerve endings marked 2; and suppose that only very faint rays reach these nerve-endings 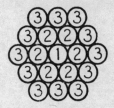 from the parts of the sky next to the star. In that case the image of the star will occupy the six spaces marked 2, and it may even occupy the twelve places marked

3, if the disturbance is strong enough to be propagated to them. Thus you see that the stars, small as they appear to be, appear much bigger than they ought to in view of their exceeding remoteness; and even if they were not perfectly circular, they could not but appear to be. Similarly, a square tower seen from a long way off looks round; and all bodies that form only very small images in the eye can form no images of their corners.

As regards judgment of distance by size, shape, colour, or light, perspective pictures show how easy mistakes are. For often things depicted in them appear to be farther off than they are because they are small, or their outlines are more confused, or their colours are darker or fainter, than we imagine they ought to be.

LETTERS

Illustrative of Descartes's
Philosophy
1630-1647

I. Descartes to Mersenne [1]

[God and the eternal truths.   The notion of infinity]

Amsterdam, 15 April 1630

. . . Mathematical truths, which you call 'eternal', were established by God, and depend on him entirely, like all other created beings.   In truth, it would be speaking of God like a Jupiter or Saturn, making him subject to Styx and the Fates, to say that these truths are independent of him.   Do not hesitate, I pray you, to assert and proclaim it everywhere that it is God who set up these laws in nature, as a king sets up laws in his kingdom.   Now there is no single one of these laws that we cannot comprehend, if our mind turns to consider it;   and all of these laws are naturally implanted in our minds, just as a king would impress his laws on his subjects' hearts, if he had power enough. God's greatness, on the other hand, is incomprehensible to us, although known to us.   But our very judgment that it is incomprehensible enhances our esteem of it: just as a king has the more majesty for being less familiarly known to his subjects—provided, that is, that they do not on that account think they have no king;   that they know the king enough to have no doubt about that.

You will be told that if God had established these truths, he could change them, as a king changes his laws;   the answer must be ' Yes, he could—if his will can change '. ' But as I comprehend them, they are eternal and immutable.'   ' That is just what I judge that God is.'   ' But his will is free.'   ' Yes, but his power is incomprehensible;   and in general we may affirm that God can do

[1] [*Corresp.*, No. 21; *Œuvres*, ed. Adam and Tannery, VOL. I, p. 145.—ED.]

everything we can comprehend, but not that He cannot do what we cannot comprehend; for it would be rash to think our imagination reaches as far as His power does.' ...

As regards infinity . . . you say that if there were an infinite line, it would contain an infinite number of feet, and also of *toises*, and consequently the infinite number of feet would be six times as great as the number of *toises*. *I fully admit it*.[1] 'So the latter number is not infinite.'—*I deny that this follows*.[1] 'But one infinity cannot be greater than another.'—Why not ? *Where is the absurdity ?*[1] especially if it is greater only *in a finite ratio ; e.g. in this case we have multiplication by 6, a finite ratio, which does not affect the infinite*.[1] Besides, what right have we to make a judgment whether or not one infinity could be greater than another, seeing that it would cease to be infinite if we could comprehend it ? . . .

II. DESCARTES TO MERSENNE [2]

[God and the eternal truths]

Amsterdam, 6 May 1630.

As for the eternal truths, I say once more that *they are true or possible only because God knows them as true or possible ; they are not, contrariwise, known to God as true as though they were true independently of him*.[3] And if men properly understood the sense of their words, they could never say without blasphemy that the truth about something is antecedent to God's knowledge of it; for in God knowing and willing are but one thing ; so that *from the very fact of his willing something, He knows it, and for this reason alone is such a thing true*.[2] We must not say, then, that *if God did not exist*,

---

[1] [Italicised words (except *toises*) are in Latin in the original, whereas the rest of the letter is in French.—TR.]

[2] [*Corresp.*, No. 22; *Œuvres*, A.-T., VOL. I, p. 149.—ED.]

[3] [These italics represent Latin words in a French context.—TR.]

nevertheless these truths would be true; [1] for God's existence is the first and the most eternal (*sic*) of all possible truths, and the sole source of all the others. But what makes it easy to misunderstand this, is that most men do not consider God as an infinite and incomprehensible Being, the sole Author of all, on whom all depends; they pause at the syllables of his Name, and think it is knowledge enough of him if we know that *Dieu* means the same Being as is called *Deus* in Latin—him whom men adore. Those who have no loftier thoughts than these may readily become atheists; and since they perfectly comprehend mathematical truths, but not the truth of God's existence, it is no wonder they do not think that the former depend on the latter. What, on the contrary, they ought to judge is that since God is a cause whose power surpasses the limits of human understanding, whereas the necessity of these truths does not go beyond our knowledge, therefore they are something inferior and subordinate to that incomprehensible Power. . . .

III. DESCARTES TO MERSENNE [2]

[God and the eternal truths]

Amsterdam, 27 May 1631.

You ask me *what kind of cause God is of the eternal truths he has established.*[1] I answer: *the same kind of cause*[1] of them, as of all things he has created: namely, *the efficient and the total cause.*[1] For he is certainly Author of the essence of creatures, as well as of their existence; now this essence is nothing other than the eternal truths. I do not conceive of them as emanating from God, like rays from the Sun; but I know that God is Author of all things, and these truths are

[1] [As before, these italics represent Latin phrases in a French context.—TR.]

[2] [*Corresp.*, No. 22 *bis*; *Œuvres*, A.-T., VOL. I, p. 151.—ED.]

something; and consequently, that God is their Author. I say that I know this, but not that I conceive or comprehend it; for we can know that God is infinite and almighty, even though our soul, being finite, cannot comprehend or conceive him. This is like our being able to touch a mountain with our hands, although we cannot embrace it as we could a tree or any other object not too big for our arms; for comprehension means that our thought embraces a thing, but for knowledge it is enough that our thought touches the thing.

Again, you ask what made it necessary for God to create these truths. What I say is that God was just as much free to make it untrue that all straight lines drawn from centre to circumference are equal, as he was not to create the world. And certainly these truths are not necessarily conjoined with God's essence any more than other creatures are.

You ask what God did in order to produce them; I say that *in the very act of willing them and understanding them from eternity, He created them;* or, if you confine the word *created* to the existence of things, *He established and made them.* For in God will, understanding, and creation are one and the same thing; none is prior to another *even conceptually.*[1]

As for the question *whether it befits God's goodness to damn men eternally,* that belongs to theology; so you will, if you please, allow me to say absolutely nothing about it. Not that the arguments of freethinkers on the matter have any force; they seem to me frivolous and ridiculous; but I think we act wrongly towards truths depending on faith, and not provable by natural demonstration, if we try to support them by arguments of a human sort, which are only probable.

[1] [The italics here and in the next paragraph represent Latin words and phrases.—Tr.]

IV. Descartes to Mersenne [1]

[God and the eternal truths]

27 May 1638

. . . As regards the question whether there would be real space, as there is now, even if God had not created anything: it may seem that this passes the limits of the human mind, and cannot reasonably be discussed, any more than infinity can; but I think it passes the limits only of our imagination, like the questions of the existence of God and the human soul, and that our understanding can reach the truth of the matter—namely in my opinion, that not only would there be no space, but not even the so-called eternal truths, like *a whole is greater than its part*, would be truths, if God had not extablished things so. . . .

V. Descartes to ? [2]

[Descartes and St Augustine]

Leyden, November 1640

I am obliged to you for bringing to my notice the passage of St Augustine [3] to which my *Cogito ergo sum* has some relation. I have been to the town library today to read it; he does, I find, really use it to prove the certainty of our existence. He goes on to show by means of it that there is in us a certain image of the Trinity; we are, we know that we are, and we love this being and this knowledge that there is in us. [4] My own use of the argument, on the other hand, was to establish that this conscious *I* is an immaterial substance with no corporeal element; these two uses are very different. To infer that one exists from the fact that one is doubting is in itself so simple and natural that it

[1] [*Corresp.*, No. 123; *Œuvres*, A.-T., vol. I, p. 138.—Ed.]
[2] [*Corresp.*, No. 219; *Œuvres*, A.-T., vol. III, p. 247.—Ed.]
[3] [*De Trinitate*, x, 10.—Ed.] [4] [*De Trinitate*, x, 12.—Ed.]

263

might have come from anybody's pen. All the same, I am very pleased to have been in agreement with St Augustine; if only to silence the petty-minded people who cavil at this principle. . . .

VI. Descartes to Mersenne [1]

[*The infinite. On the ' Meditations '*]

Leyden, 28 January 1641.

I have read M. Morin's book.[2] Its chief fault is that he treats of the infinite throughout as though his mind were superior to it and could comprehend its properties; this fault is shared by almost everybody, and is one I have carefully tried to avoid; I have always treated of the infinite only so as to submit myself to it, and not sò as to determine what it is or is not. . . . Again, he assumes that there could not be an infinite number; which he has by no means proved. . . .

I proved quite explicitly that God is the Creator of everything, and likewise, all his other attributes; for I proved his existence from our idea of him, and also because, possessing as we do this idea, we must have been created by him. But I must observe that people pay more attention to the headings in books than to anything else. That is why I thought it well to add to the title of the second Meditation, 'The nature of the human mind', the words ' it is better known than the body ', in order that people should not think I was trying to prove its immortality. So, for the third Meditation: ' Concerning God—that he exists '. So, for the fifth: ' The nature of material things—God's existence again considered '.

[1] [*Corresp.*, No. 229; *Œuvres*, A.-T., vol. iii, p. 293.—Ed.]
[2] [I. B. Morinus, *Quod Deus sit Mundusque ab ipso creatus fuerit in tempore, eiusque providentia gubernetur. Selecta aliquot theoremata adversus Atheos.* Paris, 1635.—Ed.]

So, for the sixth: ' The existence of material things—the real distinction of mind and body '. For these are the things to which I want most attention paid. But I think I have put in much more besides; and I may tell you, between ourselves, that these six Meditations contain all the foundations of my physics. But, please, you must not say so; for partisans of Aristotle would find more difficulty, perhaps in approving them; and what I hope is that readers will gradually get used to my principles, and recognise their truth, before observing that they destroy Aristotle's. . . .

VII. DESCARTES TO ? [1]

[Answer to objections]

Endegeest, August 1641.

1. It would certainly be desirable to have as high a degree of certitude in regard to the direction of life as is demanded when it is a question of attaining knowledge; but it is very easy to show that such certitude is not to be sought after nor to be expected. This can be shown *a priori*, because, whereas the mind is incorruptible and immortal, the human being as a whole is naturally corruptible; but it is much easier to give an *a posteriori* proof, from the consequences that would otherwise follow. Suppose a man chose to fast until he died because he was not certain that there was no poison in his food ; suppose he thought that he was not obliged to eat, because it was not clear and manifest that there were to hand the means of sustaining life, and it would be better to abstain and wait for death to come than to kill himself by eating. Such a man would certainly be censured as a suicidal lunatic. We may further suppose that the only food he can get is poisoned; even, that his constitution is such that starvation is conducive

[1] [*Corresp.*, No. 250; *Œuvres*, A.-T., VOL. III, p. 422.—ED.]

to his health; nevertheless, if the food does not appear to him to be poisoned but on the contrary thoroughly healthful, and if starvation seems likely to hurt him as much as other men, it will be his duty to take that food, and thus to embrace what seems advantageous rather than what really is. This is self-evident to everybody, and I am surprised that anyone should think otherwise.

2. . . . I had good reason to assert that the human soul is always conscious (*cogitare*) in any circumstances—even in a mother's womb. For what more certain or more evident reason could be required than my proof that the soul's nature or essence consists in its being conscious, just as the essence of a body consists in its being extended? A thing can never be deprived of its own essence. If a man says his soul was not conscious (*non cogitasse*) on the occasions when he cannot remember noticing that it was conscious, I think he deserves no more attention than if he were likewise to say that, during the time when he does not apprehend ⟨in memory⟩ that his body had extension, it was not extended. This does not mean that I hold the conviction that an infant's mind meditates on metaphysical truths in its mother's womb. In our experience body and mind are so conjoined that our minds are almost always being acted upon by our bodies; and although in an adult who enjoys bodily health the mind has some freedom to think of other objects than those presented by the senses, the same freedom is not found in sick men, or during sleep, or in children; and it is normally less and less as we take a more and more tender age into account. So if one may make any conjecture about this obscure matter, it is thoroughly reasonable to suppose that a mind newly united to an infant body is wholly occupied in having confused awareness (*percipiendis*), or sensation, of such ideas as pain, enjoyment, heat, cold— ideas that arise from its being thus united and intermingled with the body. At the same time, it has in itself the ideas of

God, the self, and all ' self-evident ' truths, in the same way as grown men have them when they are not attending to them; it is not that it acquires them later on, as it grows older. I have no doubt that, if freed from the shackles of the body, it would find these ideas within itself.

This view does not get us into difficulties. It is no harder for us to see how the mind, although really distinct from the body, is nevertheless joined to it, and affected by traces impressed upon it, and able likewise to impress new traces on its own account, than it is for people who believe in real accidents to suppose that they act on corporeal substance, from which they are different in kind. It is irrelevant that these accidents are called corporeal. If ' corporeal ' is taken to mean anything that can somehow affect a body, then in this sense the mind also will have to be called ' corporeal '; but if ' corporeal ' is taken to mean ' composed of the sort of substance called body ', then neither the mind nor these accidents (supposed as they are to be really distinct from body) may be called corporeal, and it is only in this latter sense that the mind is ordinarily said not to be corporeal. Thus, when a mind united to a body is conscious of a corporeal thing, certain cerebral particles are set in local motion; sometimes this takes place through external objects acting on the sense-organs, sometimes through animal spirits ascending from the heart to the brain, and sometimes again through the mind's being impelled of its own free will to a certain thought (*cogitationem*); this movement of cerebral particles leaves a trace, and it is on this that memory depends. Purely intellectual things are strictly speaking not remembered; we are conscious of them just as adequately the first time they occur to us as the second time. (Of course, they are commonly associated with names; and these names, since they are corporeal, do become the objects of memory.) . . .

6. It is assuredly the case that we do not understand the infinite by denial of limitation; and from the premise ' limitation entails the denial of infinity' it is invalid to infer ' denial of limitation entails knowledge of infinity'. That by which the infinite differs from the finite is real and positive; limitation, by which the finite differs from the infinite, is a nonentity, or a negation of existence. Now that which is not cannot bring us to the knowledge of that which is; on the contrary, the negation of a thing has to be known by knowing the thing itself. I did say that, in order to understand the infinite, it is enough to conceive of a thing not comprised within any limits; but here I was just following normal usage. In the same way, I kept the term ' the infinite'; ' the amplest of beings' would be a more correct term, if we insisted that all names should answer to the nature of the realities; but usage demands that infinity be expressed by negation of a negation—as if in order to designate a very big thing I said it was ' not little' or ' a thing with absolutely no littleness about it'. Hence I did not mean by this term that the positive nature of the infinite is known by means of a negation; and thus I have not contradicted myself. I did not deny the mind's power to add to its ideas of things; but I have frequently emphasised that the ideas so added, and the power of adding them, cannot occur in the mind unless the mind itself comes from a God in whom all perfections that can be grasped by means of such addition really exist; I proved this from the principle that there can be nothing in the effect but pre-existed in the cause. And none of those who are to be reckoned among the most subtle philosophers in this field, consider atoms as self-existent. For it is clear by the light of nature that there can be only one supreme being independent of everything else. . . .

I allow that the ideas of corporeal things, indeed, of as many things as there are in the visible universe—not, as

your objection has it, ' the whole visible universe itself '—
might be produced by the human mind; but it is invalid
to infer that we cannot know whether there is in fact anything corporeal. It is not my opinions, but only conclusions
wrongly derived from them, that lead to perplexities; for
I proved the existence of material things not from the
occurrence in ourselves of ideas of them, but from the way
they come to us; for we are thus made aware that they are
not made by ourselves but come from elsewhere.

7.   . . . If God ceased from his co-operation, everything
that he has created would at once vanish into nothing;
for before things were created, before God provided his
co-operation, they were nothing.   All the same, things are
to be called substances; for when we say a created substance
is self-subsistent, we are not excluding the divine co-
operation, which is necessary in order that it should subsist;
we mean simply that it is a thing capable of existing apart
from any other created thing—which cannot be said about
aspects of things, e.g. shape or number.   God would not be
showing his power to be unlimited if he made things such
as could exist apart from him later on; on the contrary,
this would show his power was limited, because, when once
created, the thing would no longer depend on him.
And I am not falling into my own trap when I say : ' It is
impossible for God to destroy anything except by ceasing
from his co-operation; for otherwise it would become a
non-being by a positive activity '.   For there is a great
difference between what happens by positive divine
activity and what comes about by the cessation of positive
activity; the former cannot but be thoroughly good,
while the latter comprises all evils and sins, and the destruction of a being, if any existent ever is destroyed. . . .

9. I do not remember to have ever expressed surprise
that not everybody is aware of the idea of God in himself,
I have frequently observed that what men judge to be the

case is different from their real conceptions; so, although
I have no doubt that all men have in themselves at least an
implicit idea of God, i.e. a potentiality of being explicitly
aware of the idea, nevertheless I should not be surprised
if the idea never came before their awareness or attention,
and perhaps never would come before their attention even
if they read my Meditations a thousand times. In the
same way, men judge that so-called empty space is nothingness, although they must conceive it as a positive reality;
in the same way, again, when they believe in real accidents,
they are representing them to themselves as substances,
although they do not judge them to be substances[1];
and in many other matters men's judgments differ from
their perceptions. But if people never make any judgment
except about things they clearly and distinctly conceive
(*percipiunt*)—a rule I always observe as far as I can—then
they cannot judge differently at different times about the
same matter. It is true, as you say, that whatever is clear
and indubitable appears to us more and more certain in
proportion as it is more often and more attentively considered; but I do not remember ever giving this as a
criterion of clear and indubitable certitude. . . .

10. It is self-evident that the aims of God cannot be
known to us unless God reveals them. If the human point
of view be taken, as is done in ethics, then it is certainly
true that everything was made to the glory of God, because
God is worthy of our praise on account of all his work;
and, again, that the Sun was made to give us light, because
we experience that the Sun does give us light. But it
would be puerile and absurd for a metaphysician to assert
that God had no other aim in making the Universe than

---

[1] [Clerselier's French version here adds: ' Again, in their notion of
the soul, although they do not observe it as having anything in it that
refers to body or extension, they nevertheless do not cease to picture it as
corporeal, to use imagination in conceiving it, and in fact to form
judgments and to talk about it as though it were a body '.—Tr.]

the praise of men (as if he were a very vain man); or that the Sun, which is many times bigger than the Earth, was created to no other end than to give light to man, who occupies a very small part of the Earth's surface.

11. You confound the functions of the intellect and the will. It is not for the will to understand, but only to will. True, we make nothing an object of will unless we have some kind and degree of understanding in regard to it, and so much I have admitted; but experience plainly testifies that about any given thing our desires may be more extensive than our understanding. Falsehood is never apprehended under the show of truth; e.g. those who say there is no idea of God in us do not apprehend this, though they may assert it, believe it, and argue in favour of it. As I just now remarked (point 9), men's judgments often differ from their conceptions or apprehensions.

12. . . . It does not much matter whether a man born blind has the ideas of colours or not, and it is useless to allege the testimony of a blind philosopher. Even if we supposed him to have ideas exactly like our ideas of colours, he cannot know that they are like ours, nor that they are to be called ideas of colours; for he does not know what sort of ideas we have. . . .

Although the mind is indivisible, it is none the less capable of acquiring various properties. It is not surprising, however, that it does not devise proofs like those of Archimedes during sleep; for even in sleep it remains united to the body, and is in no way more at liberty than it is in waking life. Keeping awake a long time does not make the brain better disposed to retain traces impressed upon it. In sleep and waking life alike, it is the more strongly impressed traces that are the better retained; and therefore we sometimes remember dreams, but we remember better our waking experiences (*quae cogitavimus*). . . .

13. When I say that God is his own existence, I was using a common theological expression meaning that it belongs to God's essence that he should exist. The same thing cannot be said of a triangle; the whole essence of a triangle can be correctly conceived even if it be supposed that in actuality there is no such thing.

The reason why I said that the Sceptics would not have doubted the truths of geometry if they had acknowledged a God (as one should), was as follows: Geometrical truths are quite clear, and they would have had no occasion to doubt them if they had known that everything they clearly conceived was true. Now this is entailed by an adequate knowledge of God; this is the premise not listed by the Sceptics.

Your question whether a line is made up of points or of segments has no relevance here, and it would be out of place for me to answer it. In the passage you refer to I was not talking about geometrical questions generally, but only about those proofs that the Sceptics doubted although they did clearly understand them. You are wrong to make a Sceptic say ⟨about such a proof⟩ ' Let the evil spirit deceive me as much as he can, ⟨he can never deceive me as regards this proposition⟩ '; a man who says this will *ipso facto* not be a Sceptic, because he will not be doubting everything. Of course I have never denied that even Sceptics spontaneously assent to a truth so long as they clearly apprehend it; they cannot stick to their heresy of universal doubt except verbally (though they may wish and set out to do so). Anyhow, I was dealing with our memories of previous clear conceptions, not with our present clear perception.

14. How is it that the mind is co-extensive with an extended body although it has itself no genuine extension (i.e. extension occupying a place, and excluding anything else from there), I have explained by my previous illustration of the way gravity is conceived as a real quality. . . .

You ask how one can tell which way of conceiving things is more imperfect, and more evidence of the weakness of our mind: inability to conceive (*concipere*) one thing without another, e.g. mind without body, or on the other hand our conceiving two things completely apart from each other. What we must consider is which way of conceiving things proceeds from some positive ability, the lack of which results in the other way of conceiving them. It is easy to see that there is a real power in the mind by means of which it conceives of (*percipit*) two things apart from one another, and that it is the lack of this power that leads to its apprehending the two together in a confused fashion as if they were one; just as there is a greater perfection in our eyesight when it exactly discriminates all the small parts of an object than when it perceives them all together as if they were one thing. On the other hand, a man with wavering eyes may take one thing for two, as drunken men often do; I will not say this is like the philosophers' distinction between essence and existence, because as a rule they do not assume a greater distinction here than there really is; but it is like their conception of matter, form, and various accidents as so many different things. In such a case they may readily realise, from the obscure and confused nature of the conception, that it arises not from a positive capacity but from the lack of some capacity; they have only to take the trouble to notice that they have in fact no completely distinct ideas of the things they suppose to be distinct. . . .

VIII. DESCARTES TO REGIUS[1]

[' *Substantial forms* ']

Endegeest, January 1642.

. . . First he enquires ' whether the opinion that denies substantial forms can be reconciled with Holy Writ '.

[1] [*Corresp.*, No. 266; *Œuvres*, A.-T., VOL. III, p. 501.—ED.]

Nobody can have any doubt of that; one need only know that the prophets and apostles and the others who composed the Holy Scriptures at the dictate of the Holy Ghost never thought of these philosophical entities, which are quite unknown outside the Schools. To avoid verbal ambiguity, it must here be remarked that the ' substantial form ' we are denying means a sort of substance adjoined to matter and constituting along with it a whole that is purely corporeal; something that is not less of a true substance or self-subsistent thing than matter is, but rather more, since it is called ' actuality ' and matter ' potentiality '. I do not think this substance or substantial form, existing in material things and distinct from matter, is mentioned anywhere in Holy Writ . . . The words *genus* and *species* ⟨in the Latin of the Vulgate⟩ cannot be said to stand for substantial differences; for there are genera and species of accidents—e.g. *figure* is a genus relatively to circles and squares, which nobody imagines to have substantial forms. . . .

IXA. PRINCESS ELIZABETH TO DESCARTES [1]

[On the relation of soul and body]

The Hague, 6-16 May 1643.

. . . I beg of you to tell me how the human soul can determine the movement of the animal spirits in the body so as to perform voluntary acts—being as it is merely a conscious (*pensante*) substance. For the determination of movement seems always to come about from the moving body's being propelled—to depend on the kind of impulse it gets from what sets it in motion, or again, on the nature and shape of this latter thing's surface. Now the first two conditions involve contact, and the third involves that the impelling thing has extension; but you utterly

[1] [*Corresp.*, No. 301; *Œuvres*, A.-T., VOL. III, p. 661.—ED.]

exclude extension from your notion of soul, and contact seems to me incompatible with a thing's being immaterial.

I therefore ask you for a more specific definition of the soul than you give in your metaphysics: a definition of its substance, as distinct from its activity, consciousness (*pensée*). Even if we supposed these to be in fact inseparable—a matter hard to prove in regard to children in their mother's womb and severe fainting-fits—to be inseparable as the divine attributes are: nevertheless we may get a more perfect idea of them by considering them apart.

IXb. Descartes to Princess Elizabeth [1]

Egmond, 21 May 1643.

. . . I may truly say that what your Highness is propounding seems to me to be the question people have most right to ask me in view of my published works. For there are two facts about the human soul on which there depends any knowledge we may have as to its nature: first, that it is conscious; secondly, that, being united to a body, it is able to act and suffer along with it. Of the second fact I said almost nothing; my aim was simply to make the first properly understood; for my main object was to prove the distinction of soul and body; and to this end only the first was serviceable, the second might have been prejudicial. But since your Highness sees too clearly for dissimulation to be possible, I will here try to explain how I conceive the union of soul and body and how the soul has the power of moving the body.

My first observation is that there are in us certain primitive notions—the originals, so to say, on the pattern of which we form all other knowledge. These notions are very few in number. First, there are the most general ones, existence, number, duration, etc., which apply to

[1] [*Corresp.*, No. 302; *Œuvres*, A.-T., vol. III, p. 663.—Ed.]

everything we can conceive. As regards body in particular, we have merely the notion of extension and the consequent notions of shape and movement. As regards the soul taken by itself, we have merely the notion of consciousness, which comprises the conceptions (*perceptions*) of the intellect and the inclinations of the will. Finally, as regards the soul and body together, we have merely the notion of their union; and on this there depend our notions of the soul's power to move the body, and of the body's power to act on the soul and cause sensations and emotions.

I would also observe that all human knowledge consists just in properly distinguishing these notions and attaching each of them only to the objects that it applies to. If we try to explain some problem by means of a notion that does not apply, we cannot help making mistakes; we are just as wrong if we try to explain one of these notions in terms of another, since, being primitive, each such notion has to be understood in itself. The use of our senses has made us much more familiar with notions of extension, shape, and movement than with others; thus the chief cause of our errors is that ordinarily we try to use these notions to explain matters to which they do not apply; e.g. we try to use our imagination in conceiving the nature of the soul, or to conceive the way the soul moves the body in terms of the way that one body is moved by another body.

In the Meditations that your Highness condescended to read, I tried to bring before the mind the notions that apply to the soul taken by itself, and to distinguish them from those that apply to the body taken by itself. Accordingly, the next thing I have to explain is how we are to form the notions that apply to the union of the soul with the body, as opposed to those that apply to the body taken by itself or the mind taken by itself. . . . These simple notions are to be sought only within the soul, which is naturally endowed with all of them, but does not

276

always adequately distinguish between them, or again does not always attach them to the right objects.

So I think people have hitherto confused the notions of the soul's power to act within the body and the power one body has to act within another; and they have ascribed both powers not to soul, whose nature was so far unknown, but to various qualities of bodies—gravity, heat, etc. These qualities were imagined to be real, i.e. to have an existence distinct from the existence of bodies; consequently, they were imagined to be substances, although they were called qualities. In order to conceive of them, people have used sometimes notions that we have for the purpose of knowing body, and sometimes those that we have for the purpose of knowing the soul, according as they were ascribing to them a material or an immaterial nature. For example, on the supposition that gravity is a real quality, about which we know no more than its power of moving the body in which it occurs towards the centre of the Earth, we find no difficulty in conceiving how it moves the body or how it is united to it; and we do not think of this as taking place by means of real mutual contact between two surfaces; our inner experience shows (*nous expérimentons*) that that notion is a specific one. Now I hold that we misuse this notion by applying it to gravity (which, as I hope to show in my *Physics*, is nothing really distinct from body), but that it has been given to us in order that we may conceive of the way that the soul moves the body.

Xa. Princess Elizabeth to Descartes[1]

[*On the relation of soul and body*]

The Hague, 10-20 June 1643.

. . . ⟨I cannot⟩ understand the idea by means of which we are to judge of the way that the soul, unextended and

[1] [*Corresp.*, No. 308; *Œuvres*, A.-T., vol. iii, p. 684.—Ed.]

277

immaterial, moves the body, in terms of the idea you used to have about gravity. You used falsely to ascribe to gravity, under the style of a ' quality ', the power of carrying bodies towards the centre of the Earth. But I cannot see why this should convince us that a body may be impelled by something immaterial; why we should not rather be confirmed in the view that this is impossible, by the demonstration of a true ⟨view of gravity⟩, opposed ⟨to this⟩, which you promise us in your *Physics*; especially as the idea ⟨that a body may be so impelled⟩ cannot claim the same degree of perfection and representative reality (*réalité objective*) as the idea of God, and may be a figment resulting from ignorance of what really moves bodies towards the centre. Since no material cause was apparent to the senses, people may well have ascribed this to the opposite cause, the immaterial; but I have never been able to conceive *that*, except as a negation of matter, which can have no communication with matter.

And I must confess that I could more readily allow that the soul has matter and extension than that an immaterial being has the capacity of moving a body and being affected by it. If the first, ⟨the soul's moving the body⟩, took place by ⟨the soul's giving⟩ information ⟨to the body⟩, then the ⟨animal⟩ spirits, which carry out the movement, would have to be intelligent; but you do not allow intelligence to anything corporeal. You do indeed show the possibility of the second thing ⟨the body's affecting the soul⟩, in your Metaphysical Meditations; but it is very hard to see how a soul such as you describe, after possessing the power and the habit of correct reasoning, may lose all that because of some vapours ⟨in the brain⟩; or why the soul is so much governed by the body, when it can subsist separately, and has nothing in common with it. . . .

Xb. Descartes to Princess Elizabeth [1]

Egmond, 28 June 1643.

I am most deeply obliged to your Highness for condescending, after experience of my previous ill success in explaining the problem you were pleased to propound to me, to be patient enough to listen to me once more on the same subject, and to give me an opportunity of making remarks on matters I had passed over. My chief omissions seem to be the following. I began by distinguishing three kinds of primitive ideas or notions, each of which is known in a specific way and not by comparison to another kind; viz. the notion of soul, the notion of body, and the notion of the union between soul and body. I still had to explain the difference between these three kinds of notions, and again between the operations of the soul by means of which we get them, and to show the means of becoming readily familiar with each kind. Further, I had to explain why I used the comparison of gravity. Next, I had to show that even if we try to conceive of the soul as material (which means, properly speaking, to conceive of its union with the body), we cannot help going on to recognise that it is separable from the body. This, I think, is the sum of the task your Highness has set me.

In the first place, then, I discern this great difference between the three kinds of notions: the soul is conceived only by pure intellect; body (i.e. extension, shape, and movement) can likewise be known by pure intellect, but is known much better when intellect is aided by imagination; finally, what belongs to the union of soul and body can be understood only in an obscure way either by pure intellect or even when the intellect is aided by imagination, but is understood very clearly by means of the senses. Consequently, those who never do philosophise and make use

---

[1] [*Corresp.*, No. 310; *Œuvres*, A.-T., vol. III, p. 690.—Ed.]

only of their senses have no doubt that the soul moves the body and the body acts on the soul; indeed, they consider the two as a single thing, i.e. they conceive of their union; for to conceive of the union between two things is to conceive of them as a single thing. Metaphysical reflections, which exercise the pure intellect, are what make us familiar with the notion of soul; the study of mathematics, which chiefly exercises the imagination in considering figures and movements, accustoms us to form very distinct notions of body; finally, it is just by means of ordinary life and conversation, by abstaining from meditating and from studying things that exercise the imagination, that one learns to conceive the union of soul and body.

I am half afraid that your Highness may think I am not speaking seriously here; but that would be contrary to the respect that I owe to your Highness and will never fail to pay. I can truly say that the chief rule I have always observed in my studies, and the one I think has been most serviceable to me in acquiring some measure of knowledge, has been never to spend more than a few hours a day in thoughts that demand imagination, or more than a few hours a year in thoughts that demand pure intellect; I have given all the rest of my time to the relaxation of my senses and the repose of my mind. I here count among exercises of imagination all serious conversations, and everything that demands attention. This is what made me retire to the country; it is true that in the busiest city in the world I might have as many hours to myself as I now spend in study, but I could not employ them so usefully when my mind was wearied by the attention that the troubles of life demand.

I take the liberty of writing thus to your Highness, to express my sincere admiration of your Highness's ability, among all the business and cares that are never lacking to persons who combine high intelligence and high birth, to find leisure for the meditations that are necessary for proper understanding of the distinction between soul and body. I formed the opinion that it was these meditations, rather than thoughts demanding less attention, that made your Highness find some obscurity in our notion of their union. It seems to me that the human mind is incapable of distinctly conceiving both the distinction between body and soul and their union, at one and the same time; for that requires our conceiving them as a single thing and simultaneously conceiving them as two things, which is self-contradictory. I supposed that your Highness still had very much in mind the arguments proving the distinction of soul and body; and I did not wish to ask you to lay them aside, in order to represent to yourself that notion of their union which everybody always has in himself without doing philosophy—viz. that there is one single person who has at once body and consciousness, so that this consciousness can move the body and be aware of the events that happen to it. Accordingly, I used in my previous letter the simile of gravity and other qualities, which we imagine to be united to bodies as consciousness is united to ours. I did not worry over the fact that this simile is lame, because these qualities are not, as one imagines, realities; for I thought your Highness was already fully convinced that the soul is a substance distinct from the body.

Your Highness, however, makes the remark that it is easier to ascribe matter and extension to the soul than to ascribe to it the power of moving a body and being moved by it without having any matter. Now I would ask your Highness to hold yourself free to ascribe 'matter and extension' to the soul; for this is nothing else than to conceive the soul as united to the body. After forming a proper conception of this, and experiencing it in your own case, your Highness will find it easy to reflect that the matter you thus ascribe to your consciousness (*pensée*) is not the consciousness itself; again, the extension of the matter is essentially different from the extension of the consciousness, for the first extension is determined to a certain place, and excludes any other corporeal extension from that place, whereas the second does not. In this way your Highness will assuredly find it easy to come back to a realisation of the distinction between soul and body, in spite of having conceived of them as united.

Finally, I think it is very necessary to have got a good understanding, for once in one's life, of the principles of metaphysics, because it is from these that we have knowledge of God and of our soul. But I also think it would be very harmful to occupy one's intellect often with meditating on them, for it would be the less able to find leisure for the functioning of the imagination and the senses; the best thing is to be content with retaining in memory and in belief the conclusions one has drawn once for all, and to spend the rest of one's time for study in reflections in which the intellect co-operates with the imagination and the senses. . . .

XI. Descartes to Princess Elizabeth [1]

[*The conditions of good judgment*]

Egmond, 15 September 1645.

Madame,

. . . As regards the problem your Highness was pleased to propound to me, of the way to strengthen our understanding so as to discern the best course in all the actions of our life . . . I will try in this letter to explain my opinion on the matter.

There 'cannot, it seems to me, be more than two requisites for a constant disposition to good judgment: first, knowledge of the truth; secondly, the habit of recalling and accepting this knowledge whenever the occasion

[1] [*Corresp.*, No. 403; *Œuvres*, A.-T., vol. IV, p. 291.—Ed.]

requires. Now God alone knows everything perfectly; we must be content to know what is most useful to us. The first and chief of such truths is that there is a God on whom all things depend, whose perfections are infinite, whose power is immeasurable, whose decrees are unfailing; for this teaches us to take in good part whatever happens to us, as being expressly sent by God. And since the true object of love is perfection, when once we lift up our minds to consider God as he is, we find in ourselves such a natural inclination to love him that we derive joy even from our afflictions, by thinking that his will is being carried out in what comes to us.

The second thing we need to know is the nature of the soul—that it subsists apart from the body, and is far nobler, and is capable of enjoying an infinity of gratifications that are not to be found in this life. This prevents us from fearing death, and detaches our affection from worldly things so that we regard with contempt everything that is in the power of fortune.

It may also be of great service to form a worthy judgment of God's works, and possess that idea of the vast extent of the universe which I tried to bring out in the third book of my *Principia*. If we imagine that above the heavens there is only imaginary space, and that the heavens were all made just to serve the earth, and the earth made only for man, this makes us inclined to think of the earth as our chief home, and of this life as the best; again, instead of apprehending the perfections we actually possess, we ascribe unreal imperfections to other creatures, in order to exalt ourselves above them; again, with impertinent presumption, we try to enter into God's counsel and share in his task of carrying on the world, which causes an infinity of vain worries and troubles.

After we have thus recognised the goodness of God, the immortality of our souls and the greatness of the universe, there is a further truth that it seems to me very useful to know: namely, that although each of us is a separate person and, consequently, has interests different in some measure from other people's, nevertheless each has to remember that he could not exist by himself; each is, in fact, part of the universe, or more particularly part of the Earth; each is part of this state, this society, this family— bound to it by his residence, his oath, his birth. And each must always put the interests of the whole of which he is part before his particular personal interests; within limits, of course, and with discretion; it would be wrong to expose oneself to a great evil to procure only a small good for one's relatives or one's country; and if a man is worth more, just in himself, than all the rest of his city, he would not do well to be willing to be lost in order to save it. But if a man referred everything to himself, he would have no fear of injuring other men a great deal if he thought he could derive some slight advantage; he would not have true friendship, fidelity, or in fact any virtue at all. If on the other hand a man considers himself part of the commonwealth, he takes pleasure in doing good to everybody, and he is not afraid even to risk his life in the service of others when the occasion arises; indeed, he would gladly lose his soul to save other people if that were possible. Thus this consideration is the source and origin of all the most heroic human actions; for as for those who face death from vanity, because they hope for praise, or from stupidity, because they do not apprehend the danger, I think they are rather to be pitied than admired. But when a man risks his life because he thinks it his duty, or endures some other evil so that good may result to other people, he may perhaps not reflectively consider that his reason for doing this is that he owes more to the commonwealth of which he is part than to himself in particular, but nevertheless he is acting in virtue of this consideration, which he has confusedly before his mind (*en sa pensée*). And anyone is naturally led to this consideration when he knows and loves God as a man should; for then he abandons himself to God's will, lays aside his own interests, and has no passion but to do what he thinks is God's pleasure; and from this he derives mental satisfaction and contentment worth incomparably more than the slight transient enjoyments depending on the senses.

Apart from these general truths as regards all our actions, one ought to know various truths regarding particular acts. The chief of these seem to me to be the ones I mentioned in my last letter: that all our passions represent the good they incite us to pursue as being greater than it actually is; and that bodily pleasures are never so lasting as those of the soul, and never so great when one is possessed of them as they seem to be when one is hoping for them. We must be careful to notice this, in order that when we feel ourselves stirred by some passion, we may suspend our judgment till it calms itself; and in order not to let ourselves be readily deceived by the false appearances of this world's good.

All that I can add to this is that we must specially examine the ways of the place where we live, to find out how far they are to be followed. And although we cannot have demonstrative certainty about everything, we must nevertheless take sides, and embrace, as regards all ordinary affairs, the opinions that seem most probable, in order never to be irresolute when it is a matter of action. For it is just our irresolution that causes us sorrow and remorse.

For the rest, I said just now that in addition to knowledge of the truth we require ⟨a certain⟩ habit in order to be always disposed to form good judgments. For we cannot be continually attending to the same thing; and so, however clear and evident reasons we had for being convinced of a truth, we may later on be diverted from our belief by false appearances, unless long and frequent meditations have so impressed the belief on our mind that it has become habitual. In this sense the Schoolmen are right to call virtue a habit; for in point of fact we hardly ever go wrong for lack of theoretical knowledge of our duty, but only from lack of practical knowledge—i.e. of a firm and habitual belief. And since my present examination of those truths increases my own habit ⟨of belief in them⟩, I am specially obliged to your Highness for allowing me to deal with them for you; and there is nothing in which I regard my leisure as better employed, than in professing myself,

Madame,

Your Highness' most humble and obedient servant,

DESCARTES.

XII. DESCARTES TO FATHER MESLAND [1]

[On the proofs of God's existence. On the soul. On free will.]

Leyden, 2 May 1644.

. . . As regards particular and limited physical and moral causes, we do, I admit, often find that those which produce a given effect are incapable of producing various other apparently smaller effects. Thus, a man can produce another man, but cannot produce an ant; a king, who can make a whole people obey him, sometimes cannot get himself obeyed by his horse. But when it is a question of a universal and unlimited cause, then it seems to me a self-evident axiom that *what can do more can do less*, as it is that *a whole is greater than its part*. Indeed, rightly understood, the principle applies even to particular moral and physical causes; it would be a greater thing for a man to be able to

---

[1] [*Corresp.*, No. 347; *Œuvres*, A.-T., VOL. IV, p. 111.—ED.]

produce men and ants than just to be able to produce men, and it would be greater power on a king's part to command horses as well, than just to command his people. (In order to magnify the power ascribed to Orpheus' music, the fable says that it could stir even the beasts.)

It does not much matter whether my second proof ⟨of God's existence⟩, founded upon our own existence, be considered as different from the first or merely as an explanation of the first. But just as God's creation of me is a thing he has effected, so is his putting in me an idea of himself; and any effect issuing from him gives a proof of his existence. So in any case it seems to me that all these proofs taken from effects come to the same thing. Moreover they all fail if the effect is not evident to us (which is why I considered my own existence rather than that of Heaven and Earth, about which I am not so certain); and again, if we do not associate with them our idea of God. For since my soul is finite, I cannot know that the hierarchy of causes is not infinite, except by having in myself this idea of the First Cause; and even admitting a first cause that preserves me, I cannot say that this is God, if I have not in point of fact the idea of God. I hinted at this in my reply to the First Objections, but briefly, so as not to depreciate the arguments of other people, who ordinarily assume the impossibility of an actual infinite series. I for my part make no such assumption; on the contrary, I think there is an actual infinite series in the division of matter into parts. This will be seen in my *Principles of Philosophy*, on which the printers are just finishing work.

I am not aware of having laid it down that God always makes what he apprehends as most perfect; it seems to me that a finite mind cannot judge of the matter. But when I was trying to clear up the difficulty arising over the cause of error, I did assume that God created a world of the utmost perfection; for on the contrary supposition the difficulty just vanishes.

I am much obliged to you for telling me of the passages in St Augustine, that may serve to give authority to my opinions; some of my other friends had already done this [1]; and I am exceedingly gratified that my thought is in agreement with such a holy and distinguished personage. For I am by no means of the temper that would have all one's opinions seem to be novel; on the contrary, I bring mine into accord with other people's as far as truth allows.

I allow only so much difference between the soul and its ideas as there is between a piece of wax and the various shapes it can assume. And just as, in assuming various shapes, the wax is, properly speaking, not active but passive, so also it seems to me that in receiving this or that idea the soul is passive—that it is active only in volitions. Ideas, I think, are put into the soul partly by the objects that affect the senses, partly by cerebral impressions, and partly by the soul's previous dispositions and its acts of will; just as the shapes assumed by wax depend partly on the impress of other bodies, partly on the shape it already had or other qualities already found in it (its degree of heaviness, softness, etc.), and partly on its motion (since if once disturbed it has an intrinsic power of keeping in motion).

Our difficulty in learning science and in clearly apprehending the ideas that are naturally known to us comes from the false prejudices of our childhood, and other sources of error, which I have tried to explain at some length in the work now printing.[2]

As regards memory, I think that memory of material things depends on traces that persist in the brain after some image has been imprinted on it; and memory of intellectual things on another sort of traces, which are to be found in

[1] [See above, Letter V., p. 263.—ED.]
[2] [I.e. his *Principles of Philosophy*.—ED.]

the mind itself. But the latter sort are quite different in kind from the former, and any illustration that I might give, drawn from corporeal things, would be utterly diverse from them; cerebral traces, on the other hand, render the brain liable to move the soul in the same way as before, and thus to make it remember something; just as the folds in a piece of paper or a napkin make it more apt to be folded that way over again than if it never had been so folded.

The moral error (*sic*) [1] that occurs when we justifiably believe something false because a reputable man has said so, etc., involves no privation, so long as we use our assurance only as a guide to our actions in life, in a matter as regards which it is morally impossible to know better; thus, properly speaking, it is not an error at all. But it would be an error if we were assured of it as we are of a truth of physics; for the testimony of a reputable man is then not sufficient.

As regards free will; I have seen Father Pétau's work; but from the way you explain your own opinion of the matter, I think mine is not far removed from it. For, in the first place, I would have you observe that I did not say that a man is indifferent only where he lacks knowledge, but rather that he is more indifferent in proportion as he knows fewer reasons for choosing one side rather than the other; and this, I think, nobody can deny. I agree with you about the possibility of suspending one's judgment; what I tried to explain was how one can suspend it. It is certain, I think, that *upon a great illumination of the intellect there follows a great inclination of the will ;* thus, if we see very clearly that a thing is suitable for us, then it is difficult for us (I think, even impossible), so long as we remain in this state of mind, to stay the course of our desire. But the nature of the soul is such that its attention stays hardly more

[1] [This seems to mean a view that is ' morally ' certain, but in fact not true.—TR.]

than a single moment upon a given thing; so, as soon as we cease to attend to the reasons that show a thing's suitability for us, and merely remember that it did appear desirable, we can make present to our mind some reason for doubting this; and thus we can suspend our judgment, and may even form a contrary one. So, since you make liberty consist not precisely in indifference but in a real and positive power of self-determination, there is only a difference of terms between our two opinions; for I admit that the will has such a power. So far as I can see, however, this power is just the same when it is accompanied by indifference (which you admit to be an imperfection) as when it is not so accompanied; and all that there is in the understanding, say, of the Blessed who are confirmed in grace, is light; I therefore use the general term *free* for everything voluntary, while you wish to restrict the term to a self-determinating power accompanied by indifference. But as regards terms I only desire to follow usage and precedent.

As regards irrational animals, they are clearly not free, since they have not this positive power of self-determination; in them ⟨freedom⟩ is a pure negation—absence of force or constraint.

The only thing that stopped me from talking about our liberty to follow after good or evil was my wish to avoid theological controversies as far as I could and keep within the limits of natural philosophy. I grant you that whenever there is an occasion of sin, there is indifference; and I do not think doing wrong involves seeing clearly that what we are doing is bad—it is enough to see this in a confused fashion, or even to remember having previously judged it to be bad, without seeing that it is so at all, i.e. without attending to the reasons that show it to be bad. If we saw clearly that it is bad, we could not possibly sin—not so long as we did see it this way; hence the saying *omnis peccans est ignorans.*[1] And a man does not cease to merit even if, seeing with perfect clearness what he ought to do, he unfailingly does it without any indifference as between alternatives—like Jesus Christ in this life. For a man is able not to be at all times perfectly attentive to what he ought to do; therefore it is a good act to be so attentive, and thus bring it about that our will follows the light of our understanding so strongly as never to be indifferent. For the rest, I did not write that grace completely prevented indifference, but only that it diminishes it, by making us lean more towards one side than the other. Grace, however, does not diminish our freedom; and from this I think it follows that freedom does not consist in indifference.

You raise the difficulty of conceiving how God could have chosen, freely and indifferently, that it should not be true that the three angles of a triangle are equal to two right angles, or in general that it should not be true that contradictories cannot be together. But this is easily removed by considering that God's power cannot have any limits; and also by considering that our mind is finite, and was created of such a nature that it can conceive the possibility of the things God chose should actually be possible, but not of things that God could have made possible, but in fact chose to make impossible. From the first consideration we see that nothing can have obliged God to make it true that contradictories cannot be together, and that consequently he could have done the contrary; the other consideration assures us that while this is true, we must not try to understand it, because our nature is incapable of doing so. And although God has chosen that some truths should be necessary, that is not to say that he chose them necessarily; for it is one thing for him to choose that they should be necessary and quite another for him to choose this necessarily, or be necessitated to choose this.

[1] [I.e. ' in the act of sin a man is always being ignorant '.—TR.]

I freely admit that there are contradictions so obvious that we cannot represent them to our mind without judging them to be completely impossible; e.g. the one alleged by yourself—that God might have made creatures not to be dependent on him. But we have no deed to represent them, in order to realise God's immeasurable power; and we need not conceive of any superiority or priority as between his intellect and his will; for our idea of God teaches us that in him there is only one action, supremely simple and pure. This is well expressed by St Augustine's words ' Because thou seest them, things are so '; for in God seeing and choosing are the same thing. . . .

There is a great difference between *abstraction* and *exclusion*. If I were just saying that my idea of my soul does not represent it as dependent on the body or identical with it, that would be abstraction, from which I could frame only an inconclusive negative argument. What I do say is that the idea represents the soul as a substance that may exist even after the exclusion of whatever belongs to the body; from this I frame a positive argument, and conclude that soul can exist without body. The way extension is excluded by the nature of the soul is seen very clearly in the impossibility of conceiving half of a conscious being (*chose qui pense*), as you very rightly remark. . . .

XIII. DESCARTES TO CHANUT[1]

[*On infinity*]

The Hague, 6 June 1647

. . . In the first place, I recollect that Cardinal ⟨Nicolaus⟩ de Cusa,[2] and several other doctors, have supposed the

---

[1] [*Corresp.*, No. 488; *Œuvres*, A.-T., VOL. V, p. 51.—ED.]

[2] [Descartes refers to Nicholas of Cusa's *De docta Ignorantia*, BK. II, ch. I, written in 1440; see R. Klibansky's edition and notes, Leipzig, 1932, p. 64.—ED.]

world to be infinite without ever being censured by the Church on that account. On the contrary, it is held that it is an honour to God if we make people consider his works as very great. And my own view is less hard to accept than theirs; for I do not say that the world is *infinite* but only *indefinitely great (indéfini)*. There is a notable difference here; for in order to say a thing is infinite one must have some grounds for knowledge that it is so, which one cannot have except as regards God; but to say it is indefinitely great one need only not have any grounds for a proof that it is limited.[1]

Now it seems to me that it is not provable, nor even conceivable, that there should be any limits to the matter of which the world is composed. When I examine the nature of matter, I find it to consist merely in its having extension in length, breadth, and depth; thus whatever possesses these three dimensions is a piece of matter; and there can be no space that is completely empty—contains no matter at all—because we cannot conceive of such a space without conceiving that there are in it these three dimensions, and consequently that there is matter in it. Now if we suppose the world to be infinite we are imagining that outside its boundaries there lie certain spaces; and since these have their three dimensions, they are not merely 'imaginary' (as philosophers call them) but must contain matter. Since matter cannot exist except within the world, this shows that the world extends beyond the boundaries we were trying to ascribe to it. Thus I have no means of proving, nor can I conceive, that the world is limited; so I call it *indefinitely great*. But I cannot deny the possibility that there are such grounds, known to God although incomprehensible to me; so I do not say absolutely that the world is *infinite*.

If we compare the extension of the world, thus regarded, with its duration, I think the only idea that it gives occasion

[1] [Cp. *Princ.*, I. xxvi-vii; above, pp. 185-7, § E.—Ed.]

to is that there is no imaginable time, before the creation of the world, when God could not have created it if he had willed; I do not think we are obliged to conclude that he actually created it an indefinitely long time ago. For with the real, actual existence of the world for the last five or six thousand years there is not necessarily bound up the possible existence that it might have had before then, in the way that the actual existence of the regions conceived as surrounding a globe (i.e. surrounding the world, if it is supposed *finite*) is bound up with the actual existence of the globe. Besides, if the eternal duration of the world in the past were inferable from its indefinitely great extension, this would *a fortiori* be inferable from the eternal duration it must have in the future. (Faith teaches us that though Heaven and Earth shall pass away, i.e. will change their form, yet the world, i.e. the matter of which they are composed, will never pass away. This is clear, because eternal life is promised to our bodies after the Resurrection, and consequently to the world in which they will exist.) But from the eternal duration that the world must have in the future, we do not infer that it has already existed from all eternity; for all moments of the world's duration are mutually independent.

The prerogatives ascribed to man by our religion (which seem hard to believe in, if the extension of the universe is supposed indefinitely great) deserve some explanation. We may say that all created things are made ' for us ', inasmuch as we can derive some utility from them; but I do not see that we are obliged to think man is *the* end of Creation. On the contrary, what we read is: ' All things were made for his (God's) sake '; God is the sole final cause of the universe, just as he is its sole efficient cause. And as for creatures, inasmuch as they subserve one another's ends reciprocally, each might ascribe to itself the privilege that whatever others subserve its ends are made ' for its sake '.

The six days of the creation are indeed described in Genesis as though man were the principal object of creation; but one could say that since the account in Genesis was written for man, the Holy Ghost saw fit to give particulars principally of what concerns man, and that indeed nothing is mentioned there except in its relation to man.

Preachers, in their anxiety to incite us to love God, have a way of bringing before us the various advantages we get from other creatures, and saying that God made them for our sake; they do not make us think of the other ends for which one could just as well say God made them, because this is no use for their theme. So we are strongly inclined to believe that he made things just for us. But preachers say something even stronger: that each individual man owes a debt to Jesus Christ for all the Blood he shed on the Cross, just as if he had died merely for one man. This is assuredly true; but it does not mean that Christ did not redeem, with that same Blood, a very large number of other men. Similarly, I do not see that the mystery of the Incarnation, and all the other privileges God has given to man, exclude the possibility of his having given an infinity of other and very great privileges, to an infinity of other creatures.

I do not on that account infer that there are intelligent creatures in the stars or elsewhere; but I do not see that there are any grounds on which one could prove that there are not. I always leave such questions undecided rather than deny or assert anything about them.

The only remaining difficulty, I think, is that after believing for a long time that man has great privileges above other creatures, it looks as though we lose them all when we have occasion to change our view. I must distinguish between those advantages which can be diminished through others' enjoying similar ones, and those which cannot thus be diminished. A man with a thousand pistoles would be very rich if nobody else in the world-had as much; the same man would be very poor, if there were nobody else but had much more than that. Similarly, all praiseworthy qualities give more glory to their possessors in proportion as they are found in fewer persons. This is why we habitually envy the glory and riches of others. But virtue, knowledge, health, and in general all goods considered in themselves and not in regard of glory, are in no wise lessened in ourselves from being found in many others as well; and so we have no reason to fret because they are multiplied. Now the goods that may exist in all the intelligent creatures of an indefinitely great world belong to this class; they do not diminish those that we ourselves possess. On the contrary, if we love God and for his sake unite ourselves in will to all that he has created, then the more grandeur, nobility, and perfection we conceive things to have, the more highly we esteem ourselves, as parts of a whole that is a greater work; and the more grounds we have to praise God for the immensity of his creation. The various scriptural references to the indefinite multitude of the angels entirely confirms this view; for we hold that the least of the angels are incomparably superior to men. It is also confirmed by the astronomers' measure of the stars as far bigger than the Earth. If the inference that there must be inhabitants of other places than the Earth could be drawn from the indefinite extent of the world, it could be drawn also from the extent that astronomers agree in ascribing to the world; for there is none but holds that the Earth is smaller in comparison with the whole of Heaven than a grain of sand is in comparison with a mountain. . . .

APPENDICES

APPENDIX I

DESCARTES'S ELUCIDATIONS OF 'COGITO ERGO SUM'

1. FROM THE REPLY TO THE SECOND OBJECTIONS [1]

. . . For when we observe that we are conscious beings (*res cogitantes*), this is a sort of primary notion, which is not the conclusion of any syllogism; and, moreover, when somebody says: *I experience* (cogito), *therefore I am or exist*, he is not syllogistically deducing his existence from an experience (*cogitatione*), but recognising it as something self-evident, in a simple mental intuition. This is clear from the fact that if he were deducing it syllogistically he would first have to know the major premise: *whatever experiences is or exists*; whereas really it is rather that this principle is learnt through his observing in his own case the impossibility of having experience without existing. For our mind is so constituted as to form general propositions from knowledge of particular cases.

2. DESCARTES TO CLERSELIER [2]

[*On Gassendi's Rejoinders to the Fifth Replies*]

12 January 1646

. . . The author of the Rejoinders will have it that when I say *I experience* (je pense) *therefore I am*, I am presupposing the major premise: *what experiences, is*, and have thus

[1] [First published in 1641; *Œuvres*, A.-T., VOL. VII, pp. 140-1. —ED.]

[2] [First published in the French version of the *Meditations*, with *Objections and Replies*, in 1647.—ED.]

already embraced a prejudice. In the first place, this is an abuse of the word *prejudice*. For although this term may be applied to the proposition when it is uttered inattentively, and believed to be true only from a memory of a previous judgment to that effect, nevertheless it cannot be called a prejudice upon examination; for it appears so evident to our understanding, that we cannot help believing it; even if it should happen to be the first time in our lives that we think of it, so that we have no prejudice in its favour. But the most important mistake here is that the author supposes that the knowledge of particular propositions must always be deduced from universal ones, following the syllogistic order of Dialectic. This shows how little he knows the right way of seeking for truth; for in order to discover the truth one must assuredly begin with particular notions, and then go on to general ones afterwards; although, conversely, after having discovered the general notions, one can likewise deduce further particular notions from them. For example, when a child is taught the elements of geometry, he cannot be made to understand in general that *if from equal quantities equal parts are subtracted the remainders are still equal* or that *the whole is greater than its parts*, unless he is shown examples in particular cases. It is from ignoring this that our author has been misled into so many fallacious reasonings, with which he has swelled his volume; he has simply made up false major premises out of his own imagination, as though I had deduced from them the truths I explained.

3. DESCARTES TO ? THE MARQUIS OF NEWCASTLE [1]

March or April 1648

. . . I admit that ⟨our intuitions—*connoissances directes*⟩ are slightly obscured by being mixed up with the body; but

[1] [*Corresp.*, No. 511; *Œuvres*, A.-T., VOL. V, p. 137.—ED.]

still, the knowledge they give us is primary, unacquired (*gratuite*) and certain; and we touch upon the mind with more confidence than we give to the evidence of our eyes. You will surely admit that you are less assured of the presence of the objects you see than of the truth of the proposition : *I experience* (je pense) *therefore I am?* Now, this knowledge is no product of your reasoning, no lesson that your masters have taught you; it is something that your mind sees, feels, handles; and although your imagination, which insistently mixes itself up with your thoughts (*pensées*), reduces the clearness of this knowledge, it is, nevertheless, a proof of our soul's capacity for receiving from God an intuitive kind of knowledge.

APPENDIX II

ON INNATE IDEAS

Regius, Article XII [1]

The mind has no need of ideas, or notions, or innate
axioms; but its faculty of thinking (*cogitandi*) suffices by
itself for the performance of its proper acts.

Descartes's Rejoinder

In Article 12 he seems to disagree with me only
verbally . . . For I have never written, nor been of
opinion, that the mind needs innate ideas in the sense of
something different from its faculty of thinking. I
observed, however, that there were in myself certain
thoughts (*cogitationes*) that did not proceed from external
objects, nor from a determination of my will, but only from
the thinking faculty that is in me; and therefore, in order
to distinguish the ideas or notions that are the content
(*formae*) of these thoughts from other ideas which are
adventitious or *manufactured*, I called them *innate*. It is in

[1] [From *Notes on a certain Programme, published towards the end of the
year 1647 in the Low Countries, under the title ' Explanation of the Human
Mind or Rational Soul: wherein it is explained what it is and what it can
do ';* Œuvres, A.-T., VOL. VIII. 2. pp. 345, 357. The *Explanation*, a
criticism of the Cartesian philosophy, was published in 1647 by
Henricus Regius (Henri de Roy), Professor at Utrecht, formerly a fol-
lower of Descartes. In his *Notes*, first published in Amsterdam, 1648,
Descartes takes up one by one the Articles of Regius's work, adding
his own rejoinders.—Ed.]

the same sense of the word that we say generosity is innate in certain families; or again that in others certain diseases, e.g. gout and the stone, are innate; not that infants of these families suffer from these diseases in their mother's womb, but because they are born with a certain disposition or liability to contract them.